A "Craving Vacancy"

Also by Susan Ostrov Weisser

FEMINIST NIGHTMARES: WOMEN AT ODDS
(*co-editor with Jennifer Fleischner*)

A "Craving Vacancy"

Women and Sexual Love in the British Novel, 1740–1880

Susan Ostrov Weisser
Associate Professor of English, Adelphi University

NEW YORK UNIVERSITY PRESS
Washington Square, New York

© Susan Ostrov Weisser 1997

All rights reserved

First published in the U.S.A. in 1997 by
NEW YORK UNIVERSITY PRESS
Washington Square
New York, N.Y. 10003

Library of Congress Cataloging-in-Publication Data
A "craving vacancy" : women and sexual love in the British novel,
1740–1880 / Susan Ostrov Weisser.
p. cm.
Includes bibliographical references and index.
ISBN 0-8147-9304-5 (clothbound).— ISBN 0-8147-9305-3 (pbk.)
1. English fiction—19th century—History and criticism. 2. Women
and literature—Great Britain—History—19th century. 3. Women and
literature—Great Britain—History—18th century. 4. English
fiction—Women authors—History and criticism. 5. English
fiction—18th century—History and criticism. 6. Richardson,
Samuel, 1689–1761—Characters—Women. 7. Erotic stories, English—
—History and criticism. 8. Love stories, English—History and
criticism. 9. Sex in literature.
PR868.W6W36 1996
823'.8093538—dc20   95-53139
                                                    CIP

For my mother, Betty Newman Ostrov

Contents

Preface: A 'Craving Vacancy'		ix
1	Sexual Possibilities and Impossibilities	1
2	Chastity and 'Rumour'd Heavens': 'Woman' and the Double Message of Sexual Love	15
3	The Light in the Cavern: Samuel Richardson and Sexual Love	36
4	Thornfield and 'The Dream to Repose on': *Jane Eyre*	53
5	Down the 'Forbidden Path': *Villette*	73
6	Wild Desire and Quenchless Will: *Wuthering Heights*	92
7	George Eliot and the 'Hidden Wound'	114
Conclusion		151
Notes		160
Index		188

Preface: A 'Craving Vacancy'

> We [women] have been raised to fear the yes within ourselves, our deepest cravings.... In touch with the erotic, I become less willing to accept powerlessness, or those other supplied states of being which are not native to me, such as resignation, despair, self-effacement, depression, self-denial.
>
> Audre Lorde

In a journal entry of 1836, the adolescent Charlotte Brontë identifies imaginative power with the masculine sexuality of her Byronic fantasy hero, Northangerland. Hearing the wind swelling 'wildly' – and how often wild blasts of wind appear in the writings of all the Brontës as a symbol of passionate abandon – she cries,

> Glorious! that blast was mighty it reminded me of Northangerland, there was something so merciless in the heavier rush, that made the house groan as if it could scarce bear the acceleration of impetus. O it has awakened a feeling I cannot satisfy... now I should be agonized if I had not *the dream to repose on – its existence, its forms, its scenes to fill a little of the craving vacancy.*[1]

It is this 'feeling which cannot be satisfied' in and by oneself that I propose to examine as a trope for the construction of sexual womanhood in the novels of Charlotte Brontë, Emily Brontë and George Eliot. It is a strange and contradictory construct: in the case of Charlotte Brontë, for example, the alienated heroine may be reduced to a vacuum, a literal 'vacancy', yet it would be simplistic to identify her psychological state either with Freudian absence/lack or else the passive self-effacement associated with conventional femininity. On the contrary, this is a vacancy which *actively* 'craves', i.e. longs and seeks to be filled, which names and asserts itself through seeking to be imbued with meaning and value.[2]

In her journal Brontë appears as the stranger, continually acting a role to the outside world and deprived of an inner coherence, a satisfying female identity; as such, she absolutely requires connection with the imaginative world to establish a secret, asocial 'real' self. Sexual love may also be seen as a metaphor for this forged bond; or, more accurately, the sexual and creative metaphors are blended in the act Charlotte Brontë called 'dreaming', by which she meant the creation of fantasies from which she drew her first written narratives.[3] Yet the deepest irony is that sexuality (with important exceptions) almost never appears in her novels as connection, but as an effect of power, barely mitigated by romantic love. We must look to the world she, and the other authors in this study, inhabited to see why this was (and so often still is) true.

In this journal entry, it is important to note, the fantasy character Northangerland, the power of the 'mighty blast', of wind, and the mastery of deprivation possible through the literary imagination, are conflated as masculine principles, originary to the experience of being female for both Brontës. Gender, as we shall see, the tantalizing play of the various kinds of hierarchical differences – biological, social, economic, psychological – between men and women, is an important part of nineteenth-century domestic ideology used by all the female novelists here as subject-matter for their novels. But we do not read these today only as textbook cases of Victorian manners and morals; to the contrary, their legacy to us is in the way the power of sexuality and romantic love both transform the traditional meanings of womanhood and subvert them.

The nineteenth-century authors selected for study here were chosen because they point towards the ways in which contemporary romantic ideologies are constructed from the history of gender roles in our culture. Since I believe an apprehension of these authors best proceeds from their own historical context, it is in this spirit that I begin with Samuel Richardson, a male author whose heroines, Pamela and Clarissa, provide a touchstone for romantic ideology in Victorian literature. Richardson's novels constitute a paradigm of those traits I call Moral Femininity, which serves as a kind of literary ancestry in the British novel. The ambivalence of the Victorian female authors towards sexual love as both constructive of women's freedom and destructive to female identity may be understood in terms of the models he provided.

Given the breadth of the subject undertaken here, it would perhaps be easier to detail what this study does *not* intend to do. Thus, it is not to be a panoramic investigation of a 'theme' in the large corpus of a well-defined period, since such a wide study would be impossible without large sacrifices of depth in its treatment. Nor were the novelists chosen to stand as a comprehensive selection of cultural attitudes, or, still less, selected on the basis of each one's influence, in the ordinary sense, on the next. Charlotte Brontë had a great deal more admiration for Thackeray than for Richardson, and George Eliot had far less to say about either than about numerous other Victorians, yet the bonds that link Richardson, Brontë and Eliot are more interesting than those of conscious indebtedness. Nor is it meant to be literary history: the interest of this study is not in a journey whose stops on the way constitute a tradition in the British novel, not of form nor period nor of a shelf full of geniuses in the Leavis sense. There is no direct line from Richardson to the Brontës, for example, and drawing one would inevitably shortchange a great number of women writers, including so-called 'sentimental' writers, who provided important contexts and models along the way.

Rather, this book is meant to be a representative examination of a cultural metaphor, expressed through a number of highly prestigious and influential texts, those in which sexual love appears as an overwhelming question. Specifically, this study is a close examination of the interrelations among these three ubiquitous terms – woman, sex and love – as they are exemplified in well-known works by an eighteenth-century author, Samuel Richardson, and of three typically atypical Victorians, the two most famous Brontë sisters and George Eliot, with an emphasis on seeing these large concepts as having diverse meanings while serving multiple and often conflicting purposes.

The meanings assigned to sexuality and romantic love, like those of gender, can be most confusing when they appear to be monolithic discourses, often in pairs of polar opposites: thus they may be seen as perfectly natural and universal, or cultural and historical; sexual love may be variously located in the body, in 'the spirit' or 'the heart'. Romantic love may appear far above market considerations and yet somehow also commonly available, much like a mass-produced commodity; sex may be a 'wild', mysterious, irrational force, or else a drive which has a transparent, evolutionary, not to say 'rational', function. Similarly, the values of gender are infinitely malleable: thus women can be irrational demons or else sweet and 'soothing', emotional and weak or else monstrous and consuming.

These systems in active presence with each other enormously complicate the matter: compromising understanding of any one as a separate mythos, problematizing the border between the so-called rational and the irrational which is such a comfort to the human mind, drawing other social structures (e.g. race or class) into their magic net and appearing to swallow them up. Love too is mysterious because it is supposed to be, when that is what we want from it, and sex exerts its 'rational' desires across a field mined with dark psychological holes in its terrain. It is the general thesis of this study that all ideals and practices which are the site of conflict can be co-opted by either 'side' of any social issue, as I hope to show through the examples of these texts.

These four authors were chosen because they illustrate a particular relation of gender both to sexual desire, whose site is the yearning body, and to romantic yearnings, conventionally issuing from 'the heart' or (to use Heathcliff's word) the 'soul', located for us in the body of the text. Since this is not a book about the body,[4] nor a social study of an idea, nor even a strictly literary analysis of a social ideal, its organization reflects the need to find a way to discuss sexual meanings as they appear variously in social formations, narrative (literary and non-literary) representations, and the psychic experience of gender. Thus, the first chapter begins with a discussion of how we can speak about sexual love and gender at all, and how that has affected the perception and study of nineteenth-century culture. If its language is initially abstract, it is because the subject of sexuality and gender itself is *both* extremely abstract and also historically specific, and it therefore seems appropriate to treat it in both ways, moving from the general to the concrete.

The second chapter examines the specific social and historical conformations of sexuality and romantic love for women in Victorian Britain, two sides of the same coin, which finds its exchange value in double images of womanhood. In the following chapters I look closely at the way in which sexual meanings take on specific artistic shapes, creating a problematic of sexual love from the ideals and tensions of the age. It is my premise that meaning emerges from the attempt to frame a narrative as an open question or solution to a constructed 'problem'; as such, we shall use the following chapters to find interesting questions to ask of the time. Our first task, however, is to define what we mean when we talk about sexual love.

I would like to thank the following for their contributions to my efforts: The Woodrow Wilson Foundation, The American Association of University Women and The Giles Whiting Foundation for grants during the initial writing; Michael Wood, John Maynard, Nikki Manos and Paul Mattick Jr, for their time and care in reading portions of the manuscript at various stages. To Steven Marcus, my adviser from my first days at Columbia University, I owe a unique debt as the teacher who first showed me how to go about reading novels, while to Ann Douglas I owe my focus on women and their concerns. In addition, I am grateful for the affection and encouragement of those I love during the years of work on this book.

1
Sexual Possibilities and Impossibilities

> And now that the problem of religion has practically been settled, and the problem of labour has at last been placed on a practical foundation, the question of sex ... stands before the coming generations as the chief problem for solution.
> Havelock Ellis, 'General Preface',
> *Studies in the Psychology of Sex*, 1897

> Sex is still a problem because whatever the current sexological steps to orgasmic happiness, at a more fundamental level many of the ideologies surrounding 'sex' have remained *unchanged* over the last hundred years. . . . Above all, sex remains the endorsement of gender.
> Lynne Segal, 'Sensual Uncertainty, or Why the Clitoris is not Enough', *Sex and Love: New Thoughts on Old Contradictions*, 1983

I

What is the problem of sexual love? The very concept of sexual love is an impure category, if the reader will pardon the pun: it is neither inclusive of all representations and practices of sexuality, nor is it always fully synonymous with an idealized mythos of romantic love. Rather, sexual love as desire, act or affect is constituted by the highly charged intersection of sexuality and romantic love, a space where gender is imagined and enacted. What Havelock Ellis called the 'problem' of modern Western society clearly has enormous implications for understanding the construction of gender in our culture. The focus of my study will be on representations of the relation between women and sexual love in four major British novelists because these works have revealed a particularly vexed relation between love and sexuality, between definitions of womanhood and the way these are constructed through the deadly serious play of sexual love.

Sexual love as a theme in literature is an open field for the contradictory play of metaphor. For example, it is presumed to be ordinary and supremely physical in its expression, yet it also admits broad abstraction and intellectualization; while often associated in literature with vitality, energy and being, sexuality may also signify death, complete surrender to another or a total abnegation of a character's humanity. It is 'animal' in some contexts, 'spiritual' in others. It may be conceived as the most individual human activity, and therefore the most egoistic, isolating and alienating from the community – or, conversely, it may signify connection to another as a common basis of humanity, and therefore an escape from psychic isolation. It is the most private affair of most public concern; it is the most ordinary activity with greatest individual distinctions. It is the business of society, yet it is none of society's business.

Sexuality forms one border, in other words, between our perceptions of 'private' and 'public' selves, or between Nature and Culture, or between human and not-human, borders blurred and mystified by cultural constructions of gender. Thus its representations can signify Woman's affinity with Nature just as well as they align her with a sexually repressive Culture. Moreover, it has become a metaphor for women's oppression with powerful political effect in this century, while also embodying (quite literally) exciting possibilities for women's agency.[1]

The very qualities that make sexuality fascinating in literature also make it ambiguous and unintelligible, however, for it is altogether too obviously a symbol, too psychically individualistic, and yet again, too conventional. A common assumption, in the modern age as well as in the nineteenth century, is that sexuality is 'irrational', and yet we frequently use the language of rationality to discuss and analyse it. Though sex is everywhere, the meaning of sexuality is no easier to locate: indeed, the particularities of its meaning seem to disappear into its very ubiquity.

In what way, then, can we speak of 'meaning' in sexuality at all? It is now a near-commonplace among scholars to speak of sex as always 'experienced culturally, through a translation'.[2] Even granting agreement on cold biological facts, surely the heat of sexual *meaning*, like the meaning of gender, emerges in the enactment of subjective experience and its interpretation, through the medium of that particular language of sexual discourse which unites the individual sharers in a common culture. The idea that sex is 'sexuality', i.e. *has a meaning* above the sum of physical acts and facts, is meaningful in itself.[3] But difficulties arise as soon as we attempt to decode the particularities of the discourse that characterizes sexual passion.

Although the fiction of *a* sexual 'discourse' is occasionally useful in that it allows us to speak of a time, place, class or individual at all, it is not the less simply that: a useful fiction. Narrative is one form of those useful fictions that allow us to imagine sex as a single meaningful idea attached to a particular time, place, class or character, isolated from change. But sex is a practice as well as a juncture of discourses, and that practice not only enacts ideology but in turn affirms or modifies it. Sexuality is one of the myths of culture that we live out, in the literal physical sense, and in living it, sometimes transform the social life that shapes it.

Moreover, and very importantly, in speaking of sexual love, the language of sexuality is frequently shadowed, obscured, even consumed by the vocabulary of romantic love, whose representation of experience it can secretly subvert. The discourse of love must be considered distinctly from the language of sexuality, even when, at important times and places, they seem to merge. In fact, it is all the more important, given the separateness of their origins and practices, to keep the distinction most clearly in mind at those times that they appear to be one, as when sexuality is romanticized, for example. The language spoken by lovers consists not only of entwined sexual and romantic dialects, but is intercultural as well, an ongoing conversation in which there is always assimilation and appropriation. Like the lovers, these two discourses are separate but also share the field of play (or battle), and each changes the other by making a new space that represents the two together.

The last charge in discussing this difficult subject is to preserve still another distinction always liable to slip through the hidden coils of language: we must continually remind ourselves of the doubleness of sexual discourse, which contains codes of gender as one of its hierarchies. These two meanings of sexual encodement, gender and sexuality, are also frequently so entwined as to present one face, which is, of course, an important aspect of their coding. Foucault's definition of sexuality as a 'locus of experience, one which includes a domain of knowledge, a system of rules and a model for relations to the self',[4] might perhaps be amended to include an awareness that sex can be a system of rules for relations to the Other as well.

'Woman has a language peculiar to herself,' wrote Jules Michelet in 1859. 'It is the sigh, the impassioned breath.'[5] The language of sexuality, in other words, when used to describe what Michelet called Woman, is often no-language, 'passion' that must take shape in no-words, an experience of absence. This, too, is a significant part of the sexual as well as romantic mythos, and the broken, blurred, hesitating, choked, whispered or even silent accents of Otherness is a complication and a challenge in approaching the maddening and enchanting strains of the Siren that is sexual love in our culture. The silence that is the absence of words is the female Vacancy, the no-self that longs to be moved and filled with the spirit of the wind in Brontë's own metaphor.

'The function of myth', Roland Barthes has said, connecting fact, sign and social convention, 'is to empty reality: it is, literally, a ceaseless flowing out, a haemorrhage... in short a perceptible absence.' Its function, in other words, is to establish a 'world wide open [in which] things appear to mean something by themselves',[6] but from which meaning has bled away, leaving a sort of constructed and delimited vacancy, if an eternally temporary one. Barthes notes the parallel function of bourgeois ideology; we may also note the female nature of the metaphors involved, which would suggest that the gendering, as well as engendering, of the language of sexual discourse is an important part of mystifying the subject. If myth, as Barthes would have it, 'has the task of giving an historical intention a natural justification, and making contingency appear eternal',[7] then we are left with the task of attempting to restore the 'historical intention' to which myth is directed. Since myth makes contingency appear eternal, it is only fair to ask how we will make the seemingly eternal truths about love, sex and women that emerge from the novels examined here appear to rest on contingencies.

In the last decades, several critics of importance to feminist literary criticism have done just that: to cite a few, Nina Auerbach, who identified the complex and paradoxical nature of apparently seamless stereotypes in the Victorian age; Nancy Armstrong, who demonstrated the class oppression inherent in the ideology of female virtue in the bourgeois novel; and Mary Poovey, whose work on medical, historical and fictional texts has underlined the ways in which gender ideology was an 'uneven development' in the Victorian age, contested, contradictory and continually in flux rather than monolithic, smooth or totalizing.[8] My own work, while more traditionally literary in its subject-matter, attempts also to see the ways in which ideologies of gender, romantic love and sexuality may be fluid enough to serve the interests of several paradigms of behaviour, not just official or conservative ones.

The critics Judith L. Newton and Deborah Rosenfelt have described the theoretical agenda of what they call a 'materialist-feminist criticism' of literature as a double rendering of literature and culture in order to 'explore the changing relationships among ideas, language and social conditions and relations'.[9] Newton and Rosenfelt argue that their approach differs from traditional Marxist criticism in that it foregrounds gender as a primary category of oppression and grants power to those cultural ideas usually relegated to secondary status, while it differs from other feminist criticisms in that it focuses on material conditions as the origin of multiple oppressions.[10] The theoretical edge that this dialectical analysis provides is that it avoids the double pitfalls of representing women as either entirely victims of a determined history or, conversely, entirely blessed with a free agency which they may simply empower themselves to use without any real change in the social relations of their culture. While women, like all members of society, are situated in history, and while gender is socially constructed, these critics grant that individuals struggle towards a self-construction which entails a kind of agency, allowing for meaningful social transformations.

It is somewhere between the folds of these two visions of the socially situated individual and the 'purely' subjective that literature enacts its multiple myths, its imaginary representations of both history and gender. And here we encounter a special paradox of studying Victorian novels: while a great deal of recent work has been done on the body in nineteenth-century society, there is very little actual physical connection of bodies in these narratives. There is a great deal of plot, much exposition of character and a fair amount of introspection about romantic feelings, but when it comes to the physical manifestation of sexual love, not much ever happens. The irony of Charlotte Brontë's concept of female vacancy is that it is a kind of embodied absence, which is to say a fictional body, across which desire is written in semi-invisible ink. Fictional selves yearn and withhold, tease and demand, crave and exult, yet these fictional selves do not have a simple correspondence to the historical bodies of Victorian women, or even to their authors. If these texts are mental acts of desire, therefore, an interested critic must add or even emphasize a psychological or subjective dimension to the materialist-historical awareness, and the former requires more traditional methods of close reading.

Rather than the bodily practice of sexual love, what we will examine, then, are representations of desire, and complex ones at that.[11] As such, this is a study in the fluidity of social and textual representation: if, as Regina Barreca has said, it is common for fictional characters to 'translate sexual desire into . . . ambition and anger', it is just as likely to go the other way around for women in novels.[12] Thus these novels' heroines experience sexual desire as liberating and entrapping at once, defining as well as defying their relation to the social world. My reading of the novels of Samuel Richardson, Charlotte Brontë, Emily Brontë and George Eliot views them as engaged in an ideological power struggle having to do with women and their place in material culture, and as invitations to participate in the power of the authors' images and interpretations of that struggle.

II

To talk about the representation of opposing categories is to risk being accused of operating within the system of their terms: sex as power and sex as connection, love as liberating versus love as false consciousness for women, wilful assertion as male and will-lessness as female. Yet the dilemma for the critic is that one must first burrow within them in order to open them up to analysis, since they are embedded in the language constitutive of the text itself. The difference between 'Victorian' and 'modern' is one such operational distinction. It is also important to remember that both gender and identity are categories that may appear most immutable and invariable just at the time when they are crumbling from within. Though we may exaggerate the differences between ideal types for our own purposes, the way in which ideas exert pressure contextually on each other is all the more significant for being less visible.

Perhaps the greatest enemy of any new knowledge is what we already know. In 1978 Laurence Senelick observed in *Victorian Studies*:

> The field of sexual mores during the reign of Victoria would seem to be pretty thoroughly plowed. What more is there to say amid the indictments of the Victorians as thorough-paced hypocrites who practiced a murky and pornocratic lechery while posing as apostles of domesticity and morality?[13]

Ironically, that same year saw the American translation of Michel Foucault's *History of Sexuality*, Volume I, which brilliantly advanced the thesis that in the nineteenth century, appearances to the contrary, sex began to occupy the place of high importance in Western society that it currently holds. Rather than deny or repress sexuality, Foucault proposed, the proliferation of discourses about sexuality treated the subject as if it were 'an object of great suspicion', as though bourgeois capitalist society 'suspected sex of harboring a fundamental secret'.[14] What, we might ask, was the secret which talking about sex concealed?

In 1880 the *Westminster Review*, which prided itself on being one of the most progressive journals of its day, published an anonymous article on 'Chastity', which purported to be a contribution to the infant discipline of sociology. Beginning with a respectful nod to the *Origin of Species*, the author set out to examine the question of heredity as an influence on the development of the moral sense. It is his or her particular concern, the author says, to determine whether 'moral character' – by which s/he primarily means sexual virtue – is genetically 'transmissible' to future generations.

In contrast to its inflammatory subject, the tone of the piece is self-consciously dispassionate and scientific. None the less, it embodies many of the deepest Victorian anxieties on the subject of sexuality. The author begins:

> During the discussion of our theme, 'the first thing which, in the order of Nature, forces itself upon our notice, is *the strength of the sexual propensity and the comparative weakness of the moral principle which ought to hold it in restraint.*' This propensity has an organic basis.... Whereas the power to control the emotion does not arise till later in life. It resides in the will, and the conditions which preside over the coordination of this will are so variable, that it is less certainly entailed than the passion which it has to govern.[15]

There are several features in this excerpt which show that the author, though what used to be called an 'advanced thinker', shared the important cultural myths of this age, namely that humanity in general is engaged in an uphill battle against a force of Nature, which is arranged most irrationally and inconveniently for humankind. It is obvious to the author of this article that a greater balance between the sexual 'propensity' and the restraining 'will', the power to control desire, 'ought' to be the natural order of things. Yet not only is the principle of restraint inherently weaker, subject to uncertain conditions and influences, but the sexual emotions, as representatives of the 'organic', hold sway earlier and with more constancy.

A striking sense of underlying tension pervades this rational and scientific examination of human sexuality. This tension is the by-product of a familiar and quintessentially Victorian dilemma: that living with or without our 'natures' – which is sometimes the same as our bodies, sometimes equated with our 'real' or whole selves – is equally impossible.[16] It derives from the nineteenth-century paradox that sexual energy is both essential and destructive to the construction of 'society', and that it is necessary to struggle constantly with this problem against nearly insuperable odds.[17] It was the belief – or hope – of many Victorians that a human 'will' existed which was inherently in opposition to the 'instinctual' power of passion, and it was their concern to determine the social conditions which best produced and strengthened this phenomenon.

But as we shall see repeatedly, the will itself became a problematic concept in the nineteenth century. Its very nature was contradictory. It was not only that it too often failed, though by definition it was the essence of power and strength. More disturbing, 'the will' was believed capable of excesses of its own.[18] Indeed, the very progress of material civilization seemed to lead directly at times to increasingly destructive social forces, and in ironic reversal, the gentle, 'will-less' woman came to embody for many Victorians the best hope for the protection of values that seemed steadily to be losing ground.

Because the author was a self-consciously 'advanced thinker' and an admirer of the scientific, 'detached' attitude, this essay may be said to represent one strain in Victorian culture which did not accept as given the immutable spiritual origin of morality. Yet a very different theme, which is also characteristically Victorian, is heard in the firm assertion that there is an 'order of Nature' upon which we must base our discussion of sexual morality. Certain thematic words emerge as notes in the Victorian polyphony: 'the *power* to control', 'the passion which the will has to *govern*'. Further on in the paragraph the author states:

> The essential character of chastity implies active mastery over appetite, not the negation of appetite, and this mastery is a

constituent of character capable of being entailed. But such is the vacuity of our language that . . . it denies to the heroism of self-conquest a single active transitive verb to denote that the English-speaking race can conceive of a masterful will which rules.[19]

Words like 'mastery', 'govern' and 'rules' work as metaphors to construct a coherent world in which an explanation of behaviour – and therefore also of misbehaviour – is possible. The images are social metaphors of a class-based society, of a stability which is won at the cost of holding tightly to an unequal and easily unbalanced hierarchy, where one either masters or is mastered, governs or is governed. It is no accident that the term 'entailed' is borrowed from the legal language of land inheritance in order to suggest the genetic inheritance of 'character', or rather, of moral characteristics: this is, we remember, a society in which landed property, a form of value declining in economic if not yet social importance, has become a problematic issue in an era of rapid commercial change. What is notable is the application of these terms to the individual psyche: it is the human will that is entailed, the self that is conquered, sexual passion which must be governed and ruled. It is as though the author must bravely assert that there *is* a hierarchy of the self which parallels that of society, in order to confess the overwhelming force of sexual desire. This cultural myth, accessible even to advanced thinkers in the Britain of 1880, satisfied the need to impose order, to coordinate the disharmonious, even irreconcilable elements of moral experience. It is not simply that the discourse of sexual morality serves the structures of power, as Foucault tells us: the discourse of power serves the cause of morality as well, organizing Victorian culture's thinking about its own meaning and importance.

As feminist critics have long pointed out, however, Foucault's influential analysis tends not to differentiate between prescriptions or experiences of male and female sexualities.[20] While male sexuality was associated with an active-aggressive mode of being in the world for which men are most frequently socialized, women's sexuality was constructed as opposite but complementary to the male. That is, the sexuality of women could be either secret, withheld, absent, i.e. 'pure', *or* seen as excessive, consuming and dangerous, with the two extremes often varying according to class.[21] We may see the gendered distinction when the anonymous author of 'Chastity' suggests the direction of the wish for protection against the encroaching dangers of moral disorder by coining the new word 'astriction' to suggest what is called the *active* sense of chastity, i.e. chastity as a heroic act of 'the will'. This neologism is defined in the article as the binding fast or confining of passional impulse.[22]

By literally closing off the most characteristic passage of a woman's body to entry by menacing forces, the author seeks to unite the promise of contained but available passionate energy with the exercise of the 'masterful will that rules' in one happy solution.[23] The power associated with male rule and male sexuality may then be left intact, while the female body, i.e. whether it was closed or open to penetration, could be metaphorized as 'the problem'.

While the author's suggested term 'astriction' was not universally adopted into the English language, images of restraint, binding and holding on, all associated with femininity, permeated Victorian culture and literature. But the gendered nature of the concept of 'will' gives it a double meaning that frequently places the fictional nineteenth-century heroine in a double bind: if the will is associated with an aggressive (male) thrust for power, how can it be the source for (female) self-control? Is the human will naturally aligned with a sexual desire gendered as masculine, or participatory in a 'feminine' control over that power?

Since, following Marx, the sexual relationship may be taken as a 'sensuous manifestation' of all other social relations,[24] sexuality became for many writers the stage on which the dilemma of the 'human' in its relation to a problematized 'self' is imagined in modern society. The theme of man's sexual relation to woman as a metaphor for the exploitation of the humanity of others in Western literature similarly reflects a deeper, less acknowledged fear that reaches beyond merely sexual anxiety: that the core of all social relations in modern, commercial society *is* exploitation. This is a sexuality based on personal gratification and an ethic of self-interest which cannot be controlled by a society whose first principle is the freedom of the individual to acquire. The self-gratifying drive for individual entitlement and acquisition in a swiftly developing capitalist culture is both acted out and contained in representing it as either an impure but fascinating sexual desire, or a pure but obsessive desire for romantic love. The construct of sexual love as a kind of double-natured sexuality charged with heightened meaning and emotion is, especially, one which marks off a distinction between the genders.[25]

The late eighteenth and nineteenth centuries were a time when gender oppositions, i.e. cultural constructions of masculinity and femininity, intersected favourably for some authors with an agenda of political/social protest against the relatively new commercial ethic of self-interest. Among these were novelists whose subject was the sexually restrained domestic heroine. Feminisms change: the idea of an inherent 'essential' opposition between masculine and feminine natures which is anathema to some modern feminists, who see as inevitable the asymmetrical ranking of those values associated with 'femininity', was stressed by many nineteenth-century feminists as a way of correcting an immediate and pressing social inequity, the brutality of masculine power in the marketplace and workplace.

The possibilities thereby imagined for the cultural ideal I will call Moral Femininity are only a part of the story, however. The woman as Lady, successful counterpart of the upwardly mobile bourgeois male, has less appeal to the modern feminist reader, and for this reason, I would submit, the latter ideal has been neglected as a subject of serious study. But concentrating on the more accessible and attractive aspects of female power envisaged in Moral Femininity implies that there was a homogeneous view of sexuality even among a relatively small and privileged group of women. It is more useful to see both gender roles and sexuality as a dialogue between fluctuating and multiple viewpoints, rather than as fixed or stable entities which are unambiguously available for choosing. The female authors in this study in no way 'reflected' or 'expressed' the cultural ideals discussed in Chapter 2 in any simple manner, but responded to them also as constraints on desire, conditions of oppression to be worked in or around, or possibilities to be played with or on.

III

While literature surely takes part in the regulating functions detailed by Foucault, it also just as surely has the power to resist.[26] As literature makes the familiar strange as well as the strange familiar, it exposes as well as delineates ideologies, opening the web of power relations for inspection. My own predilection in the enterprise called literary criticism is for the close reading of texts, which I would argue still imparts best the pleasure of seeing a narrative unfold according to its own principles of construction. Literature, while closely related to, even perhaps inseparable from, theory and history, is neither equivalent to theory nor entirely congruent with history. Rather, it has a pleasure in itself which ought, I believe, to be valued on its own terms. To this end the reader must passionately enter into the intimate pleasures of the text, feel its pull, even risk the danger of falling in love with it, as well as maintain the theoretical-historical (which is to say, critical) distance necessary to valuation.

Felicitously, in these particular novels, the pleasure of the text is in part learning to read about pleasure. Though few modern literary critics believe any longer in the Eternal Verities of the literary enterprise, this pleasure is not entirely ephemeral. The works here endure because the issues themselves endure. Then, as now, sexual love can appear as a 'problem', a symbolic way of thinking aloud about being a woman and a self in a particular society of highly problematic values in high tension with each other (not unlike our own).

The struggle to come to terms with the paradoxical implications of sexual love was particularly pervasive in Victorian culture and literature, as was the question which obsessed nineteenth-century writers, i.e. the ways by which women were or were not sexual 'by nature'. But the novelists who appear in this study were chosen because their concern went beyond this popular preoccupation into a more radical area of investigation: the ways in which sexuality could be defined by women themselves. One of the mythic paradigms of women's sexuality in nineteenth-century British literature is one I call Moral Femininity, in which a heroine is empowered and achieves self-definition by restraining her own strong desires, as well as those of her lover. Yet in such works as Charlotte Brontë's *Jane Eyre*, Emily Brontë's *Wuthering Heights* or George Eliot's *The Mill on the Floss*, this particularly 'womanly' power to change a social order marked by greed, aggression and unrestrained self-interest is seen as equivocal or problematic, and another view is represented in tension with the first: to repress female sexual desire is to forfeit some essential measure of female selfhood and autonomy.

The critic Martha Vicinus has observed that in Western culture, 'the dominant paradigm for sexuality is overwhelmingly male and heterosexual'.[27] But while sexual desire remains a primary metaphor for a masculine capitalist ethos of self-assertion and self-aggrandizement in the above novels, it also attains an authentic female shape as a force against male domination of the body. Thus heroineship in these works consists of engagement in a personal as well as political struggle in the form of a double bind: how to validate female sexual desire as authentic without submitting to the sexual demands of the desired male. Especially when in combination with the emotional ties and yearnings of romantic love, female desire appears to be dangerous because it can be used against women as a form of domination. It is no wonder that the impossible presence of desire is finally dissolved in these narratives by such devices as a sudden, irrevocable decision to remain chaste, or else the destruction of the problem-causing heroine herself. In Eliot's *The Mill on the Floss*, for example, Maggie Tulliver both makes the decision to restrain her own wild desire *and* is punished by the author for her sexual craving at the novel's end.[28]

Whereas the home with the moral woman in it was seen as humanizing the selfish and aggrandizing will of men in an amoral public sphere of power, sexual love filled the vacancy that a woman was, humanizing her by acknowledging her secret craving. The fictional women of this study 'experience' sexual passion as both a dangerous and repressive force *and* as a means for acknowledging a suppressed capability for private rebellion and even social change.[29] These two messages stood in dialectical tension in nineteenth-century bourgeois society, fuelling the growth of what literary critics traditionally called a 'theme'. The engagement with the problematics of passionate love turns the metaphor of women as 'craving vacancies' into a complex paradigm of growth. It reifies the absence which is the beginning of desire into a selfhood that confesses its own desire, that wills itself and its objects into being through imaginative understanding.

From penny-newspaper fiction to the highest of privileged culture, a great strain in Victorian society was represented through the cultural metaphor of the will-less Virgin, vulnerable to emotional as well as physical assault, yet at the same time a vacancy craving to be filled with meaning through romantic love.[30] Yet as we shall see, the Virgin of the novels we will examine is not necessarily the Virgin of the popular press. A paradigm is not merely a literary or social convention; it is also a strategy through which the practices of reading and writing and even living take place. The Virgin heroine in these texts is neither truly will-less nor asexual. On the contrary, she is often a rebel, secretly or otherwise, a potential not yet fulfilled, becoming rather than fixed as an absence. I hope to show that the much maligned ideal of Moral Femininity, like its supposed cultural opposite, the Lady, constitute formidable representations of a legitimate and assertive state of wilfulness in women.

For all the female characters in the novels after Richardson examined here, passion may be inimical to the moral life, but it is also absolutely necessary for the survival of women.

In the popular as well as literary response to the system of sexual ideologies in Victorian culture, we frequently encounter sexual love as a dangerous, destructive, sometimes uncontrollable force. It is associated with the worst abuses of self-interested behaviour in an unchecked commercial economic system, even as we force the text to give up its second secret – that self-fulfilment through gratification of desire is necessary to (female) freedom. Not surprisingly, in the Brontës we will notice a concern, amounting at times to obsessiveness, with forbidden knowledge, with the dark and empty spaces of life, with portents and messages dreaded or longed for, with secrets not quite written fully into the texts or clearly understood. And increasingly, we will see the growing significance of a sexual love that is 'wild', 'free', even 'strange', on the part of heroines strongly attracted to the aggressive, ambitious, self-asserting values associated with masculinity in Victorian society. It is sexual love which thickens the texts of these novels; it is a woman, a heroine, a Virgin, who defines and carries the burden of its problems outward into the world.

2

Chastity and 'Rumour'd Heavens': 'Woman' and The Double Message of Sexual Love

> Woman deck'd
> With saintly honours, chaste and good
>
> Coventry Patmore, 'The Angel in the House'
>
> What rumour'd heavens are these
> Which not a poet sings
> O, Unknown Eros?
>
> Coventry Patmore, 'The Unknown Eros'

I

What *is* a woman? If you have to ask the question, you might say, you will probably never find an answer; or, as Simone de Beauvoir has said, in asking the question we have already suggested an answer, since the very fact of having asked is significant.[1] I may as well confess at once that I *will* not answer it, that in fact there is no answer to this question which obsessed nineteenth-century writers. Another way of putting this refusal is to observe that there are too many answers which cluster around this question, too many hopes for certainty and, finally, too many representations, a plenitude of forms and values which constitute an impenetrable thicket of meanings. Moreover, there are thickets in at least two forests: one we might label essentialist, in which the term draws its definition from immutable, ultimately biological conditions, and the other constructivist, in which no a priori trees are presumed to exist in the forest at all.[2] This is not to say, however, that there are no paths through this density. One path is to observe a connected series of representations, such as are constituted by those novels we will examine.

In this process of looking at cultural products, we cannot, of course, speak of what women *are* because they are, in one sense, whatever they are said to be. In order to tell a story about women, it is, however, paradoxically necessary to posit a (more or less) coherent entity which appears full-blown with its own thoughts, feelings and intentional states – a woman and her desire, in other words, or a woman with a 'will' to act or not act on that (frequently, but not always specifically) sexual desire. Such a woman *character* – the subject of the story, in the rhetorical sense, as well as figuring as a subject in the philosophical sense – especially when authored by a male in a male-dominated society, can thus be seen as part of a strategy for concealing the social values of the narrative, for imposing hidden definitions of who a woman should be. The critic's presumption of such an overdetermined subject then allows us to look *through* texts, for example, as many have, at the oppressive ways by which women have been defined through their sexuality, or lack of it. There is, needless to say, an entire corpus of feminist literary criticism built upon this perspective.

But if we grant agency to women as authors, we must also look at the ways in which sexuality was defined and shaped by women themselves through the medium of their literary surrogates. The first view presupposes women as passive objects, shadows of their supposed subjectivity in the literary work, constituted solely by the dominant discourses in their social order. The second implies that women may and do take an active role in manoeuvring around or imposing alternative meanings within the constraints of these discourses. Indeed, it is through the act of writing that these women authors find ways to redefine the very conditions of their oppression so as to conceptualize freedom through desire.

In each text, the circumstances that foster a 'strong will' in a woman may also obliterate it; the same ethos that justifies her very existence as a moral agent will be used to punish her for desiring or even for having been desired. In the end she is in an impossible position: the novels allow us only to imagine a heroine who must either disintegrate as a self or change the world by Romance.[3] The males in the story, we are relieved to observe, fare little better. They too must be changed, broken or cut to size to fit these pages – if they survive at all (Emily Brontë's Heathcliff and Charlotte Brontë's M. Paul do not). All are caught in a web of contradiction, in which the pleasure of sexual love, which constitutes a kind of freedom for a woman, is revealed to be complicitous with the social order that formed the heroine's prison and necessitated the escape to freedom in the first place. Thus passion is found to be both inimical and indispensable to character, just as, in Freud's view, sexual energy is both indispensable and inimical to society. The only saving grace is that both 'character' and 'society' are disposable commodities at the end of a novel.[4]

This is the structure of each story, but it is not the full story itself. Like most models, it is an oversimplification, and ignores both the nuances and variations, not to mention the great ambiguities, at work in the pattern. Working with the same structure found in innumerable popular works of fiction from Samuel Richardson's time through the soap operas and romance magazines of our own day, these novels construct female sexuality as a battle zone. Within this field of conflict the line of action is drawn between the self-interested principle of modern capitalist society which endorses the amoral power of the self, and the larger claims of a patriarchal 'moral' community which traditionally requires female self-denial and obeisance to authority.

In this construction the narrative seems to require of its hero (but really of the reader) that a choice be made between the values of an attractive but dangerous modernity and a threatened, increasingly weakened traditionalism. But then another story seems to take its place within the first, realigning the values which appear to be so clear in the above structure. In this latter configuration, desire appears to be the sign of a strong, authentic, 'real' self liberated from domination, and self-denial is equated with an oppressive demand for submission. Disconcertingly to a postmodernist reader, the belief in the idea of a 'real', essentialist self may be intrinsic to the narrative of 'craving vacancy'. Moreover, it is absolutely essential to the workings of this double-edged story that the two sides fight their war in the arena of the female psyche.

The female psyche was of course a favourite topic of the Victorian age, and a great many scholarly works have already been written on such well-known nineteenth-century dissections of it as Tennyson's 'The Princess', Ruskin's *Sesame and Lilies* or Patmore's collection of poems, 'The Angel in the House'. Patmore's domestic angel elicits nearly universal distaste today as an expression of misdirected idealism overlaying a priggish and patronizing misogyny. Yet asking why the image of chaste womanhood was elevated to new levels of moral significance leads directly to still more interesting questions. How was it that this imagery touched the collective hearts of so many readers? What does it mean that women themselves were the most ardent admirers of Patmore's poetry? It was women, in fact, who were the chief consumers of the entire literary industry built around the myth of romantic love in the nineteenth century and beyond. Can this be explained entirely by false consciousness?

Patmore's Angel in the House became for feminist critics, beginning with Virginia Woolf, a kind of eponymous literary antiheroine, while the study of living female angelhood has been extended to what I call, for lack of a more consistent term employed by social historians and literary critics, Moral Femininity.[5] Moral Femininity is the idea that women inherently possess a redemptive power (or to use the nineteenth-century term, 'influence') through the restraint of their own desire, a power which is capable of transforming a morally disintegrating society. This ideal is based on a moral authority which is conceived as originating in private (female) life and radiating outwards, instead of emanating from a 'natural' or divine (male) spiritual source and flowing downwards through the larger structures of the social and political orders. The paradigm of Moral Femininity is to make an indivisible link between sexual desire and morality on the one hand, and female withholding/suppression/absence on the other.

This, as numerous studies have attested, is not a simple description of an actual change in gender relations or even a cultural myth about all women everywhere. To the contrary, the ideology of Moral Femininity, even in Victorian Britain, was confined mainly to the middle class and even there was not accepted unproblematically.[6] Nor is the concept quite as simple as it first appears as a prescription for sexual behaviour. First, there are a great many possible varieties of the Moral Feminine. Desire may be represented as either lacking in women, or as 'weaker' than in men, or as present, even dangerously so, but restrained by higher considerations. There are also quite specific differences in the social implications of each of these theories.

Second, a closer look at the sources reveals a surprising awareness in the Victorian age of a very striking gap between the ideal and its efficacy in practice. Even Coventry Patmore pauses to reveal a yearning for meaning through a sexual love barred from 'The

Angel in the House'.[7] When he does so, as in 'The Unknown Eros', the result is surprising in a literary figure so largely identified with the idylls of middle-class sexual purity:

> What rumour'd heavens are these
> Which not a poet sings,
> O, Unknown Eros? ...
> What portent and what Delphic word
> Such as in form of snake forbodes the bird
> Is this?

'The Unknown Eros' is an odd, enigmatic poem, in which sexuality has become a message of 'portent', one with a heavy burden of significance to bear. It speaks now as a 'Delphic word', an oracle capable of telling us more than we already know, so that the poet's inability to read or place this message is all the more frustrating. Most importantly, in direct contradiction to the ethos of Moral Femininity, the erotic is said to be heaven-like, but the poet qualifies this judgment by calling this heaven a 'rumour', a displaced sign whose truth-value is in question.

Patmore suggests that the 'unknown Eros' in us 'forebodes' something, but exactly what is not clear. Sexuality embraces, to use Foucault's words, a great secret, yet its significance for our lives is a frightening Unknown. The outward sign of this dilemma is that the poet – and his culture – literally do not know where to place this portentous signal; we are pointed vaguely up to the transcendent zone of a rumoured heaven, but it is not much to go on, given the implied consequence of the trip. Yet, as the anthropologist Julian Pitt-Rivers once remarked in an essay on Mediterranean social values, 'traffic lights are not found where there are no automobiles'.[8] Here is one place where we can, as Pitt-Rivers suggests, direct our attention to the congestion of automobiles implied by a proliferation of signals.

Near the end of Patmore's poem he expresses the power of Eros in an enigma:

> There lies the crown
> Which all thy longing cures.
> Refuse it, Mortal, that it may be yours!

There are two contradictory messages in this directive: first, the assumption of a state of 'longing' similar to an illness that may be 'cured' by sexuality, and second, a slap to the hand that reaches for this cure. Yet in a bewildering reversal, the reward of the panacea goes *only* to those who 'refuse' it – i.e. remain chaste. It is as though, to return to Pitt-Rivers' metaphor, the green, red and 'left turn only' traffic signals were all activated at once during a traffic jam.

Existing simultaneously in the Victorian era, then, were *two* quite opposite messages for women, and the interest of the present study is in the relation between the two: the official didactic pronouncement that society required the will-lessness of chastity, and the powerful secret of a 'rumour'd heaven', in which true meaning could only be found in the individual self-fulfilment of sexuality. While it has become a scholarly commonplace that middle-class women in the nineteenth century were valued through their supposed absence/restraint of sexuality, this observation is rarely linked to this second strand of romantic (and Romantic) ideology gaining force in the rapidly changing world of the industrializing West.

As we shall see, the radical gap between these two was eventually filled by the mythos of romantic love as it was reshaped and redefined in the age of companionate marriage as the right of every man and woman.[9] One might point to several key features of the idea of romantic love in its particularly modern version. First, it expresses the individualistic freedom of the self-assertive will valued in a liberal, commercial society, while still retaining the aura of quasi-mystical sanctity that was a product of the Middle Ages. Second, romantic love appeals particularly to women because it promises agency and self-definition through sharing male power. Finally, the highly ambiguous relation between romantic love and sexuality has permitted the co-optation of sexual love by both radical and conservative elements of society, those who seek the erasure of hierarchical distributions of power and those who benefit from keeping oppressed groups (such as women) within their traditional places.[10]

It was the erotic side of romantic love, the rumoured Victorian 'heaven', that in the end broke through the defences represented by Moral Femininity, the containment of power built around, for – and by – Victorian women. Eros may imply want, lack, a 'desire for that which is missing', says Anne Carson, but it can also represent more than that. It may be conceived as a form of appropriation, which implies a kind of entitlement.[11] Then again, the very act of wanting suggests a 'knowledge of what is lacking in the actual'; that is, the awareness of oneself as a 'craving vacancy' confers a sharpened consciousness of an external social reality that is defective or insufficient in supplying what one needs. From this awareness, the conditions for a kind of rebellion may grow.

II

The reading of masses of popular articles on the 'education, rights and condition of women', as the *Westminster Review* phrased it, reveals neither assured unanimity of opinion nor unquestioned ideals, but rather a strained effort to be authoritative in the face of contradictory opinion.[12] The tone of these articles is often openly argumentative, as if the writer expects to be vigorously opposed:

> Man is intellect, woman is love. Man is mind, woman is heart. Man is truth, woman is goodness ... so it has been from the foundation of the world, and a thousand women's conventions cannot make it otherwise,

defensively cried the *Monthly Religious Magazine* in 1862.[13] Similarly, and with unusual candour, the anti-feminist Eliza Lynn Linton remarked in that same year: 'The man to work, the woman to love; the man to earn, the woman to distribute; the man to protect, the woman to cling – ah! that is the ideal life, which, unhappily, *so few ever attain*' (my italics).[14]

One cannot help but be struck, in reading this literature, by the massive attempt to force into consciousness distinctions between men and women that are posited as essential and natural, while at the same time loudly claiming that they are utterly self-evident. The active need to create a myth of simple dichotomies in the two genders which could embody the dualities of modern culture is evident in the two quotations above. Masculinity and femininity are a matched pair of horses pulling the cart of culture, whose heavy burden is a cluster of multiple values which do not sit comfortably with one another. Of these matched pairs the most revealing is 'truth' placed in radical opposition to 'goodness': women were 'good' (except when they were wicked), i.e. necessary carriers of the seeds of morality, but men's lives expressed the 'truth' of capitalist practices, meaning both its materialistic ethos and advancing technico-scientific knowledge.

In order to emphasize these distinctions, it became habitual for writers to refer to the nature of 'Woman' or 'the Sex', as though individual variation were a strictly male prerogative. It is this conceptualization of woman as a blank space, a vacancy, an empty page on which the drama of the desiring/constraining will could be rewritten, that was the foundation for her role as the self-creating literary heroine.

Two strikingly different models in both privileged and popular culture developed new significance to fill the vacancy of personal meaning for women after the mid-eighteenth century. There was the ambitious, self-interested Lady, whose assertiveness was not at this time expressed as sexual behaviour, and the sexually restrained and restraining ideal of Moral Femininity.[15] Though sexual reticence was enormously valued in both models, the sexual withholding by the Good Woman had distinctly moral overtones and implications, while the virtue of the Lady was primarily a social status marker. This disparity is of enormous importance to understanding the nature of feminist thought predominating in the era: Moral Femininity actually encouraged the recognition of female sexual desire, in so far as its presence shed more glory on the power of the woman to shape or restrain it.[16]

Together these two formulas for personal fulfilment reflected the two sides of the cultural crisis of nineteenth-century capitalism. While there were rising opportunities for comfort, material gain and individual freedoms, these were achieved at the expense of diminished moral certainties. In this context, the dichotomy of Lady versus Moral Femininity allowed women to choose either to concentrate on the rewards of the material comforts and social mobility newly available, or to assert their own personal value through moral superiority. Within the extremely narrow range of these two ideals, middle-class women were granted the limited freedom to stand on the side of 'truth' *or* 'goodness' – but never both. Poised on the threshold of established society, yet positioned outside 'real' society, women perfectly embodied in their doubleness the separation between capitalist material practices and bourgeois morality.

While the idea of the Lady pre-dates the nineteenth century as a term of social class, a consciousness of the new significance of the Lady as a set of values, psychological attributes and controlled behaviours accessible to a wider swath of social strata reached unprecedented heights in the British and American press after 1800. 'The women and females are all gone,' groaned the *Athenaeum* in 1847, 'instead we have *ladies*, always *ladies*.' Similarly, in 1846 a popular magazine declared that 'This word *lady* has forced its way into all our vocabularies.'[17]

This popular literature on the subject of the fashionable Lady clearly points to an affluent idleness as one of the most important aspects of this ideal. 'The Way to Spoil Girls' (1866), an article satirizing social fashion, advises parents to tell their daughter she is beautiful, dress her in rich and fashionable style and prepare her for visits rather than 'home duties', so that 'she will grow as useless as modern fashionable parents delight that their daughters should be.' Further, the author recommends impressing on such a child that 'it is vulgar to do anything for yourself or to learn how anything is done in the house.' As mistress of a house, it will be her chief duty 'to sit on the sofa all day long, in the midst of a pyramid of silks and flounces, reading the latest novel, while her domestics are performing the labours of the house.'[18] While the tone of this piece is wryly condemnatory, the magazine in which it appears is full of articles and advertising on those same useless and silly pursuits it condemns. Indeed, the very next article in the magazine is an admonishing 'Word to Female Servants', who are urged to perform those very 'home duties' whose neglect by young, middle-class women the author of the satirical article deplored. Apparently female readers did not mind being scolded for their trivial aspirations, since they were encouraged to take them seriously in the next breath.

Another important aspect of the 'Lady' ideal was its emphasis on the symbols of gentility, which intensified a sense of personal identity and self-worth through class. Though defined in part by her idleness, the *absence* of money-making activity, the Lady was said to be imbued with the same ambition to gratify the self that characterized her achieving husband. Indeed, her ethos was perfectly complementary to his, since her preoccupation was with the results rather than the process of acquisitive gain. It is significant that the conservative journalist Eliza Lynn Linton, in her notorious attack on 'modern' women, *The Girl of the Period*, accuses the mid-Victorian girl, whose 'sole idea of life is fun', of being 'bold and masculine'. She vividly depicts a class of women dominated by their love of 'unbounded luxury', attention-getting finery and personal pleasure.[19] Like the figure of the masturbator in the Victorian era, the modern 'girl of the period', free to seek the gratification of her will (and by implication, a 'masculine' will to sexual gratification), was a caricature of antisocial self-indulgence. Yet in her resolute pursuit of individualism, she mirrored the very essence of modern, commercial society to a degree heretofore reserved for her male counterpart.

A typical and important criticism levelled against the 'modern girl' in her quest to be a Lady was her anti-maternalism, which implied the use of her sexuality for other than selfless purposes. Eliza Linton was not alone in pointing out the growing reaction, accompanied by rapidly declining birth rate in England and America after 1850, against both maternity and breast-feeding.[20] *The Saturday Review* (1877) accounts for this trend by connecting anti-maternalism to new female attitudes towards personal freedom and acquisition, which it calls a 'desire to go forth and play with men in the mart and on the platform the more bustling and exciting games of life'.[21]

Materialistic, consumption-oriented, guided by the dictates of private desires, the idea of 'modern' young ladies who, in the words of a mid-century American journal, 'live but for themselves and seem to see nothing beyond this', supported the values of the male capitalist world through indirect participation in its system of beliefs and practices.[22] For those on whom birth had not conferred a privileged existence, the ideal of fashionable Lady at least held out the possibility of material reward by a profitable marriage, however unlikely such a prospect was in reality.

In contrast to the ideal of the Lady, the other alternative available to the middle-class woman in her search for identity was a regressive model of femininity deliberately borrowed from a fantasy of the 'traditional' home, reshaped into a kind of radiant domesticity. Where the Perfect Lady was idle, the 'womanly' woman was active in order to be useful. Whereas the hallmark of the Lady was her preoccupation with self, the 'womanly' woman was heralded as the very type of the constitutionally unselfish sex. If the values of the affluent ideal led to anti-maternalism, the 'womanly' woman was best known for her instinctive love of motherhood, or what one cynical male observer called 'baby-worship'.[23] Most striking of all is the rejection by 'moral womanhood' of the Lady's attempt to entice men with her finery, cosmetics and coquettish ways, the use of her sexuality as a commodity. 'Woman is a being made by God', asserted Mrs Martyn, the American editor of the *Ladies' Wreath* in 1847, and is thus demeaned by a role in which she is cast as 'a plaything – the toy of sensualism, valuable only for her external attractions'.[24]

When the same author undertook to define for her readers 'What Constitutes a Lady?' in the journal's first number, she began with the common contrast between the modern idea of 'the lady', who 'commands our respect and admiration', and the 'good old Saxon term *woman*', permanently enshrined 'in the heart's inner sanctuary'. 'With *woman*', declares the author,

> we associate the idea of the home, with all its fond recollections and innocent enjoyments, and of love with its thousand gentle ministries, strewing life's pathway with flowers from the cradle to the grave.... No such hallowed associations cluster around the term *lady*.[25]

The moving force behind domestic womanhood was the centring of feeling in the face of the wage relationship; it was the hope that under the false glitter of the cash-nexus (the 'truth' of society) real gold could still be found.

These nuggets of 'goodness', like the family itself, had to be isolated, protected, insulated in a separate, private sphere from the 'truth' of the male entrepreneurial world.[26] But the appeal to those women incapable or undesirous of achieving the ideal of Lady was a direct one. The role of moral guardian conferred on women the dignity, purpose and identity felt to be lost with the passing of the traditional community. By 1830 women were widely spoken of as 'different' rather than 'inferior', presiding over their 'true sphere', a carefully preserved utopia where the cumulative meaning of small daily tasks was suffused by the light of private emotion. Abruptly, the 'womanly' woman found herself propelled, in the words of *Sharpe's London Magazine*, to 'the centre of the whole moral world'.[27] The result of the new moral division between men and women was that unlike the ideal of the Lady, it organized social discontent into 'natural' divisions of sex rather than divisions of class.

The idea of Moral Femininity, then, was closely allied to the contemporaneous 'cult of the home', a cluster of values which defined family life as a sort of negative space in a society illuminated by the strong glare of self-interest.[28] What the home – or at least the idea of a home – was expected to deliver was no less than a world whose values were those of the pre-industrial community before, as Carlyle wrote, 'cash-payment was the sole relation of human beings'.[29] In the nineteenth-century version of this community, a stable familial hierarchy contrasts favourably with the social climbing and general mobility of Victorian society; authority, patriarchy, loyalty and religion all exist in their supposedly innocent, unquestioned state. Most appealing of all, the bonds between persons – and between the genders – are those of mutual dependence, 'mutual helpfulness', to use Carlyle's phrasing again, along the lines of the model of pre-industrial culture that the historian E.P. Thompson has called the 'moral economy'. The reciprocity of desire and need that romantic love presents as its founding principle for courtship, marriage and the family appears in this nineteenth-century version as a kind of balanced emotional economy, the loophole in the web of contradictions generated by gender as well as class hierarchies.

It was, most importantly, the woman's alleged tie to emotion which particularly suited her for the mission of guarding the home which was, in the words of the *Monthly Religious Magazine*, 'an enclosure – a secret, separate place'.[30] Noted and justified by contemporary studies was what Havelock Ellis called the 'affectability of women', their supposed susceptibility to emotional response, which was opposed to the more 'hardened' egoism of men.[31] One aspect of this 'affectability' was the famous female capacity for sympathetic feeling, leading to altruism or religious devotion; another, with very different consequences, was the greater female susceptibility to the irrational emotions of romantic love. 'The power of sensibilities and emotions...is woman's, not man's,' stated the *London Review* in 1865; while earlier, Stendhal had hardly found it necessary to remind his readers that 'nineteen-twentieths of [woman's] ordinary dreams are relative to love.'[32]

The liability of women to emotion of all kinds was invariably contrasted with the supposed sexual avariciousness of men, marking out an important border between 'irrational' emotion whose object is service in the interest of others, and the 'rational' (though not officially legitimated) pursuit of one's own desires in or through the body of another. 'Love...has become more spiritualized in woman than in man; her temptations to sensuality are generally conceded to be less, and compliance with the law of chastity on her part easy,' declared the *Westminster Review* in 1879.[33] The individual selfishly pursuing sexual gratification seemed totally irreconcilable with the woman whose role was giving humane support and sustenance. Sexual energy was identified with the aggressive values of a male-dominated society, a society based on an ethic of acquisition. Thus, sexual desire as the motivator for sexual conquest was classed as one form of the general 'will' to achieve and acquire. To put it simply, in a society based on a free market, sexuality is one of the goods. Therefore the seduction of a young, innocent female by a powerful male figure became a nineteenth-century prototype for the 'inevitable' exploitation of personal relations that constituted modern society, for a type of evil rationalized as understandable, or in other words, eminently narratable.

A contemporary British journal called man 'the architect' in society. In the public imagination, he was literally the erector, in both the social and sexual senses of the word.[34] The presence of the sexual urge as the corporeal symbol of the 'free' individual will was incompatible with the soothing syrup of womanhood and home; it is in this context that the sexual purity of Moral Femininity can best be seen. The achieving ego of the male 'architect' of society was openly celebrated in the popular press. While its unchecked capacity for excess continually and thrillingly threatened to break out of the realm of the 'rational', the idea that the will must remain unchecked in order to be 'free' was recognized as the cornerstone of so-called free enterprise. The privileging of its freedom ensured its perpetration. The construct of Moral Womanhood thus contained within itself a contradiction which ensured its own demise. Women were told to submit to men, to have decisions made for them, to be childish and will-less, except in the realm of sexuality, the source of their own power as sexual objects and 'innocent' instigators of male desire. There they were urged to suppress male desire as an assertion of their own control.

A mid-century 'letter of advice' to a daughter in a popular American periodical will illustrate:

> There is one point, my daughter, which is too important to be omitted; I refer to the deportment which it becomes you to maintain toward the other sex. . . . On the one hand, it has much to do with forming your own character; and I need not say that every lack of prudence in this respect even for a single hour, may expose you to evils which any subsequent caution could enable you to repair. On the other hand, the conduct of every female who is of any consideration, may be expected to exert an influence on the character of every gentleman with whom she associates; and that influence will be for good or evil, as she exhibits or fails to exhibit, a deportment which becomes her.

The advice of this father, who goes on to judge the character of a community, if not the world, from the standard of female behaviour, is simply *not* to act:

Let me counsel you, then, never to utter an expression, or do an act, which even looks like soliciting any gentleman's attention. Any wish on your part, whether directly or indirectly expressed, to make yourself a favorite, will be certain to awaken the disgust of all who know it.[35]

Through their will-lessness, women derive their moral 'will-power'. Through sexual restraint women could control the personal excesses of the private desires of *both* sexes without impairing the natural, 'essential' and necessary ego of the male. The sense of anxiety and ambivalence in the enormous quantity of writing about both the conventions of chastity and the nobility of home derive from precisely the same paradox: both the source of the threat *and* the only possible defence against it reside in the individual. The concept of Moral Femininity thus absolutely depends on its association with a male sexuality assumed to be 'naturally' aggressive and aggrandizing: the world of the soft and weak and humane is always about to be penetrated, sexually and otherwise, by the menacing force of the 'hardened'.

But Moral Femininity proved neither enduring nor practicable as an idea. While the sentimentalization of domesticity was directly related to the values associated with the lost traditional community, for example, the picture of domestic life that emerges in popular literature and essays in the Victorian period is often far from idealized. For every sentimental paean to the heavenly enclave of peace and devotion, a note of discontent and disillusion is heard in the magazines and newspapers read by the literate masses.[36]

'The poetry of belief makes the English home the very ideal of sweetness, peace, love and security,' remarks *The Queen* in 1874 in a 'realistic appraisal'; there, supposedly, 'all are enclosed in a golden web of affection, which keeps all the good spirits and shuts out all the bad.' But in reality, the article continues, 'instead of love, confidence and security ... we have ill-tempers and selfishness, back-biting and quarreling, and anyone abroad preferred to everyone at home.' Fathers devoted too much time to their businesses, brothers were sent away to school too early, while too many women spent afternoons 'mainly in a sustained state of waiting'.[37] The contrast between the new intimacy and the traditional household was not favourable: 'The home of today, in both city and village,' commented another contemporary journal, 'is more sorely beset ... than the homes of our fathers. *Capable of giving more, it is constantly liable to give less.'* The typical husband 'knows he neglects his home, but calms his conscience by pleading the inexorable will of his business.'[38] While the ideal of the Moral Feminine held out the promise of a kind of power and dignity for the 'womanly', moral, sexually restrained woman, the attitudes embodied by a Samuel Smiles or a Horatio Alger were at least as pervasive, and certainly more concretely and materially rewarded, than those of the magazines for women whose philosophy of domesticity proposed to stand in opposition to their values.

Moreover, unlike Moral Femininity, which offered emotional bribery to counteract the discontent and restlessness of women, Ladyhood promised more pragmatic and material rewards. Patricia Branca, in her study of the social conditions of nineteenth-century British middle-class women, has shown that the ideal of Ladyhood was unattainable for the vast majority of hard-working middle-class women.[39] Nevertheless, inaccessible ideals can exert a strong negative pressure, at once tantalizing and demeaning. Even while she provoked gentle ridicule or loud indignation, the Lady still elicited admiration for her single-minded ability to acquire the social status and material luxury she wanted. While the ideal of the Lady was less openly articulated as official ideology, it spoke to women through the silent but eloquent symbols of affluence, and therefore needed the written organs of persuasion far less. Most important, it presumed the radical proposition that such women could pursue a goal with highly rational single-mindedness, not subject to the vagaries of 'weak' emotion or 'pure' altruism, a premise that twentieth-century feminists themselves would later share and apply to sexual behaviour.

By contrast, the moral possibilities of restraining man's egoistic, brutal nature seem to have appealed most to the intellectual and sentimental popularizers. Even the redoubtable Sarah Ellis called the notion of woman's moral superiority 'merely fashionable'.[40] Indeed, much of the writing on Moral Femininity is obviously prescriptive in tone and intention, rather than descriptive. When *Sharpe's London Magazine*, for example, undertook to define 'womanliness' in 1866, it contrasted a woman's ability to bear 'danger with calmness, suffering with patience, injury with forbearance', plus 'dependence, gentleness and gracefulness' to the masculine qualities of 'courage, strength, vigour, energy and dignity'. Yet in the next breath it felt obliged to castigate a good portion of the very sex whose 'intrinsic' nature was praised. Those conventional feminine virtues characterized by humane, passive behaviour were said to be ignored, not only by those genteel Ladies whose will was anything but passive and selfless, but also by another faction: 'The numerous and constantly increasing body of females... those dangerous, extreme reformers who... would have women step from and exceed their sphere.'[41] Who, then, was enacting these virtues?

Several studies have linked the rise of the feminist movement in the nineteenth century to the movement of Moral Femininity, particularly in its role of raising women's self-esteem and sense of sisterhood.[42] It is less common to associate a feminist political agenda with the attitudes of the Lady, whose material ambitions and assertion of her individual will were more assimilated to her culture than were the values of Moral Femininity. If the 'moral' woman wanted men to be more like women, the Lady wanted to be more like men and have what men could have. In 1870 Eliza Linton worried over the question of whether modern women wanted to be treated seriously or simply have 'a share in that which men have appropriated'.[43] Later, in 1891, when she wrote of the New Woman, she was to write with more decisiveness: 'The frantic desire of making money has invaded the whole class [of women].'[44]

Sexuality constituted an important part of the pie that men had appropriated and divided amongst themselves. The fashionable Lady supposedly had always known how to exploit her sexuality to attain the material comfort and social status she sought. This interest in self-fulfilment and the covertly sexual route to it was in fact one of the distinguishing hallmarks of the Lady as opposed to Moral Femininity. 'Whoever lives in the world with his eyes and ears open', remarked Eliza Lynn Linton in 1870, 'uses these organs to little purpose when he frequents the watering-places, fashionable churches, hotels or promenades, if he does not find very many ... identical individuals: Grecian band, false hair, padding, paint, enamel, nudity and all.'[45]

By the end of the century the legitimacy of sexual allure had begun to prevail as part of the triumphant doctrine of individualism that superseded communal restraint as the dominant ideology. The 'modern gospel of divine right of self-development', as the novelist Mrs Humphry Ward called it, triumphed over order, purity and self-sacrifice at last.[45] Feminist attitudes towards sexuality remained ambivalent for some decades after new sexual attitudes began to supplant sexual purity around the turn of the century, but the more attractive doctrine of equal rights to sexual gratification eventually won out.[47]

I would argue that this outcome was deeply affected by the ambiguous role that sexual desire played in the stories that nineteenth-century society told about women. At the same time that sexuality seemed to subvert one temporary solution to the problem of the principle of self-gratification in nineteenth-century society, i.e. the myth of home and moral womanhood, it had already begun to form the basis of another, very different solution. Sexual love as personal elixir and social panacea proffered a bigger and better promise of personal meaning to women which proved fatal to Victorian sexual ideology. Though sexual purity received a great deal of exposure in the didactic press, the romance of sexual love had quietly crept into the popular media, especially books and journals addressed to women. By the mid-Victorian period the philosophy of individual gratification through romantic love stood side by side with the moral and social selflessness of sexual purity as two powerful and contradictory cultural messages to young women. Chastity now had to compete directly with 'rumour'd Heavens'.

A striking bifurcation appeared in the popular press at this time: the didactic literature remained for the most part anti-sexual, asserting the importance and power of the moral 'will', while a great deal of popular fiction celebrated romantic love in courtship as its theme. A most significant problem at issue was whether or not 'falling' in love was an act of the will or beyond individual control. A didactic article on 'Falling in Love' in 1861, for example, concluded that: 'To love ... is an act of the human will, not a mere instinct or uncontrollable desire. ... "To fall in love" with a woman or man is, strictly speaking, as absurd as to talk of falling in love with your neighbour's house, or to yield to any other covetousness, as if it were uncontrollable.'[48]

Yet in the same year, a penny-newspaper of broad popular appeal, the *London Journal*, like numerous others in England and America, was publishing love stories in which a sympathetic young lover could righteously claim to his objecting father that his love is 'unconquerable'.[49] While one heroine, a paragon of beauty, wit and virtue, could 'sob' of a man who has insulted her that 'I hate myself for a selfishness ... so unwomanly' in wrongly pursuing her love, the secret admission that such passion was both right and characteristically womanly was supported by the outcome of the tale, in which the heroine captures the love of the unregenerate fellow and follows him into marital bliss.[50] Everything in the capitalist ethos supported this view; one had only to look about Victorian society, after all, to see that people could and did fall in love with their neighbours' houses, metaphorically speaking, and considered it their right to acquire them as well.

The relationship of romantic love to the sexual impulse was ambiguous and shifting in the nineteenth century and continues so into the present day. On the one hand, the values of an idealized romantic love seemed clearly *opposed* to the 'animal' passions of sexuality. Thus a mid-century periodical typically characterized first love as 'the sweetest, tenderest, most genuine and unselfish of human passions'.[51] This supposedly unselfish and pure side of romantic passion led to its appeal even among 'moral womanhood', who were fond of describing the 'influence' of an innocent maiden over her impressionable young lover.[51] But while Moral Femininity used the appeal of romantic love as a corollary to the moral power and significance it promised the Victorian woman, the sexual side of passionate love was more directly compatible with the model of the Lady, who could use beauty, fashion and status to attain the object of her desire.

The problem of whether romantic love could be 'pure' or was simply sexual desire in disguise, whether it was a 'holy' passion or a selfish indulgence, derived from its peculiarly dual nature as it appears in the history of Western culture. The mythology of sexual love in Western society encompasses both the submergence of one's own will (thereby leaving one open to the influence of the beloved), and, simultaneously, the desire to possess the other. Perhaps, then, the wonderful appeal of romantic love in the nineteenth century and beyond is the way that it seems to 'solve' the problem of the desiring will by obliterating it and legitimizing it at once. Roland Barthes, in *A Lover's Discourse*, records as one of the signifying messages of love that 'I am engulfed, I am consumed.'[53] Sexual passion is experienced as somehow independent of the self, even 'against one's own will'.[54] Yet the will to possess the beloved, which Barthes calls the drive to 'absolute appropriation', appears equally valid: I am my beloved's, and so he must also be mine.[55] Thus the modern expression of romantic passion appears in a highly palatable form as a communal right (and a rite) of *ordinary* life, rather than as the extraordinary and privileged experience of elite culture in former ages.

Thus romantic love as it begins to take its modern form is seen as democratic, if not democratizing: no longer only for the socially elite who can afford it as a luxury, or the pure at heart (i.e. morally privileged) alone, it is, with the sharp rise in companionate marriages after the eighteenth century in England, supposedly available – as a part of our 'nature' – to everyone. Moreover, we might speculate that romantic love succeeded as ideology because it implies a sense of absolute connectedness in an alienated society, a mutual power of self-generated meaning that appears to erase gender distinctions. Not only the isolation of the individual, but the relatively powerless position of women in the social order is corrected by the perception that one person can satisfy all one's needs, thus forming a tiny island of humanity, an equable community of two. 'You're my whole world', as countless popular singers have crooned, or as Erich Fromm remarked, 'One forms an alliance of two against the world . . . an egoism *à deux*.'[56] It is the myth of home and womanhood in disguised form once again, but without the cumbersome convention of selflessness. Whereas the home with the moral woman in it was a microcosmic haven of human needs, the modern message of sexual love, as it arose with companionate marriage, is that the rumoured 'heaven on earth' is constantly available and universally accessible.

This myth was particularly directed to, perpetuated and even partially self-created by women, who stood to lose more from the dissolution of traditional social ties with the onset of industrial capitalism. Romantic love, for the heroines of many nineteenth-century novels, is a way of appropriating male sexual power through an identification with the object of desire, of participating, by proxy as it were, in the 'potency' of the acquisitive, aggressive, even violent, will, identified as masculine 'by nature'.[57] But such is the multiple construction of sexual love that it can coincidentally also seem, through the power of what one heroine, Lucy Snowe, will call '*being* loved', a means to reining in those very elements that threaten 'conscience'. The location of this threat is also the acquisitive male. To men, Sarah Ellis observed, 'belongs the potent – (I had almost said the *omnipotent*) consideration of worldly aggrandizement; and it is constantly misleading their steps, closing their ears against the voices of conscience, and beguiling them with the promise of peace, where peace was never found.'[58] Sexual love, in other words, offered to women the promise of a freedom and meaning not usually available to them, while at the same time fostering a sense of immense personal control over another, of new definitions of self which could fly above the constraints of gender difference, of the hope of a symbolic renewal of meaning lost from traditional economic relations and social order.

Havelock Ellis tells an anecdote in his *Studies in the Psychology of Sex* which naturalizes the relation between women and passion in our society:

> 'But when I am not in love I am nothing!' exclaimed a woman when reproached by a French magistrate for living with a thief. There are many women who could truly make the same statement, not many men. That emotion which, one is tempted to say, often unmans the man, makes the woman for the first time *truly herself*.[59]

Similarly, just as the Victorians envisaged man as somehow becoming 'human' through the restraint of his selfish sexuality, they believed that a woman must, in equally mysterious fashion, become *herself* only through the self-defining powers of romantic love. We are left to wonder exactly who she was before: by implication, someone quite self-less. Love filled the sexual space, the vacancy that a woman was, 'humanizing' her by recognizing a craving seen as sympathetic, if not quite legitimate.

The era from the mid-eighteenth century on, when the apparent opposition and secret alliance between sexuality and romantic love appeared most critical, was also the great era of the English novel. The works of Richardson, the Brontës and Eliot, which we now turn to, engage those questions that arose in the wake of this dilemma, both narrativizing irresolvable contradiction and representing specific strategies for being at once human and female. Haunting the nineteenth-century novel in particular is the need to discover a 'real' female self, which these authors see as an essence or identity ideally free of oppression, repression or social and economic restraint. Women begin in these novels (and begin writing novels) as 'unauthorized, illegitimate' objects of social discourse and must attain and prove themselves as speaking subjects through desire, in a historical context that does not want to hear the terms of such desire.[60]

In each case we are invited to consider sexual love as the mediator between the modern division of 'truth' and 'goodness', between the necessity for a social order requiring an essential, traditional womanhood and an individual freedom authorizing a self-created identity – between, in fact, female vacancy and female craving for meaning, power and definition. The yoking of the concepts of vacancy, which is the absence of self, the lack of wholeness and meaning for women, and of craving, the recognition of which provides the source and sense of self, the wellspring of intention and 'will', is what this study is about. Sexual love is, here, alternately, the hero(ine) and the villain of the piece.

3

The Light in the Cavern: Samuel Richardson and Sexual Love

> When a woman's sex is in itself dynamic and alive, then it is a power in itself, beyond her reason. And of itself it emits its peculiar spell, drawing men in the first delight of desire. And the woman has to protect herself, hide herself as much as possible. She veils herself in timidity and modesty, because her sex is a power in itself, exposing her to the desire of men...
> D.H. Lawrence, 'A Propos of *Lady Chatterly's Lover*', 1930

> From this elementary iconography may be derived the whole metaphysic of sexual differences – man aspires; woman has no other function but to exist, waiting.... Between her legs lies nothing but a zero, the sign for nothing, that only becomes something when the male principle fills it with meaning.
> Angela Carter, *The Sadeian Woman and the Ideology of Pornography*, 1978

Clarissa, as she tells her own story, was once woven of whole cloth: her public and private selves were one before the cloth was rent. After fleeing the scene of her rape, however, Clarissa speaks poignantly of a new self-perception, one she recognizes by naming it only after its loss. 'Once more have I escaped – but, alas! *I*, my *best self*, have not escaped!' she cries.[1] This 'best self' is her Virgin self, the enclosed and empty space of moral virtue, penetrated in the course of the novel by sexuality defined as male. Consequently, the character of Clarissa came to personify for many readers the vulnerable, the passive, the penetrable, the physically and socially powerless female figure.[2] She is characterized most frequently as a creature out of balance with her physical body, place and time, whose textual life consists in marking and reproaching that imbalance: an exemplar.

Clarissa's term 'best self', however, naturally implies its correlative, and her character, unlike that of most exemplars, possesses a divided selfhood. Along with the 'best self' there is also a secret Other, a nether Self if you will, dark and mysterious as a sealed cavern, which, with the force of its unspoken cravings, 'draws men on', to borrow from D.H. Lawrence. To tell a different story about Clarissa, we have only to see her as the agent of this force as well as (or even more than) of Lovelace, and Lovelace himself as likewise a victim of its hold on him. This, of course, is the story as Lovelace himself would tell it.[3]

To Lovelace, Clarissa is a sexual space, but above all an empty space, violable only in the absence of her consciousness. She is for him a gap whose boundaries are defined most clearly by an *absence* of will and selfhood; like a poem, Clarissa must not mean, but be. Yet, a true heroine, Clarissa's textual space is more than the sum of her sexual parts. For Clarissa, though an 'absence', is full of presence, discovering sex everywhere even while denying it bodily to her lover, eternally virginal yet signifying sexuality to all around her. To be 'dynamic and alive' in Lovelace's and D.H. Lawrence's sense is to come to full life only in the secret presence of desire, or to put it another way, in its apparent absence.

This mystification of a symbolic subject is hardly unique in literature: Lionel Trilling once pointed out that the idea of money in Western civilization exercises the fascination of an 'actual thing' that is 'both real and not real, like a spook. We invented money and we use it, yet we cannot either understand its laws or control its actions. It has a life of its own which it properly should not have...'[4] This same bewildering energy, conceived variously as the power to corrupt and destroy, or to reform and create, also belongs to the category of sexual love as it is presented in the English novel, beginning with Richardson. The focus of *Pamela* and *Clarissa* is on a deliberately narrowed and intensified sexual struggle, out of which arises a mystified historical and social conflict. Like that of money and materialism, to which it is inevitably related, the theme of the Virgin struggling against sexual love in the novels of Richardson and after is made to bear a heavy burden of meaning which forms one battle-line between imaginary categories marked as the individual and society, self and other, or human and animal.[5] The dark secret of the Richardsonian novel is not sexuality, but the salaciousness of gender difference.

In creating his novels, Richardson was able to draw on, and react against, an abundance of contemporary popular writing by women about the 'problem' of seduction. The first decades of the eighteenth century in Britain saw a surge of interest in exotic and stylized tales of erotic love, 'scandal novels' and amatory tales such as Mary Manley's *New Atlantis* (1709) and Eliza Haywood's *Love in Excess* (1719), which revolved around heroines, helpless, hapless and innocent, attacked and/or swept away by overpowering, sexually amoral men.[6] The stock figures of these early erotic tales nearly always included a corrupt and lustful aristocrat and a virgin whose continually heaving breasts betrayed the ripeness of unawakened passion within. Some ended in rape, but most were likely to include at the very least a successful seduction, in which the heroine yielded, as in Eliza Haywood's *Memoirs of a Certain Island Adjacent to the Kingdom of Utopia* (1725), out of 'absence of mind', 'excess of softness', or 'unknowing that she did'(!)[7] While both male and female protagonists in these proto-novels could be purely lascivious, it was women who were most often susceptible to the mysterious and irresistible 'force' of sexual love.

This treatment of sexual love legitimized first, the power of 'irrational' sexuality over reason, and second, the weakness of women, in whom 'virtue' resided only long enough to melt into the soft recesses of 'Nature'. The problematic relations of the sexual impulse to reason, of women to virtue, and of virtue to sexual love, were therefore themes not unique to the novels of Richardson,[8] but his originality in dealing with them was immediately recognized by his readers. For example, the setting of these early popular tales in exotic locales and distant, vaguely heroic times, a tradition which has persisted in the romantic and Gothic novel, contrasted sharply with the middle-class, here-and-now world of Richardson's works.[9] The exotic setting of popular fictions joins an identification with voluptuous sexual surrender to the comforting knowledge that the moral choices involved are at a safe distance. A contemporary review of *Clarissa* in 1749 stressed the revolutionary possibilities of combining imaginative, romantic themes with plausible characters: the power of *Clarissa*, said the reviewer, derives from its being the first romance to deal not with 'the illustrious actions of illustrious persons', but the private life of a character 'in the same situation as ourselves'.[10]

Richardson's strategy as a 'serious' novelist involved the restylizing of chastity in the novel. From a more or less open invitation to sexual or emotional stimulation, Richardson made use of that desire to dramatize sexual and social exploitation in a newly emerging commercial society. His heroine Pamela's repeated cry of 'I am honest!' signals her social and moral decency *as well as* literal virginity. Pamela uses the word consistently to mean chaste, an alternative definition which was becoming archaic even in Richardson's time.[11] But Mrs Jewkes tries to persuade Pamela that 'ne'er a lady in the land may live happier than you if you will [be Mr B.'s mistress], or be more honourably used', by which she means that Pamela would be well repaid for compromising her moral principles in the coin of material comfort.[12] The result is a complex literary world in which an anomalous personal passion exists in a fine tension with a network of 'ordinary' social rules and moral prudence.

In Richardson's day it was most unorthodox for a serious male author to focus an entire novel on the consciousness of a woman in love. Where moral choice was critical, even in the tradition of medieval courtly love, it had appeared almost exclusively in the context of male action. Diderot's famous eulogy to Richardson, that 'It is he who carries the torch to the depths of the cavern . . .' refers to the interiority and complexity of psychological motives that Diderot believed entered the novel with Richardson.[13] But the cavern is also the darkly unexplored and undefined recesses of a woman's sex, to which an 'enlightened' Richardson attempted to bring the clarity of reason and the coherence of Puritan morality. The difference between Richardson and his predecessors is that for the first time in the English novel the female voice is central: his heroines tell it themselves, quite wonderfully, so that the narration of a female consciousness and sensibility – the centrality of what Genette has called 'focalization' – constructs a potent illusion of a speaking female subject with authorized (in more than one sense) power.[14] The power that the heroine is granted, however, is part of what we may call the *gendering* of a problem: when and how desire may ever be valued in a world corrupted by unrestrained pursuit of private gratification, both bourgeois and aristocratic. It is her presence as representative of Woman in the text that provides both the problem and its solution.

In *Pamela* a 'realistic' social context for the problem of sexual conflict is established from the very first page. By contrast, in the amatory tales popular in the decades before Richardson wrote, the aristocratic cad preyed upon a female whose social position was usually left deliberately vague; it was enough to know that she was virtuous, and therefore helpless. Pamela's first letter, however, presents us with a young virgin of the servant class at a double remove from parent figures. She is literally at a distance from her parents, and then deprived of surrogate parental authority and protection by the death of her mistress.[15]

Yet Pamela does not encounter an openly hostile society, as does Richardson's later heroine Clarissa. Rather, she is surrounded by a degree of admiration and affection that David Copperfield or Maggie Tulliver might justly have envied. Her experience of modern society is limited to her master's two estates, just as her eye-opening experience of sexual exploitation is narrowed to the seduction attempts of this master, the attractive, egotistical and strong-willed Mr B. The chief irony of this situation is that according to the custom of the traditional community, the servant Pamela owes her upper-class employer a passive submission to his will, just as he owes her his benevolent protection.[16] It is extremely important to the ethos of *Pamela* that a mutually understood ideal of reciprocal obligations in a traditionally hierarchical social order is violated by the self-interested sexuality of one male.[17]

As we have seen, one of the ways in which materialistic social values in the eighteenth and nineteenth centuries affected women is that two choices of personal behaviour became defined as ideals beginning in this period. Women, especially those of the rising middle class, could either choose to identify with the attitudes towards acquisition and status of the more aggressive male by aspiring to the role of the fashionable Lady, or they could see themselves as making an individual, if largely fruitless, resistance to these values by asserting the 'power' of Moral Femininity and home. Though both *Pamela* and *Clarissa* are concerned with presenting the first literary definitions of such 'moral womanhood' and its connection to chastity, *Pamela* in particular also examines the question, 'What makes a lady?' in the hope that the two ideals could still be conjoined – and women could win dignity, respect and power both ways. One of the most striking characteristics of *Pamela* is the repeated suggestion that there exists a state of 'true' ladyhood which has nothing to do with birth or class and is distinguishable from a moneyed fashionability. In this respect Richardson decisively broke from the conventions of the many amatory tales in which the heroine is discovered to have been a lady by *birth* in disguise all along.

In Richardson's only published essay, which appeared in the *Rambler* in 1751, he deplored a 'change in the manners of women' who, no longer 'contented with domestic duties', aspired to the condition of ladyhood through marriage. He portrays these young women as given to 'idle amusements' in which 'forwardness', i.e. assertive egotism, prevails, and to frequenting the newly fashionable 'markets for women' to attract men.[18] Richardson especially disapproved of the emphasis on sexual attraction as a means for those ambitious girls

> in haste to make their fortunes, to catch their fish. . . . What shall become of the delicacy of the sex when a fair face and fine features, without any other merit, shall allowably push girls into public life, and declaredly with a view to captivate – to make prey, I should rather say – of the first man they shall think considerable enough to support them in their glare and vanity?[19]

The loosening of parental control over dowry and choice of spouse in the eighteenth century pushed those women who aspired to the ideal of the Lady into the aggressive, self-seeking behaviour conventionally associated with masculinity. *Pamela* keeps this double image before us of women's 'power' to evoke and limit desire – the sexually provocative would-be Lady versus sexually restraining Moral Femininity – by showing the heroine through two mirrors held up to her nature: those of her allies and her antagonists, especially the doubled housekeepers of official estate and hidden retreat, Mrs Jervis and Mrs Jewkes.[20]

Pamela can end happily because romantic love, presented without its component of self-seeking sexuality, functions to provide human benevolence as glue to a society increasingly rent by shifting and problematic power relations between classes and genders. Though *Pamela* demonstrates that the disruption of traditional communal values by uncontrolled male sexuality leads to the exploitation of virtuous (i.e. moral and feminine) women, it simultaneously underwrites another result of the unrestrained will and another kind of excess, the delightful irrationalities of romantic love. Thus sexual love for Richardson is founded on the power differentials of gender, while it is represented as the force that erases the evil consequences of dominance. In the end, social class, authority and sexual morality are threatened yet not divided in this first novel, though they show dangerous cracks in *Clarissa*.[21] Society, or a reformed corner of it, can still potentially be a 'palace', whereas for Clarissa only the kingdom of Heaven is the palace no longer possible on earth.

'Love is not a voluntary thing,' states Pamela firmly, if somewhat defensively, 'I know not *how* it came, nor *when* it began, but crept, crept it has, like a thief, upon me' (p. 260). Mr B. soon follows with *his* casting down of arms: 'In vain, my Pamela, do I find it to struggle against my affection for you'.[22] The personification of love as a thief implies the separation of the emotion from one's will, and thus from one's sense of self. 'Love' as an abstract, mystified force therefore represents an attractive solution to the dilemma of the moral soul which longs to enter the realm of experience and self-gratification while guarding against the aggressive incursions of others. For the ideology of romantic love holds that *involuntary* self-gratification can be unselfish, even reformatory, through the mutual act of trust that is the submission of each lover's will to the other. The result is a narrative of courtship, the transformation of the seducer/ seducee relation into quite another story: the story of a marriage.[23]

In *Pamela* the strength of Moral Femininity derives directly from the heroine's ability to poach emotionally on the preserve of the sexual aggressor, just as her greatest danger lies in her own susceptibility to emotion, i.e. the source of power is identical to its greatest threat. The resolution to this smoothly constructed paradox is that the ability to surrender to this 'weakness' (p. 260) is construed as a kind of strength in itself. Consequently, in *Pamela*, as contrasted to Richardson's later *Clarissa*, the unreliable bonds of society are in the end cancelled out by achieving a dyad of mutual protectiveness, a kind of 'moral economy' of two, in which the inequality of gender relations is tempered by the equal reciprocation of desire.

Pamela thus raises radical questions about the value of the rising ethos of self-interest in modern bourgeois society and its role in shaping gender, only to put them to bed again within the status quo. But though, like all romances, it resolves conflict within an idealized imaginary space, serving in this case to support a social ideology about women and sexuality, it also contains a disruptive subtext: women are powerful, their vacancy a sort of magic transformative container for social meaning, though women's desire is only as powerful as their limits on men's desire. One may speculate that *Pamela* appealed to female readers because it drew on a romantic fantasy with an uncommon heroine at its centre, one with the wit, dignity and strength to beat the class and gender systems, not merely because of the material rewards at its end. At this time, in that place, the message of *Pamela* was a revolutionary cry, a sense of the living presence of possibilities for women.

It is significant that *Clarissa*, Richardson's second novel, does not contain a model of ladyhood like Mr B.'s mother for its heroine to pattern herself after. The construction of a conflict between the ideals of Lady versus Moral Femininity and the problematics surrounding sexuality and love are once again the focus, but this time without a refuge in romance as a solution. In *Clarissa* Richardson explored similar questions of sexual morality and power, of distrust and acquisitive freedom, but his treatment of these themes contain a harsher indictment of eighteenth-century bourgeois society and the way in which it informed the gender identities of its members.

In addition, in *Clarissa* the heroine's home and family are no longer, as they were in *Pamela*, a stronghold of old-world morality and a shelter from sexual exploitation just out of the heroine's reach. On the contrary, Clarissa's relation to her family is carefully analysed so as to reveal the subtle complicity of its values with the sexual aggressor himself.

Clarissa begins, as *Pamela* does, with an evocation of a traditional community based ideally on bonds of mutual affection and obligation which is then violated by the selfishness of individual desire. But whereas Mr B. was the exception in Pamela's ordered community of bonds with mistress and parents, friends and fellow-servants, most of whom sympathized with her plight, Clarissa herself is shown to be an anomaly in a family whose ruling principle is narrow self-interest. As Clarissa reaches the age at which women become sexual property to trade on, she is pressured with increasing frenzy by her kin into a marriage based on neither sympathy nor respect nor sexual satisfaction, but only on the principle of family aggrandizement. Clarissa's indignant friend Anna Howe describes the bourgeois acquisitiveness of Clarissa's family as a kind of moral sickness from which Clarissa herself has somehow escaped:

> None of your family but yourself could be happy were they *not* rich. So let them fret on, grumble and grudge, and accumulate, and wondering what ails them that they have not happiness when they have riches, think the cause is want of more, and so go on heaping up till Death, as greedy an accumulator as themselves, gathers them into his garner.
>
> (I, pp. 41–2)

Just as Pamela countered the 'sinful pride of high estate' with her assertion that 'we were all on a foot originally' (p. 271), Clarissa, referring to her brother's ambition to gain estates and his hope 'that my own at least may revert to the family', similarly muses: 'And yet, in my opinion, the world is but one great family. Originally it was so. What then is this narrow selfishness that reigns in us, but relationship remembered against relationship forgot?' (I, p. 34). The context for the entrance of the sexual intruder Lovelace is Clarissa's growing realization that her brother acts not for 'the family' but for his own interests alone, whereas Clarissa conceives of humanity as 'one great family'. Her spiritual dwelling, in other words, is the home ruled by bonds of mutual affection and moral obligation in a society which is rapidly losing ground to the Lodging House of which Carlyle spoke in *Sartor Resartus*.

This sense of separation from her society makes Clarissa one of the first alienated heroines in the English novel. As Anna Howe remarks to her friend, 'What would you have of them? Do they not act in character? And to whom? To an alien. *You are not one of them*' (I, pp. 282–3, my italics). It is exactly at this point, when the authorities in Clarissa's world endorse the power-seeking and selfish possessiveness of Clarissa's suitor, Solmes, that the virgin is cut loose from the community and offered an alternative identity through sexual love.

The next part of the novel, after Clarissa runs away with Lovelace and before she is raped by him, is her (and our) education in the nature of sexual love. In order to make Lovelace, the tempter, as attractive as possible, Richardson makes very clear from the start that Lovelace has no other common flaws but an aggressive sexuality. An inquiry into his character by Clarissa's family reveals that he is a 'generous landlord', 'clear of the world' financially, and not overly fond of liquor – but a 'sad gentleman as to women' (I, pp. 16–17). He is as single-minded, unswerving and constantly lustful in his pursuit of Clarissa as if the rest of the world did not exist.[24]

Lovelace is a more dangerous opponent than Mr B. was to Pamela because the 'nature' of his sexuality is presented as aggression. The more Clarissa struggles in his grasp, the more her kin assert their authority, the more he is driven by his self-characterized 'triumph in subduing' (I, p. 172) for its own sake. Lovelace's sexuality is a mode of acquisition or consumption, as when he makes reference to his desire to 'devour' Clarissa's hand in the act of kissing it, or in his description of himself as a 'notorious womaneater' (II, p. 496).[25]

By establishing the basis of Lovelace's violent desire as a compulsive will to possess, Richardson makes a radical connection between male sexual energy and the selfish, ambitious acquisitiveness of the family Lovelace despises. To Lovelace, Clarissa's body is a commodity to be fought over, just as it is to her kin and to his arch-enemy, the suitor Solmes. Thus Clarissa is surrounded by men who view women's sexuality as synonymous with tradeable goods.[26]

The very language of male–female relations is appropriate to a society in which life is a struggle for power as moveable property. If Clarissa submits to the illicit attractions of sexual love she will, her sister informs her, be 'the *property* of an infamous rake' (II, p. 171). Yet, if she succeeds in forcing Lovelace to marry her, he will become, in her lover's words, 'rather *her* prize, than she his'. To the end, Lovelace never wavers in his overpowering interest in possession: after Clarissa's death he cries in the midst of his agony: 'Living and dying she is mine – and only mine. Have I not earned her dearly? Is not damnation likely to be the purchase to me?' (IV, p. 342).

Lovelace's mounting anger towards Clarissa's resistance has none of the playful tone of the 'angry' love-exchanges in *Pamela*. In the paradigmatic romance, the structures (and strictures) of the form ensure our knowledge that the trajectory of the narrative is towards a resolution of reward/recognition, encouraging the reader to view humiliation or aggression as a preliminary to that closure. But Lovelace, like Clarissa's family, uses his power over Clarissa's sexual fate to wage a war of humiliation which has become an end in itself. 'I must keep my anger alive,' Lovelace notes, 'lest it sink into compassion' (II, p. 514). We could almost say that where Mr B. melts, Lovelace hardens in attitude, until he is more concerned with Clarissa's submission *against her will* than with sexual pleasure itself. The theme of persistent humiliation so prominent in *Clarissa* constructs the sexual impulse as an assertion of the male self as pure 'will', which must penetrate, 'encroach' (to use Clarissa's word) and subdue another in order to exist; it is as if Lovelace must continually grow larger in power in order to threaten Clarissa or else melt into nothing at all.

When Lovelace snatches Clarissa's hand and presses it to his lips 'in a strange wild way' (II, p. 80), the English novel is introduced to the darkly attractive nihilistic passions, prefiguring the later fascination with the male lover who is 'wild', 'free' and 'strange', in the Brontës and beyond. In *Clarissa* and later novels, such as *Wuthering Heights*, the meaning of the 'strange and wild' male will can only be fully understood by its effect on a woman for whom desire is a problematic issue. Clarissa begins by rejecting an attitude of self-seeking; she refuses from the start to 'act like a lady' and seek aggrandizement of any sort in marriage or otherwise. At no time is she given the easy expedient provided for Pamela in the ideal of the 'true lady' who deserves her privileged position. Instead, she is forced to choose between Moral Femininity and the values of her sister Arabella, who demonstrates the false breeding and self-interested motives of the fashionable Lady. In *Clarissa* Moral Femininity could never be reconciled to the wry description that Mrs Thrale, the eighteenth-century memoirist, gave of her daughters:

> When all is said they are exceedingly valuable girls: beautiful in person, cultivated in understanding and well principled in religion ... wishing to raise their own family by connections with some more noble – and superior to every feeling of tenderness which might clog the wheels of ambition.[27]

While Clarissa's family attempts to bribe her with wealth and status into a fashionable marriage, Lovelace, on the other hand, tries for his own reasons to make Clarissa behave like a 'woman'. He cannot believe that she is not resisting him out of pride rather than principle, because in his experience of ladies, 'Pride is perhaps the principal bulwark of female virtue.' On this assumption, supported by conventional society, Lovelace follows with a crucial question: 'Is then the divine Clarissa capable of *loving* a man who she ought *not* to love? And is she capable of *affectation*? ... Must she not then be a *woman*?' (II, p. 38). The definition of femininity that Lovelace would force upon Clarissa is a cultural veneer of purity, all the better to mask the same principle of self-interest that is assumed to motivate all of humanity. Thus it is the ideological assumptions about 'human nature' underlying the burgeoning growth of the new social system which dictate the story of sexuality for each gender.

Yet if Clarissa's kin and lover have the same view of women as sharing men's ambitious nature (though covering it with 'affectation', and therefore without even the virtue of honesty), they also share a willingness to limit the female power to fulfil this ambition. Clarissa's parents play on her traditional obligation to obey her father, and would deprive her of the privilege of choice. Lovelace's relationship with Clarissa, on the other hand, is a caricature of conventional male–female relations: he wishes her to be in his power, 'lying under pecuniary obligations' (II, p. 67), yet she draws him on by her withheld sexuality and his unwilling emotional response to her – the last two being closely connected, of course.

Yet in her very rejection of fashionable Ladyhood in favour of a moral definition of femininity, Clarissa must exhibit an enormous strength in order to maintain her integrity in the face of superior power. Appearance and rhetoric to the contrary, she is neither passive nor weak, but tough with the strength of self-respect. In this she strongly anticipates Jane Eyre. 'I find', she asserts with self-assurance early in the novel, 'that they have all an absolute dependence upon what they suppose to be a meekness in my temper. But in this they may be mistaken, for I verily think, upon a strict examination of myself, that I have almost as much in me of my father's as of my mother's family' (I, p. 37). Nor is Clarissa above using performance and deception when it serves her purpose: like Pamela, she unabashedly describes her attempts to escape as 'cunning' and 'artful' (I, pp. 466, 467).

At times the boundary between self-respect and self-will seem thin indeed. Clarissa insists on infusing sexuality – and the rejection of sexuality – with a meaning of her own, in defiance of her lover, family and society. In this way her very refusal to assert her self-will leads to the passionate assertion of her moral will and the ambitious desire to impose her interpretations on others. 'Virtue thus becomes a spontaneous impulsion,' Mme de Staël was to write in 1800, 'a motive which passes into the blood, and which carries you along irresistibly like the most imperious passions.'[28]

Adding to the problematics of passion, which is both inimical to the moral life yet necessary for personal survival, is the allure of romantic love. It is one thing to oppose a Solmes or a Mrs Sinclair; it is quite another to place in this scheme a Lovelace, who prides himself on being, in contrast to Clarissa's family, above considerations of money or status. Lovelace, with his personal attractiveness and his frequent protestations of 'love', is a far more formidable adversary to Clarissa. It is interesting that in indignant response to the sentimental reaction of many readers to Lovelace, Richardson in later editions increased his brutality and lack of compassion, but never made him less physically attractive, charming, witty or courageous. Lovelace must be appealing because Clarissa cannot be entirely a victim: she must have desire, or there is no struggle. The compelling question, and one that is never rendered in clear terms as it was in *Pamela*, is whether romantic love has legitimate claims on the individual as an inevitable impulse of 'nature', or is merely another expression of illegitimate and anti-social desire.

On the one hand, Clarissa's adherence to traditional values of authority and self-sacrifice is so strict that her plight is materially worsened by her unwillingness to breech them; e.g. her rejection of Anna Howe's offer to run away, or her refusal to litigate against her father for her estate. On the other hand, Clarissa's unbending rejection of Solmes, her parents' choice of spouse, on the grounds of personal dislike only, presumes her equally strong belief in the right to pursue private happiness. 'Justice', writes her friend, Anna Howe, in her defence, 'is due to ourselves, as well as to everybody else' (I, p. 245).

One of the appeals of romantic love as ideology in the eighteenth and nineteenth centuries was that its values were in direct opposition to those of propertied marriage. But the point where duty ends and the right to private satisfaction begins is not so clear when Clarissa must go beyond a veto of her parents' selection to an insistence on independent choice based on personal preference alone. Lovelace himself slyly dissects his own attractiveness to women: 'If she call me *ungenerous*, I can call her *cruel*. The sex love to be called cruel. Many a time have I complained of cruelty, even in the act of yielding, because I knew it gratified the fair one's pride' (II, p. 102). Choosing a Lovelace, with his unusually forceful demands for the satisfaction of his individual desires, amounts to an identification with the power and aggression associated with men.

The difficult question of whether sexual love is a private right or a personal indulgence was usually obscured in popular literature by a conventional vocabulary of romantic impulse, which implied that agency was mysteriously obliterated in the special case of love. In the amatory tales of the early eighteenth century, the heroine often fell in love 'against her will', thereby avoiding entirely the problem of whether or not sexual love represented a yielding to pure self-interest. In *Love in Excess* (1719), for example, the novelist Eliza Haywood declares firmly, 'Love is what we can neither resist, expel nor even alleviate, if we should never so vigorously attempt it; and tho' some have boasted, "thus far will I yield and no farther," they have been convinced of the vanity of forming such Resolutions by the impossibility of keeping them.'[29]

Richardson's frequent reference to this subject reveals his deep concern with the religious view that sensual love could be resisted and overcome, in direct opposition to the romantic idea that it was subject only to its own laws which are above those of society, or the 'pretty idea' that 'real' love is unselfish by nature. In his letters and, to a lesser extent, in his novels, Richardson was at pains to locate self-gratification as the true source of sexual love, no matter how idealized. 'Do not all men and women pretend to this sort of love?' he wrote to his idealistically romantic friend, Miss Mulso, in 1751, '... And yet what means the person possessed, but to gratify self – or self and proposed company? Is a man who enters into a partnership to be regarded, who declares that his ardent thirst after accumulation is not for himself, for his own sake, but for his partner's, whom he loves better than himself?'[30]

It is interesting to compare this letter to a passage in Richardson's earliest printed work, *The Apprentice's Vade Mecum* (1733), in which he advises that a young man 'should *principally* pursue your own *Interest*, and prefer your*self* in all *lawful* Cases, to *everyone* else', as the proper attitude of a 'gentlemanlike' businessman.[31] *Enlightened* self-interest, within the bounds of legal propriety, appeared as the guiding principle to Richardson the prosperous printer in 1733. Yet the novelist Richardson who later connected the self-gratification of sexual love with the pursuit of self-interest in society in general was not so sure. Whereas the more worldly Anna Howe offers her friend the defence that 'it is no manner of argument that because you would not be in love, you therefore are not' (I, p. 49), Clarissa chooses instead to consider the moral implications of personal freedom: 'Those passions in our sex which we take no pains to subdue, may have one and the same source with those infinitely blacker passions which we used so often to condemn in the violent and headstrong of the other sex; and which may be only heightened in *them* by *custom*, and their *freer* education' (II, p. 236).

Richardson's technique is to engage our sympathetic identification with his heroine in her struggle for selfhood and freedom of choice against tyrannical parents who would mould her into the conventional ideal of womanhood in the first part of his narrative. The tone of the first part of the novel is imbued with the inalienable right to pursue one's own private good as a moral given: 'I *ought* not [to marry Solmes],' insists Clarissa. 'For surely, my dear, I should not give up to my brother's ambition the happiness of my future life' (I, p. 93).[32] Yet *Clarissa* is structured so that no sooner is this sympathy established than we are led to explore the hidden 'nature' of sexual love through the heroine's greater struggle with Lovelace, who is the incarnation of unbridled self-gratification. For the crux is that, as Lovelace himself assures us, 'An *acknowledged* love sanctifies every freedom; and one freedom begets another' (II, p. 102).

Too late, Clarissa is trapped by an increasing awareness that the fulfilment of the unfettered individual will often requires robbing others of *their* freedom. As the object of Lovelace's desire, Clarissa becomes, in her words, 'your prisoner, rather than a person free to choose for myself, or to say what I will *do* or *be*' (III, p. 266). Moreover, we are not allowed to forget that it is a young woman of the rising upper middle class, the first to embrace the ideology of economic individualism, who is thus systematically isolated and imprisoned. The sexual plight of the middle-class virgin, at once a privileged and constrained woman, provides a unique occasion for contesting the boundaries of the self and the legitimacy of its (sexual) impulses.

In the context of this struggle for position and power, we can see more clearly why there is a fascination with forcible confinement throughout the novel. Clarissa is successively trapped in a series of prisons: her room at home, a brothel in the midst of a crowded city, and finally, the jail to which she is confined before her death. In part the growing isolation of the heroine is a concrete representation of her radical estrangement from the values of her family, lover and society, the same attitude that was contained in Anna Howe's pronouncement, 'you are not one of them.' But the sexual obsession with purity and the punishment of the virginal inspirer of lust also invites the reader (and most of Richardson's admirers were women) to identify with the suffering and indignation of the victim, while simultaneously 'experiencing' the role of the aggressor. The Lovelace who is 'hardened', emotionally, sexually and morally, is thus perceived as if he were a *genderless* part of us all, a caricature of the 'human' desire for power and possession that can no longer be controlled by traditional social constraints because it is increasingly essential to the workings of modern society itself.

Writing to her sister, who had formerly accused her of wilfully encouraging Lovelace, Clarissa begs her to 'pity the humbled creature whose foolish heart you used to say you beheld through the thin veil of humility which covered it. . . . You penetrated my proud heart with the jealousy of an elder sister's eye' (III, pp. 206–7). After the rape, ultimate proof of Lovelace's motives, it is impossible for Clarissa to trust even her own concept of self. In her own words, she is 'no longer what I was in any one thing' (III, p. 205), as though in receiving his sexuality she had absorbed it and become it, taking on herself the despised character. In popular romances the heroine is often told by her lover that he has put his 'brand' on her: in the mythology of romantic love, the first is always best. If the first is also intolerable, there *is* no place, no life possible thereafter, except perhaps in the Hereafter.

Clarissa's death represents the judgment that the only purely consistent self is no-self. In the end she wills herself into a totally will-less state, engenders in herself a virginity so fierce that it nullifies the problems of human gender: she becomes, in other words, the *ultimate Moral Feminine*, finding transcendent presence through absence of desire, willing the denial of Will. She expires, dressed in 'virgin white', with her cheek on a motherly friend's bosom, 'saying ... she would delight herself in thinking she was in her mamma's arms' (IV, p. 332) – regressed to an infantile asexuality as she dies.[33] Clarissa's textual body asserts that sexual love confers meaning on a woman's life, but mainly by giving her the opportunity to reject it.

It is Clarissa who penetrates in the end, to Lovelace's heart and through the terrible silence of God who allowed her victimization, but only after the fact. 'There she lies, weltering in her blood!' cries Lovelace, 'Her death's wound have I given her! But she was a thief, an imposter, as well as a tormentor. She had stolen my pen' (III, p. 146). At the last, Clarissa steals the power of the pen/penis by becoming the Word. Like Catherine Earnshaw, she goes wilfully out to Silence, leaving behind only her haunting story.

Richardson's contribution to the theme of sexual love in the novel was his popularization of the Moral Feminine, combining to powerful effect the mystique of hidden female sexual power, the withholding of desire which signifies a woman's presence, with a deep concern for the social issues of his time. Because his readers are forced to enter this moral and social criticism through an obsessive focus on the problems of sexual love, we may say that Richardson was the first, but hardly the last great novelist to be, in V.S. Pritchett's words, 'mad about sex'.[34]

Beginning with Richardson, sexual love became a pivotal issue in the British novel, a fault-line locating the rising tension in modern culture between Christian self-restraint and capitalist market freedoms, political authority and the newer authority of the individual, old-world community and the interests of an ambitious and acquisitive class. The problem of sexuality was bound to increase in importance as these issues intensified in the industrializing nineteenth century, as the place of women became more controversial and the role of romantic love continued to ascend in private life. In *Pamela* and *Clarissa*, Richardson invented the terms of Moral Femininity in the English novel, not merely as a theme, but as an expression of a certain kind of relationship between the novel and society, a relation which promised both criticism and hope between the covers of one book.

Clarissa constitutes a lesson and a heritage for the novel: she must withhold sexual love to allow the survival of her selfhood, yet her very withdrawal drives the male ever wilder, until he destroys that 'best' self. In effect the very purity of Moral Femininity destroys itself in the end. But though Clarissa cannot win, she can triumph. Pamela is transmuted into a Lady, and is lost as an autonomous identity as she is reabsorbed into the traditionally hierarchical community, but Clarissa burns through the fire of sexuality altogether, past social bargains. As powerfully imagined women, both get what they want in the end through (rather than in spite of) their lack of power. And in the emblematic coffin of Clarissa, Lucy Snowe, Catherine Earnshaw and their spiritual kin of the nineteenth-century novel lay lurking, haunted and haunting, ready to walk.

4
Thornfield and 'The Dream to Repose on': *Jane Eyre*

> The paths of vice are sometimes strewed with roses, but then they are forever infamous for many a thorn.
> John Cleland, *Fanny Hill*, 1748

Though I have said that the meanings of desire cannot be separated out from historical context, the reader of Charlotte Brontë's novels must engage with fictional texts which present Desire precisely the opposite way. In *Jane Eyre*, Desire is originary to the search for a psychologically contained 'self' – one's own or other – powerful enough to fulfil or restrain it. For Charlotte Brontë both sexual love and the art of creating fiction itself are figured as 'dreaming', acts of imagination which represent virtual survival. 'The dream' is, in fact, almost the only resistance – the other is anger – against the condition of 'vacancy', the emptiness and smallness of the female self in a society in which there is no place for meaningful work or social gestures. Through the love she both espouses and exposes as a fiction, and the fictions she writes about sexual love, the very blankness of existence is transformed by the author: the 'vacancy' of womanhood becomes the creatively open, blank slate of the imagination, on which can take shape the story of what can be done with a woman's life.

In this sense sexual love to a Brontë heroine is an assertion of her mastery and strength, a felt power. Yet it also contains its own contradiction: it is represented as an overwhelming force in its own right, one which subordinates and contracts female identity to the strictures of social conventions of femininity. By casting Desire as a state of craving vacancy, a reification of the traditional idea of feminine absence and passivity, Brontë reconceptualizes sexual love as a 'power' which *must itself be resisted*.

In this and the following chapter, Charlotte Brontë's two best-known novels will be examined as an evolving attempt to represent, and by reaching towards an accommodation, resolve these contradictory positions, i.e. sexual love as both liberatory and oppressive. To do so, love must be presented fictionally and then re-presented as a fiction, which is to say first mystified and then clarified as an ideology. It is very important, therefore, that all Brontë's novels, as well as those of her sister Emily, begin with a realization of the conditions of oppression, the overwhelming estrangement of the heroine from her society as the one radical fact of her existence. But whereas novels about besieged young sexual innocents from *Clarissa* to *Tess of the D'Urbervilles* begin by depicting a stable, seemingly ideal social world, then slowly build an atmosphere of injustice, suspicion and danger caused by the unchecked male will marauding in virgin territory, the plots of Charlotte and Emily Brontë, by contrast, frequently begin with images of helpless, rebellious or suffering children in an oppressive adult world.

The children bereft of protective parents who appear in *Jane Eyre*, *Villette* and *Wuthering Heights* represent a sense of estrangement from the bonds of nurturing love, presaging the powerlessness, vulnerability and social injustice which are the conditions of falling in love for the heroines in these novels.[1] A sense of the loss of traditional community, with its ties of morality and economic interdependence, precedes the Brontë heroines' sojourn in the Carlylean Lodging House, that site of commercial, self-interested relations between humans, or more to the point, between men and women. Charlotte's heroines, especially, are literal Lodgers – either in homes where they are not at home, like the Gateshead of *Jane Eyre*, in boarding schools or in foreign lands. It is from this starting point – the inability to find a meaningful place in the social community – that the Brontë heroine is impelled to find an alternative home in sexual love.

The relationship of sexual love to the anger caused by the heroine's isolation from society is an especially complex one in Charlotte Brontë novels. Unlike the paradigm of Moral Femininity, with its saint-like resignation and calm, Jane Eyre, Lucy Snowe and Catherine Earnshaw are decidedly not 'sweet'. Matthew Arnold's famous characterization of Charlotte Brontë's writing as full of 'hunger, rebellion and rage', could equally well be applied to both Jane Eyre and Catherine Earnshaw, furious and rebelling from the first scene in which we are introduced to them, while Lucy Snowe's apparent calm is relentlessly dissected and found to be utterly false.

From 1835–7, Charlotte Brontë, in the adult world for the first time as a very young teacher at the girls' boarding school Roe Head, kept a remarkable journal in which she articulated that sense of estrangement from 'insipid' society which was to fill an important function in her novels.[2] Early in 1836 she notes that her ability to detach herself imaginatively from her surroundings sets her apart from the others at the school. When 'the school room is quiet' she can

> assume my own thoughts; my mind relaxes from the stretch on which it has been for the last 12 hours, and falls back onto the rest which nobody in this house knows but myself.... It is strange I cannot get used to the ongoings that surround me. I fulfil my duties strictly and well [but] it is the still small voice alone that comes to me at eventide... which takes up my spirit and engrosses all my living feelings, all my energies which are not merely mechanical.[3]

Similarly, in a letter from Charlotte Brontë to her very conventional best friend, she cries, '*I am not like you*', by which she means 'my thoughts, the dreams that absorb me, and the fiery imagination that at times eats me up, and makes me feel society, as it is, wretchedly insipid'. These are 'qualities which make me very miserable, some feelings you can have no participation in, that few, very few people in the world can at all understand... they burst out sometimes, and then those who see the explosion despise me.'[4] The heroines of her novels, it should be noted, are also not merely outside and superior to society, but also inadequate to it in some way. This difference is the permanent Byronic limp of the potential artist.

By the summer of 1836, Brontë's dreamy detachment reveals itself as a secret contempt for the stupid conventionality of the 'ladies' around her. After 'toiling for an hour with Miss Lester, Miss Marriott and Ellen Cook, striving to teach them the distinction between an article and a substantive', she explodes,

> Am I to spend all the best part of my life in this wretched bondage, forcibly suppressing my rage at the idleness, the apathy, and the hyperbolical and most asinine stupidity of these fat-headed oafs, and on compulsion assuming an air of kindness, patience and assiduity?[5]

She 'longs to write', but again and again a distinctly inferior reality intrudes: 'Miss W. came in with a plate of butter',[6] or 'the ladies were now come into the room to get their curl-papers';[7] when a 'dolt came up with a lesson', interrupting her fantasies, she writes, 'I thought I should have vomited . . .'[8]

The constant humiliation and rage that Charlotte Brontë recorded resulted from her secret sense of inner superiority and frustrated capabilities, combined with a strong suspicion of persecution: repeatedly, as the journal progresses, the others are 'talking about her',[9] or 'staring, gaping', while she is lost in the 'divine unseen land of thought'.[10] As Charlotte admitted in a letter of 1836, 'things that nobody else cares for enter into my mind and rankle there like venom'.[11] Yet the scorn she evinced towards the 'ladies' was often mixed with a covert envy of their smooth air of assurance and strength of self-will. Her own sense of social incompetence only added to her humiliation and led her to the admission in a letter to Ellen Nussey that 'I have a constant tendency to scorn people who are far better than I am.'[12]

In Brontë's journal we can see the development of the persona of the Lodger, the female boarder, as it takes on its characteristic elements: the feelings of secret superiority to and contempt of others, the rejection by others in turn, the consequent humiliating necessity for mask and disguise: 'It is the living in other people's houses – the estrangement from one's real character – the adoption of a cold frigid apathetic exterior that is painful,'[13] she writes of her experience as a governess in 1841. The idea that there is a self more 'real' than the social persona was extremely important to her and would pervade both Charlotte and Emily's work. This 'real' identity is conceived as an experiential self, living deeply 'inside' superficial physiognomy or determinate social behaviours and yet 'outside' the conditions of oppression: the self that experiences Desire.

Just as she had *assumed* an air of kindness and patience' at Roe Head, the estranged heroine is shut out from ordinary 'feminine' virtues and must act a role continually. The 'real character' of which Charlotte spoke does not – *cannot* – fit either of the prescribed conventional roles for women: she is *neither* the type of Moral Femininity – passively self-denying, kind, pious and patient – nor successful in the role of the cold but socially adept Lady.

More and more in Charlotte Brontë's journal, the so-called 'real' self exists only in her inward capacity to plunge with dizzying boldness into the empirically *unreal*, to connect with the buried imaginative life she had fashioned as a bulwark against her estrangement. Eventually Charlotte herself feared that the increasing reliance of her 'real' self on the inner life for its identity was becoming a source of further social isolation. In 1839, when she made a conscious decision to abandon the melodramatic fantasies which had grown to 'a system strange as some religious creed',[14] she noted that she felt 'as if I stood on the threshold of a home and were bidding farewell', while the concrete world of which she intended to write was 'a distant country where every face was unknown'.[15] The *literal* search for a home in this 'distant country' was, of course, to become the theme of her two best novels, which were to use the materials of her 'dream world', an imaginative social order which was a projection of this internal 'real' self, integrated with the demands of novel-writing in the actual social world of mid-Victorian England.

Yet Brontë's heroines are not conventional orphan-victims who will make good and enter the society from which they were excluded, after teaching it or being taught a lesson or two. They are not, in other words, either alternative forms of Dickens' Oliver Twist or Pip with the gender reversed, nor even a nineteenth-century version of Richardson's Pamela, but are, in some elemental sense, *different* from others of both genders – at once superior and inadequate to the role of Lady to which every woman around them aspires, both forcibly excluded and deliberately aloof from the solid rewards of conventional society. The innovative mysteriousness of a Charlotte Brontë heroine is that though there is so much more to her than meets the eye, in terms of her imaginative and emotional capacities, there is virtually no bodily self to speak of. So often is she described as small, thin and plain, that the heroine seems about to disappear entirely, were it not for the enormous strength of her desire and imagination.

Charlotte's adolescent writings already reveal the imaginative fusion of sexual and social metaphors that is characteristic in her major novels, where her rendering of 'sympathy', for example, acquires ever-widening circles of emotional, social and moral connotation. The juvenilia are wonderfully lurid: in 'Caroline Vernon', for example, one of the last of the early novelettes, and probably written soon after the Roe Head journal in 1838 or 1839, we may see how the primitive armature of a love-fantasy provided the material for tying together Charlotte's concerns with artistic superiority and female humiliation, identity, will and self-interest, albeit in immature and rough form. Caroline Vernon, the heroine, small in size like Charlotte herself, is nobly born: 'distinguished', 'patrician', 'ladylike' by nature. Yet she is not a conventional Lady: like the Brontë persona of the journal, 'something might remain behind which she did not choose to tell or even to hint at ... she'd sensations somewhere that were stronger than fancy or romance.' Caroline is different from the start by virtue of this mysteriousness, her superior capacity for feeling and her strong will, which is signalled by 'impetuousness of manner'.[16]

When the tale begins, Caroline's father has come to release her from the virtual captivity in which he had placed her, 'where she had been reared like a bird'. In Brontë's later novels the caged bird image comes to represent an important conflict between the prison of feminine selflessness and the demands of the desiring will. When Caroline, the bird poised for flight, is told about the romantic, 'powerful' Zamorna, with his 'vicious, passionate past', and his 'feelings stronger than his reason' (p. 323), the pattern is set for the wild, strong father-figure to arouse great feeling in the young girl seeking her 'real' self.[17] The man who will fill the vacancy that craves is also 'different' and unconventional. In fact, Caroline almost seems attracted to him for what he is *not*. Like Rochester, he does *not* appear 'good, kind or cheerful'; like M. Paul, he is neither witty nor 'complimentary' (p. 337).

Unlike Jane Eyre or Lucy Snowe, however, Caroline Vernon acts purely because 'her Will urged it' (p. 341); her feeling for Zamorna is said to be 'restless' and 'devouring' (p. 349). Sexual love is frankly depicted as a form of the aggrandizement of the devouring will, devoid of the altruism of Jane Eyre's love for Rochester or the intellectual admiration of Lucy Snowe's for M. Paul.[18] The passionate nature of this love story seems to derive from its strongly familial setting. Caroline 'wished her sister [Zamorna's wife] dead and herself his wife' (p. 349), while her own father, angered by their affair, wishes Zamorna a 'withered hand and foot' (p. 357), in an interesting anticipation of Rochester's fate.

Here, then, in very rough and juvenile form, is the love-myth of Charlotte Brontë's later novels, with one notable distinction: its entire lack of concern with questions of morality. Caroline Vernon does not judge; she has no conscience. There are no moral issues in the imaginary Angrian world of Charlotte's apprenticeship because there is no society, only pure passion and will thwarted or fulfilled, whereas in actual society, as Charlotte perceived it, passionate feeling was castigated, while moral restraint was not necessarily rewarded. Conversely, the 'strong will', while clearly the only means for the uprooted individual to survive, had to be hidden behind the mask of feminine passivity at all costs. We recall that at the formative time of her apprenticeship writing, Charlotte began with a negative definition of self: 'I am *not like you*', i.e. *not* calm, restrained, 'moral', passive – or conventional.

In her novels, Charlotte attempted to forge a heroine of the negative materials of this estrangement of the so-called 'real' self from social recognition or power. Emptied of definition, the female outsider will successively try on all the roles available to women: the wilful Lady, the Moral Feminine who renounces her own will, child/mother, pupil/teacher, slave/mistress/wife. The novels rise above these sentimental models because they evolve into the means through which to re-evaluate social definitions of womanhood by imagining a strong female selfhood capable of uniting desire, power and morality.

In only the second paragraph of the novel, Jane draws the reader's attention to her 'physical inferiority' (p. 39) to these proto-gentlemen and ladies, her young cousins. This very plainness is symbolic of her utter unfitness for conventional Ladyhood. Nor can Jane be successful in the role of submissive femininity: her aunt finds her repugnant precisely because of her strong will. In sum, Jane Eyre at Gateshead is 'not one of them', as was said of Richardson's Clarissa, the outsider in her family. 'I was a discord in Gateshead Hall,' she tells us, 'I was like nobody there.'[19]

The same 'no-win' attitude dominates the emotional worlds of the early family scenes in both *Clarissa* and *Jane Eyre*. Just as Clarissa's attempts to propitiate her mother cause her further rejection on the grounds of hypocrisy, Jane's very act of questioning why she has been excluded from fireside and family love becomes further proof of *her* unworthiness to be loved because of an unbecoming forwardness. Yet Jane contends at all costs against putting on a pretence of resignation, which represents to her literal self-obliteration. Imprisoned in this vicious circle, Jane sees that asserting the will which is the only means to survival causes her oppressors, as it did Clarissa's, to wilfully misinterpret her as a monster of self-interest, a projection in fact of themselves.

In such a home, only lying, role-playing and calculating would overcome Jane's reputation for dishonesty. The double point of view of this section – the Jane as others see her as opposed to the person she thinks she is – establishes the particular nature of Jane's estrangement in this novel. Jane's tenacious clinging to a belief in a 'real' self, lying dormant until 'discovered', i.e. affirmed, by others, is her chief strength. This kernel of elemental self, protected from social oppression, is kept alive for Jane only by the sheer heat of her anger. When Mrs Reed judges her 'not worthy of notice' (p. 59), Jane's sudden reckless cry of protest, 'They are not fit to associate with me', emerges 'without her will consenting', from a voice over which she 'has no control' (p. 60). So important is Jane's passionate anger to her sense of selfhood that when she next engaged in a violent argument with Mrs Reed, 'shaking from head to foot, thrilled with ungovernable excitement' (p. 68), her soul is said to 'expand, to exult' (p. 69), as it later does in sexual exaltation. Anger, like sexuality, is viewed as an expression of the necessary will to individuation; yet like sexual love, it is also dangerous to a self conceived as an essential nature, prior to the creation of others or the pressures of the social order. Both anger and sexual love consume and eventually obliterate the will because they are 'ungovernable' once let loose (as Jane is said to be by Mrs Reed), and therefore self-devouring if not imprisoned.[20]

In this plight, her schoolmate Helen Burns' potent calm under suffering is meant to offer an alternative point of view to Jane, but it is a stance that is presented as highly problematic. Helen's is the role of Moral Femininity, which seems to create a self-contained meaning and humanness by an individual spirit of submission in a haven apart from the self-seeking ethos of society. By contrast to Jane, Helen flies in the face of power and its ethos of self-interest by her saint-like trust in goodness. Her absolute rejection of anger, like Jane's submission to it, is considered a rebellion in itself: thus, when Helen calmly allows herself to be unjustly whipped, the cruel Miss Scatchard is doubly infuriated and calls her 'a hardened girl' (p. 86).

Helen's creed of universal forgiveness and salvation makes the universe, and even death, a 'mighty home' (p. 91) for her so that she can bear the world's evil. But neither she nor the kind Miss Temple, who spreads goodness by small acts of personal benevolence, are the models of behaviour for Jane that some critics have contended.[21] In part this is because neither can be ultimately effective, since Miss Temple's power in the school community is very limited and Helen, though armed with a coherent vision of selfhood, is soon literally extinguished as an individual amidst the oppression and deprivation against which she struggles. More importantly, this critical portion of the novel, while sympathetic to Helen as an individual, at the same time bitterly parodies the very concept of self-denial as a useful social or ethical category and reveals it as potentially self-interested through the character of Mr Brocklehurst and the principles of Lowood School.

While accompanied by overdressed and pampered ladies, Mr Brocklehurst expostulates on the virtue of allowing as little food, clothing and pleasure as possible in order to 'mortify in these girls the lusts of the flesh' (p. 96). Again and again, the dignity of the individual and of physical need is asserted in this part of the novel, as is the absolute necessity for human love. While Helen wins their rhetorical argument with the conventionally religious speech that begins, ' "Hush Jane! you think too much of the love of human beings" ', her success in calming Jane's turbulent emotion is quickly undercut by a surprising qualification. 'In the tranquillity she imparted,' notes Jane, 'there was an alloy of inexpressible sadness' (p. 100). It is significant that Jane questions Helen's religious beliefs virtually until the latter's death; she never verbally accepts them. What Jane most seems to absorb from Helen and Miss Temple is the nourishment of their affection, and the importance of an *appearance* of feminine calm.

When we next see Jane, she is on the verge of womanhood and still seeking 'liberty', which is the release of the imprisoned 'real' self into the social world. From the beginning of Jane's experience at Thornfield, where she takes up her new role of governess, the doubleness of Jane's character is emphasized.[22] As she herself advises us when she has arrived at her destination, 'Reader, though I *look* comfortably accommodated, I am not very tranquil in my *mind*' (p. 125, my italics).

Thornfield itself is a place of the imagination, an old Gothic mansion, whose name derives from its 'mighty old thorn trees, strong, knotty, and broad' (p. 131); this image is a wonderfully connotative fusion of masculine sexual energy and imaginative power. When Jane meets Rochester, her new master, on the road, he is 'puzzled to decide what I was' (p. 146). Through Rochester, in other words, we are able to see Jane as a self not yet generated (or even, given the use of 'what' instead of 'who', gendered). The heart of the matter (so to speak) has been reached: the reader is observing Brontë in the act of creating a male character who, as the product of her own imagination, will empower her to do what imagining itself is a trope for: the creation of a female identity out of sheer desire.[23] Jane begins to live as a woman because Rochester does not know how to fix and imprison her in a social context. She is nameless, new, unformed, not yet placed in a genre: is she the Rose among the Thorns, the romantic heroine she feels she could be, or the plain, calm, romance-debunking 'servant' she is at pains to appear to be? Does she, in other words, both literally and metaphorically, belong to Thornfield or not?

Rochester himself is described by the narrator again and again, as though Charlotte Brontë were struggling to pin down the exact qualities which will do their work on the as yet unexpressed 'real' self of Jane Eyre. We are told he is like a 'mass of crag' or 'a great oak' (p. 143); 'dark, strong and stern' (p. 147), like God the Father, but 'cynical' and 'self-willed' (p. 174). His eyes are 'irate and piercing' (p. 152), his features are 'all energy, decision, will', his look one of 'genuine power' (p. 204). The strength of desire and will which is the primary characteristic of Rochester's 'masculine' sexuality calls to mind the image of the thorn trees surrounding the mansion, in which physical size and 'might' evoke imaginative and sexual power.

Even before Rochester appears on the scene, Jane was told that he is 'peculiar' by the down-to-earth housekeeper, who has only a vague sense that 'you cannot always be sure whether he is in jest or earnest, whether he is pleased or the contrary: you don't thoroughly understand him in short' (p. 136). It is absolutely essential to Rochester's sexual attractiveness that he is moody, hard to 'read', an intensely private and convoluted hero who presents no surface smoothness or conventional blandness on which to depend: he constitutes a secret. Like the thorn trees on his property, he is, we may say, knotted; in his own characterization, he is 'hard and tough like an india rubber ball; pervious, though, through a chink or two still' (p. 163). Rochester is penetrable: There is a private, even a 'female' entrance to this secret, available to the adventurer willing to undertake the risk of enduring the full power of masculine sexuality. And Jane, as we know, is ready for 'vividness'.

At their first meeting, Jane is 'set at her ease' (p. 145) by Rochester's physical ugliness, ill-humour and total lack of gallantry. They are the emblems of his own estrangement from conventional society: under no other circumstances could she trust him. Jane feels 'no fear' (p. 145) of the angry, frowning Rochester because no *conventional* romance seems possible under such conditions.[24] If the stranger is not playing the Gentleman, Jane feels no challenge to rise to the role of the Lady. Whereas the conventional Lady would see the polite formalities of society as a protection from unwarranted sexual intimacy, this vulnerable and guarded heroine presents them as hypocritical pretexts for self-interest and exploitation.

Though a good deal of their early conversations turn on the theme of hierarchy and power – his 'claim to superiority' and 'right to be a little masterful' (note the qualifier) versus Jane's status as 'a paid subordinate' (p. 165) – this parody of the customary master/servant relation is itself part of the sexual game. Here the issue is introduced early in order to declaw the potentially dangerous difference in class power; it is exposed as a joke rather than as part of the sexual appeal of the situation. Similarly, Rochester's irrational ill-humour parallels the attitude of the Reeds towards Jane as a child, but the anger is here reduced to the delicious tyranny of love, rendered innocuous by the promise of a 'real' kindness underneath. Yet it is this promise of kindness, this hope of a relation of trust, which the next part of *Jane Eyre* proposes to examine. In the love relation of Jane and Rochester we will see the hope and promise of sexual love stripped away to reveal the dangers, as well as pleasures, of individual gratification in a self-interested society.

Jane recognizes that she is in love when she feels understood: Rochester, she says, can 'dive into her eyes' (p. 164), 'read [her] glance' (p. 166) and 'interpret its language' (p. 167). She is named and therefore created in a new private social order: 'I felt at times as if he were my relation rather than my master . . . [so] that I ceased to pine after kindred. . . . The blanks of existence were filled up; my bodily health improved; I gathered flesh and strength' (p. 177). She willingly becomes Rochester's 'diary' (p. 167), and believes she 'understands the language of his countenance and movements' because she is 'akin' to him, 'assimilated' (p. 204) to him.

In identifying with the assertive will and defiant individualism of the male who can act on desire, Jane's 'real self', constituted by the desire confined behind a conventional representation of calm, is released like the bird from the cage in which Rochester imagines her: were the 'restless, resolute captive' but free, he says, 'it would soar cloud-high' (p. 170). Not least important for Jane's sense of selfhood is the opportunity for aggression conferred by her 'assimilation' with her masculine counterpart. But like the tyranny of Jane's oppressors, the quality of Jane's own aggression has been altered by the corrective of love. The uncontrollable and impotent rage of Jane's childhood is replaced with Jane's metaphorically 'stick[ing] a sly penknife under my ear' (p. 162), as Rochester laughingly complains, and keeping her lover at bay with this 'needle of repartee'

(p. 301). The impotent anger that was a problem in childhood is thus reduced to a part of coy sex-play: role-playing phallic self-assertion *and* feminine submission 'by turns', as Jane knows 'the pleasure of vexing and soothing by turns' (p. 187), trying her skill in argument by keeping Rochester on the verge of retaliation.

During the period of the growth of her love for Rochester, Jane is also given the opportunity to define herself partly through comparison with other women. In Blanche Ingram, the Lady as Bitch, Jane observes female self-assertion in the service of self-interest: 'I must have my will' (p. 221), cries Blanche coldly and imperiously. Significantly, the only wedding Blanche can have with Rochester is in the form of charades, the game in which one assumes another's identity. Blanche has no 'real' female self, because her 'will' is not dictated by the uncontrollable emotions of sexual love.

Jane's visit to Gateshead with her now grown cousins, Eliza and Georgiana Reed, frames a contrast between the two which is still more significant to Jane in defining herself as a woman who spurns the ideal of Ladyhood. The younger of Jane's former oppressors, Georgiana, who was always the beauty, has become 'weak, puffy and useless', existing to be stylish, enter society and marry a 'prospect' (p. 264); the sight of her 'full-blown' figure 'fallen asleep on the sofa over the perusal of a novel' (p. 265) is a comic portrait of vapid and self-indulgent Ladyhood.

Eliza, on the other hand, is the type of Moral Femininity gone wild: she would 'seek a retirement where punctual habits would be permanently secured from disturbance, and place safe barriers between herself and a frivolous world' (p. 263). Eliza takes Moral Femininity to its logical extreme – namely, to a nunnery, where she will 'take the veil' (p. 270). Whereas the Moral Feminine restrains her sexual feelings, Eliza rejects the importance of feeling entirely; and whereas the ideal of Moral Femininity seeks to inspire order in a chaotic moral world by renunciation, Eliza seeks a rigid celibacy out of a desire for selfish isolation, which she calls being 'independent of all efforts, and all wills, but your own' (p. 264). Eliza's is a type of isolation from society which Jane inevitably must compare unfavourably to the sympathetic communion of lovers, who at least live with and for the other. If Georgiana is the super-feminine, '*craving*, whining and idling' (p. 264, my italics), Eliza represents the dangers of frigid self-control, where celibacy is another name for self-will.

Jane Eyre builds, then, through the invocation of *Bildungsroman* and the emphasis on the search for a positive female identity, to an apparent assertion of the innate, lawful power and dignity of sexual love. The argument from nature – that the 'natural' self, with its necessary urges, should be the 'real' self – underlies Rochester's pronouncement to Jane, that 'I think you will be natural with me, as I find it impossible to be conventional with you' (p. 170). Similarly, to think of Rochester as only her 'paymaster' would be, according to Jane, 'blasphemy against nature' (p. 204); passion sets the natural at war with the merely commercial, the relation of trust with the relation of self-interest.

Consequently, when Rochester proposes marriage to Jane, the 'nightingale's song', the song of passionate love, 'was then the only voice of the hour' (p. 282). Jane, formerly the caged bird, is now happy in her imprisonment. But the freedom conferred by the release of a confined sexuality proves a deception, just as the power of the individual lover is qualified by the submergence of the lover's will into the beloved's. Rochester's features are 'full of an interest, an influence that quite mastered me', says Jane, 'that *took my feelings from my own power and fettered them in his*' (p. 204, my italics). Particularly for a woman, presumed to own the weaker will, 'real' passion is constructed as involuntary – 'I *must* love him' (p. 204, my italics), declares Jane. It is in this sense only 'a new servitude', like her work.

Jane has experienced two self-defining aspects of sexual love: one is a wish for a father-like figure who will punish and master with cruelty, render one will-less, swallow one's identity up, and the other a kind of mother-longing, in which the lover creates, nurtures and props the self with kindness, so that one can 'repose on what I trust'.[25] Such trust is the final hedge against the heroine's life-long loneliness. But the protection of Rochester's love requires, as Jane will find, the absolute dependence of a child, an image which will recur with new significance.

Rochester's 'kindness', in which she trusts, proves oppressively paternalistic. Just as his tyranny was sexually provocative rather than threatening because it was based on loving desire, the 'power' to make 'unheard-of-rules' (p. 169) – i.e. to make Jane his mistress – should be his, according to Rochester's dictum, because it too is based on right motives, 'to guard, cherish and solace her' (p. 284). His passionate pronouncement to Jane, ' "Let it be right" ' (p. 169), stands alongside the argument from nature as the credo for self-gratification and the importance of individual desire.

Once again, Jane's identity is revealed as unstable and fluctuating as she is forced to try on one of the roles available to women with her 'new name'. To her dismay, Rochester, in his 'kindness', attempts to mould her into a Lady, 'dressed like a doll' (p. 297), on whom he may bestow jewels and lavish money. During their engagement she is variously called a fairy, a 'peer's daughter', or an angel, all of which she deflates, Pamela-like, with the self-deprecating remark, '"Don't address me as if I were a beauty; I am your plain, Quakerish governess"' (p. 287). But Jane perceives her new status as a fall from the dignity of honest self-employment to the dependence of the Lady who parasitically feeds from the material wealth of her host. The reality of the Lady is that she is a well-kept courtesan, 'slave' of a fond sultan.

As Jane finds herself losing 'the sense of power over him' (p. 294), the restraining influence which is the essence of Moral Femininity, she again takes up the weapon of sarcasm which served her during their first encounters as both sexual defence and allure. But she now has a new enemy: her own desire for the submergence of her self, as Rochester becomes to her 'my whole world; and more than the world; almost my hope of heaven' (p. 302). Whereas the heroines of *Pamela* and *Clarissa*, or numerous Gothic novels, were literally imprisoned by their lovers, Jane Eyre has stepped willingly into the prison of love, and will pay the price of further diminishment.[26]

Dressed for her wedding morning, Jane is forced literally to look her own departure from her 'real' self in the face: the mirror reflects only 'a robed and veiled figure, so unlike my usual self that it seemed almost the image of a stranger' (p. 315). Exactly who is this 'stranger'? Significantly, Jane has recounted to Rochester, the day before, disturbing dreams in which she is on an 'unknown road' or in the 'dreary ruin' of Thornfield Hall, 'burdened with the charge of a little child' (pp. 309–10), which shivers and wails as she half attempts to comfort it, half wishes to lay the burden down. The symbology of this pining, protesting child has naturally been the subject of a good deal of critical speculation.[27] Yet all along, one of the most vibrant metaphors animating the novel is that of a dependent, powerless child set against a selfish but powerful woman. Repeatedly, we are told that Jane, who even in maturity looks 'almost like a child' (p. 453), is attractive to Rochester partly *because* he perceives her as vulnerable and childlike.

Rochester is attracted, not only to Jane's dependence on him, but also to the uncorrupted integrity associated with her pre-sexual self. Jane, on the threshold of consummation of a highly sexual love, carries the burden of this helpless yet necessary childishness in her role as the Moral Feminine. She must, she believes, be childishly innocent in order to counteract the immoderation of Rochester's own sexuality. Moreover, Jane has been asked to abandon this unresolved identity for the role of the Lady, who is also dependent, like a child, but with disturbing overtones of the wilful self-seeking inherent in sexuality. Caught between these two roles or definitions of self – the childishly 'helpless', i.e. ineffectual, Moral Feminine, and the forceful but self-willed Lady – Jane has become a stranger to the 'real' sexual self she thought she had just discovered.

In the catastrophe that follows, the promise of sexual love to create a viable identity will prove to be a 'mere dream', as Jane prophetically terms her lover, despite the solidity of the 'rounded, muscular and vigorous hand' and 'long, strong arm' (p. 307), he laughingly – and provocatively – holds before her. The strength in that masculine hand is not nurturing as Jane has hoped, but potently destructive, like the secret strength of Rochester's mad wife, Bertha, the hidden impediment to their marriage, whose fiery rampages follow each mention of Jane's wailing-child dreams. Bertha, 'savage' like Rochester's look when he proposes, is the dark self of *both* Jane and Rochester. In the 'vampire'-like Bertha, the lust for aggrandizement, whether for material or sexual acquisitions, is horribly revealed as the corollary of the desire for self-creation.

Jane's abortive false marriage has removed the pretext which conveniently prevented her from confronting the central problem she has avoided: how to create a strong female identity in an oppressive social world. She can no longer be a Lady, thereby merging the components of sexuality, ennobling romantic love and social respectability in one legally and morally sanctioned union. Her alternatives are now bifurcated into a Victorian woman's other essential roles: as Rochester's mistress, she may become the purely sexual being she has thus far denied and evaded, or by leaving him entirely, she may choose to create meaning through the self-sacrifice of the Moral Feminine.

In her last turbulent scene with Rochester, Jane is the bird in the cage again, as Rochester sees in her eyes a 'resolute, wild, free thing looking out of it'. But the cage is now self-protective and of her own making: '"Whatever I do with its cage,"' groans Rochester, '"I cannot get at it"' (p. 344). Passion has moved her as its passive victim, and Jane sees that her only chance of selfhood lies in opposing

Rochester's 'frenzy' and 'wild licence' with her own inward power. But although she is now 'honest', she is not at all certain what she is 'free' to do. She and Rochester do not speak the same moral language; therefore, Jane has become once more the Lodger, the inarticulate stranger in a foreign land. Having left Thornfield, wandering without money or connections of any sort, Jane is also the helpless and starving child of her dream, a nightmare repetition of her own childhood state.

In the passages which describe Jane's homeless wanderings, we are aware of a community all around which is closed to her. This exclusion is all the more poignant to Jane because she is conscious, as she says, of 'having no claim to ask – no right to expect interest in my isolated lot' (p. 354). In an era when individual charitable solutions to social problems were popular, Jane affirms the true ethic of a commercial society: 'As to the woman who would not take my handkerchief in exchange for the bread, why, she was right, if the offer appeared to her sinister or the exchange unprofitable' (p. 355). The mistrust Jane has learned from her encounter with sexual love is writ large in society as a whole, where it is only necessary and proper precaution to be suspicious of the Lodger who comes and goes in one's Lodging House.

Familial adoption becomes Jane's mediated state between the utter estrangement from an unnatural/impersonal society and the perilous ecstasy of belonging in a bond of sexual love with a man. It is St John Rivers, the clergyman she meets at the cultured home into which she is adopted, who becomes the means through which Jane will complete her search for self-definition.[28] He does so by harking back to an earlier stage in Jane's quest, her struggle against Mr Brocklehurst, another clergyman whose rigid ethic of anti-sensualism and renunciation enforces the self-sacrificing values of Moral Femininity.

St John, a devout Christian like Helen Burns, the Angel in the boarding school, castigates Jane, as she did, because 'human affections and sympathies have a most powerful hold on you' (p. 382); like Helen's, his message of conscious renunciation of passion and self-will leaves Jane with 'an inexpressible sadness' (p. 378).[29] But there the resemblance ends. While both Helen and St John resolutely control their own strong wills, Jane senses that the core of St John's passionate renunciation of passion is another kind of urge towards gratification: 'It seemed to me ... that the eloquence to which I had been listening had sprung from a depth where lay turbid dregs of disappointment, where moved troubling impulses of insatiate yearning and disquieting aspirations' (p. 378). In his ambitious will and repressed 'impulses', in his 'restlessness' and need to fulfil special 'faculties' (p. 382), St John clearly resembles an aspect of Jane herself, pacing passionate and restless for 'a new servitude' in her chamber at Lowood.

The servitude St John chooses, however, is not the service of romantic love, but like Jane's convent-entering cousin Eliza's, a logical extension of the values of Moral Femininity into the foreign arena of the 'primitive': a life of personal renunciation spent morally influencing and restraining passionate natives as a missionary. Like Eliza Reed, St John would purposefully isolate himself from 'human affections', because he is incapable of seeing earthly love in any terms but the carnal, a 'mere fever of the flesh' (p. 400), as he calls his feelings for Miss Oliver. St John is like a 'guardian angel', as Jane says later, ever watchful, restraining and purifying, and he thus plays the same role to Jane as Jane herself, the womanly Angel of Moral Femininity, has played to Rochester.

St John's demand that Jane follow him to be 'a wife: the sole helpmeet I can influence efficiently in life, and retain absolutely till death' (p. 431), provokes another crisis. Jane is challenged to live out the values of Moral Femininity just as she begins to comprehend that the renunciation of passion necessary to this social ideal will signify 'abandon[ing] half myself' (p. 430). St John wishes to 'retain' Jane, to form her to his tastes as absolutely and selfishly as the most possessive lover. In a parody of self-definition through sexual love, Jane sees that St John would create a new selfhood for her, 'give to my changeable green eyes the sea-blue tint and solemn lustre of his own' (p. 424). But unlike Rochester's, St John's despotism is not sexually attractive. His is the self-will and urge to possession of romantic love, without its 'sympathy' and mutuality. Thus, if Rochester's masculinity was imaged in a thriving mighty tree, St John is 'a cold cumbrous column' (p. 419), as the more malignant Rev. Brocklehurst was perceived by the child Jane as a 'black pillar', oddly phallic in the way it is said to stand 'erect on the rug' with a 'grim face at the top ... like a carved mask above the shaft' (p. 63).

In the last remarkable scene between the two, St John attempts to force Jane's decision by 'claiming' her. Like Rochester, St John sees himself as a 'pastor recalling his wandering sheep' (p. 443). In a close parallel between religious and sexual ecstasy, this and other metaphors from Jane's last passionate scene with Rochester are repeated in her desire to lose herself in St John's will to absolute renunciation. Jane had responded to the temptation to submit to a purely sexual gratification by navigating the flood like 'the Indian in his canoe'; now Jane is 'tempted ... to rush down the torrent of his will into the gulf of his existence, and there lose my own' (p. 443). The referent of 'my own' could be either 'will' or 'existence', and the interchangeability of terms is telling: without will there is no Self and no life.

Jane's 'real' self emerges as she physically and metaphorically breaks from St John's grasp: '*My* powers were in play and in force,' she tells us. Desire has literally willed Selfhood into existence. Jane's 'faculties', by which she seems to mean both an imaginative/intellectual capability and the life of the senses, including sexual desire, must somehow be incorporated into a definition of what is possible for women. In a sense, the imaginative production of the narrator Jane's novelistic story becomes her halfway house.

Two alternative modes of being for women have been measured and found wanting: the loss of social supports in abandoning the sexual morality of the traditional community, and the loss of selfhood in restraining or renouncing private will and sexual passions. But the balance is not perfectly equal, for sexual love has come to be seen as a necessary source of strength for a woman if she is to preserve herself in a social context that wants to obliterate her into self-sacrifice.

When Jane returns to Thornfield Hall as she resolved, she finds that both Bertha, the impediment to her marriage, and the mansion itself have been destroyed, self-devoured in a conflagration, the 'natural' end of unrestrained (i.e. 'natural') desire. Rochester is living in near-total isolation, cut off from all community, having lost his left eye and hand in a selfless effort to save others, including his mad wife, from the fire. In an ironic variation of earlier female caged-bird imagery, Jane compares him to a 'fettered wild beast or bird', a 'caged eagle' (p. 456), a 'royal eagle chained to a perch' (p. 464) in his woman-like helplessness and passivity. Certain of the strength and validity of her own impulse, Jane sets out, in her own words, to 'rehumanize' Rochester (p. 461) by liberating his will as he earlier did hers.

But Jane Eyre's own description of her love clearly abjures the conventional catchwords of Moral Femininity, its 'nobility' and 'selflessness'. Jane vigorously denies Rochester's analysis of her motive for loving him as 'delight in sacrifice' (p. 470) for its own sake; indeed, as she herself emphasizes, her new economic independence as her 'own mistress' (p. 459) gives her the ability to pursue her own will and pleasure. Though she soothes him, her own 'spirits' are said to be 'excited': with him, there is 'no harassing restraint, no repressing of glee' (p. 461). Her usefulness to him, so far from signifying the noble self-restraint of Moral Femininity, frees her to express sexual excitement because it brings their relation to terms of equality in power at last.

'Humanizing' Rochester has meant taking the infectious 'frenzy' – i.e. the tyranny and greed for possession – from his sexuality. It cannot be denied, therefore, that the nature of this sexual love is transformed.[30] Rochester is diminished but certainly not entirely emasculated or asexual in his helplessness; he seizes Jane with his 'muscular hand' as soon as he knows her, and she pointedly alludes to him as a 'green and vigorous tree' (p. 469). The masculinity which, as the housekeeper said, 'you do not thoroughly understand' is rendered coherent, however, and therefore narratable: you *do* thoroughly understand him by the novel's end, in short.

Rochester is tamed into a narrative with closure, but the point is that Jane has not only reformed a rake (the Byronic rather than eighteenth-century version) and won a husband, but also has achieved something for herself: the fulfilment of her own sexuality. Rochester's sexual desire and appeal are altered in quality, not quantity, in order to ensure the fulfilment of Jane's own desire. Charlotte Brontë thus makes use of the paradigm of Moral Femininity, in which the crown is refused so that it may in the end 'be yours', while deforming and reforming it to her own purposes. We can see the difference in emphasis from an author like Richardson when Brontë has Jane herself use the same argument for individual fulfilment pleaded by Rochester during their last feverish meeting before separation: 'Nor did I refuse to let him, when seated, place me on his knee. Why should I, when both he and I were happier near than apart?' (p. 464). But this scene of physical intimacy can take place only after Jane has 'led him out of the wet and wild woods into some cheerful fields' (p. 464), when 'nature', whether the physical world or man's intrinsic character, is accepted as beneficent as well as 'wild'. This is, after all, sexuality in the context of 'real' love, i.e. courtship leading to marriage.

Sexual love, then, is seen by Brontë as properly a form of life, not the 'real' and essential thing; an affirmer, not the creator, of the female self. But in their oneness after reunion, in which 'in his presence I thoroughly lived; and he lived in mine' (p. 461), sexuality has a definite, if controlled, place as part of 'thoroughly living'. The observation about St John which closes the novel is filled with admiration for a near impossibility, a remote ideal: 'His is the exaction of the apostle, who speaks but for Christ, when he says "Whosoever will come after Me, let him deny himself"' (p. 477). To deny the self and the desire for sexual love is to be like Jesus, but in the end it is not an ideal for a woman of feeling and imagination.

At an emotional moment early in their relationship, Rochester cried out to Jane, 'My little friend! I wish I were in a quiet island with only you' (p. 232). At the conclusion of *Jane Eyre*, Jane does not so much take her place *in* society, radiating influence all around as does Richardson's Pamela or Austen's Fanny in *Mansfield Park*, or find certain values in rejection of society, like Clarissa, as form an isolated strong bond in the midst of society, a 'quiet island', on the order of Dickens' Little Dorrit. Threatened by the growing power of self-interest as an ethic in a commercial society, only an individual solution seems possible to Charlotte Brontë.

Jane Eyre, in spite of its religious-mystical vocabulary, is an attempt at a private morality, in which one 'cares' for the sake of one's selfhood, as Jane cried, 'I care for myself' (p. 344).[31] Sexual passion is found to have a dignity of its own, but it seems valid only for the unconventional, socially estranged individual with special needs and 'faculties', not in the context of a society of self-indulgent Ladies or aggrandizing males. By the end of *Jane Eyre*, some of the passionate energy of the sexual imagination must be ritually sacrificed through the act of fiction to gain a greater good: that of membership in a microcosmic 'moral economy', whose peculiar conditions allow one, in Jane's words, 'to repose on what I trust' (p. 470), in 'the dream' of sexual love, a pure connection beyond social power.

5

Down the 'Forbidden Path': *Villette*

> The Angel [in the House] was dead; what then remained? You may say that what remained was a simple and common object – a young woman in a bedroom with an inkpot. In other words, now that she had rid herself of falsehood, that young woman had only to be herself. Ah, but what is 'herself?' I mean, what is a woman?
>
> Virginia Woolf, 'Professions for Women', *Death of the Moth*, 1931

In spite of very different ideas on the question raised in the foregoing epigraph, Harriet Martineau and William Makepeace Thackeray came to remarkably similar conclusions concerning what being a woman meant to Charlotte Brontë: her obsession with sexual love. Thackeray, in a letter of 1853 to a friend about *Villette*, characterized Charlotte as 'the poor little woman of genius! ... I can read a great deal of her life as I fancy in her book and see that rather than have fame, rather than any other earthly good or mayhap heavenly one, she wants some Tomkins or another to love her and be in love with.'[1] So much for *Villette*.

In the same year, Harriet Martineau had objected to *Villette* in an otherwise positive review on the grounds that 'All the female characters, in all their thoughts and lives, are full of one thing ... – love.' This subject, 'incessant' and 'dominant' in *Villette*, countered Martineau, 'is not thus [pervasive] in real life. There are substantial, heart-felt interests for women of all ages, and under ordinary circumstances, quite apart from love: there is an absence of introspection, an unconsciousness, a repose in women's lives ... of which we find no admission in this book.'[2] Brontë's furious rejoinder to her friend Martineau does not dispute her observation, but claims that the latter severely underestimates Brontë's definition of love: 'I know what love is as I understand it; and if men and women should be ashamed of feeling such love, then there is nothing right, noble, faithful, truthful, unselfish in this earth.'³

In her reply, Charlotte Brontë was directly addressing the implications in Martineau's criticism that the 'introspection' and lack of 'repose' in her female characters constituted a subterranean celebration of the individual, of self-indulgence, and more specifically, of sexual desire. While not disagreeing with Martineau's description of her emphasis on love, Brontë evaded its implications by side-stepping this covert issue, taking refuge, one might say, on the safe side of romantic love: in its obsessive concern with the Other, in its possibilities of good influence over the beloved, such a love, she reminds us, can *deny* the Self. But by retreating behind the pious conventions of the nobility of romantic love, Charlotte also minimized the subversive genius of her work, although in a different way than Thackeray and Martineau did.

Between these two skewed evaluations and Brontë's own self-evaluation lies an art whose sexual values are shifting, difficult to place, even, at times, in apparent contradiction. Charlotte Brontë is an artist who speaks powerfully through what is held back, who arouses us, then 'vexes and soothes by turns', as Jane Eyre does (p. 187). Sexuality is represented as a struggle for power between unequal partners, yet the conclusion of *Jane Eyre* suggests that sexual love contains the possibility of a human connection that is a mutual fulfilment of pleasure rather than the fulfilment of a lack or the exertion of control. In *Villette*, her final novel, Charlotte Brontë once again mapped the interior of a woman's heart in crisis, striving to bring a relentless and self-mocking truth to the painful questions arising from *Jane Eyre*: does exploring the forbidden path of sexual love affirm the 'real' self, by legitimating 'natural' impulses which give vivid life to womanhood, or does the need for completion through another corrupt the quest for a powerful female identity?

In making the text do the work of representing these issues, however, Brontë was forced to call into question the very concept of 'real', essential selfhood that had formed the basis for the romantic solutions in her previous novels. Lucy Snowe is far more problematic than Jane Eyre in that she begins with neither the raw materials of strength nor anger nor even desire in her quest to find her 'real' self, but only with the eye of observation. *Villette*'s heroine, Lucy Snowe, presents a most harrowing separation, not merely of self from society, or of public image from private self, but of character's concept of self and the reader's expectations of what constitutes selfhood as a category.[4] Her beginning as a blank slate is turned into an advantage: without personal attractions or the temptations of a male's overwhelming desire, she is able to reformulate the relation of sexuality and romantic love so as to build a more powerful model of female selfhood. Rather than representing sexual love as a force which either undermines or affirms the 'real' female self, Brontë here sees it as the substratum of all selfhood, in a way that (ironically enough) anticipates D.H. Lawrence.

Jane Eyre may have been robbed of her 'real' self as a child, but she always had her 'faculties', her strong capacity for feeling and imagination, and the reader is allowed to discern this hidden, superior self from the beginning. The hallmark of Jane Eyre's character was self-respect: 'They are not fit to associate with me' (p. 60) was her reckless cry, even in mental agony. But in the character of Lucy, Charlotte Brontë posed the Victorian question, 'What is a woman?' in a new way; the heroine begins by being no more than, in the words of Charlotte's own youthful journal, a 'craving vacancy', a female sexual space, which is an empty blank until filled up with a power and meaning which is defined as 'male'.

In a novel which is 'a perfect cabinet of oddities', as one character in it describes another,[5] the first oddity which strikes the reader is that its entire opening section is devoted, not to the heroine-narrator, but to an intense observation by the narrator of the actions and feelings of a small, temporarily abandoned child, a little girl who is then abandoned in turn by the narrator as a focus. Polly, at age six, has already learned to wear a cloak of socially appropriate behaviour. Lucy observes that 'she never showed my godmother one glimpse of her inner self; for her, she was nothing but a docile, somewhat quaint little maiden' (p. 26).

But if Polly reveals her 'inner self', the passionate will which craves love, only to Lucy as a defence against pain, Lucy for her part seems to be false even to herself. Her responses to Polly's hungering love for the boy John Graham, for example, are conventionally 'wise' and cool, yet this love, in both its grief and joy, obviously had a singular importance to her. As she traces its beginnings in Polly's 'home sickness' (p. 7) for her father, Mr Home, Lucy is haunted by the longing and worship of Polly, the 'precocious fanatic', for a male as an antidote to her state of exile.[6]

The child as a figure of helplessness, needing protection and love, yet naively irrational and wilful, is an appropriate and typical trope for conventional Victorian womanhood. But Polly is a also child who is 'most unchildlike' (p. 5). Through Lucy's assumed neutrality, we examine how a woman, miniaturized in Polly, is made 'interesting' by love. When Polly is 'tractable' and sits on a stool all day learning to sew or draw, Lucy 'ceased to watch her ... she was not interesting' (p. 18). We are given, in Polly, a small portrait of noble Moral Femininity in the act of self-sacrifice: loving Graham means waiting on him and maternally looking after him. Whether refusing a treat for herself because 'girls ... don't need treats, but *he* would like it', or adapting herself 'to such schemes as interested him', Polly is the sort, as Lucy drily notes, who 'must necessarily live, move and have her being in another' (p. 19).[7]

Like the character of Lucy as we know her so far, Polly acts as though she 'had no mind or life of her own' (p. 19). Such submergence of identity, however – 'herself ... forgotten in him' (p. 18), which was after all the accepted ideal of both Moral Femininity and romantic love – is shown through Polly to be at bottom a craving for affirmation of self, rather than denial of self. Polly may deprive herself of prizes and treats, but she is infinitely demanding, as we soon discover: 'To stand by his knee, and monopolize his talk and notice, was the reward she wanted.' Like a small, invading ghost, Polly haunts Graham's presence with a monstrous desire, which is no less than to 'exist in his existence' (p. 19).

Polly imagines a future with Graham 'climbing Mount Blanc', an image of the heights of sexual love and, like the other pictures in Graham's book, a metaphor for the participation in the active life such love promises. But the danger of such vicarious existence is clear too: when Polly is not noticed by Graham, she feels that she has ceased to exist. The bitterness of her wound when she is very slightly rejected by him awes and frightens Lucy. It exposes for her the utter vulnerability of the craving soul open to love in bearing the 'shocks and repulses, the humiliations and desolations' (p. 28) of needing others to get on in life.

Bereft of Graham on the eve of their parting, a desolate Polly can't sleep for shivering: 'My bed is cold,' she complains, 'I can't warm it' (p. 27). Polly knows what Lucy cannot admit: sexual love is the spark of life. While a leap into a conflagration of feeling such as Polly's is, as Lucy comments, 'strangely rash' (p. 22), it is the only means to melt the dead frosts of selflessness in a Victorian woman, whose life is seen as without other value.

Polly's craving appears not to rest on mere self-interest or indulgence, partly because as a child she is accorded immunity to 'real' sexual desire. But Polly is also allowed a dignity of her own: she exercises enormous self-command and restraint while admitting, unlike Lucy, that she has a self-will to command and passion to restrain.

'I am going,' says the child Polly, and in fact disappear she does from the novel. We are then left alone with a narrator who resists characterization as she has so far denied herself the heroineship of the novel. Lucy both has and is nothing. She looks, she tells us, like a 'placeless person in debt' (p. 35), the flotsam of society. Yet, thrown back on her resources, forced to 'look to herself' in both the economic and emotional senses, Lucy must assume a disguise which implies the possibility of a buried selfhood. Like Polly playing the demure maiden, Lucy makes deliberate use of 'a staid manner of my own . . . as good to me as a cloak and hood of hodden grey' (p. 36).[8] Thus equipped for survival, the coward who had quailed before 'stimulus' now makes a bold leap into the very centre of excitement and risk, the city of London.

In the great metropolis, Lucy feels, as have so many before her, that 'my inner self moved; my spirit shook its always-fettered wings half loose' (p. 39). Choosing a book from a shop, she feels she momentarily partakes of the culture of the city, in an 'ecstasy of freedom and enjoyment'. Drawn to the 'heart of city life' – i.e. its commercial heart – with its 'perils of crossings' and eager rush in getting its living, she feels deeply excited (p. 40); the public world seems momentarily full of high promise.

Yet the other face of this ethos of freedom and enjoyment soon confronts her on her crossing to the Continent. Cast adrift, friendless and penniless, Lucy is abandoned at night by the coach driver, who 'offered me up as an oblation, served me as a dripping roast' (p. 41) to a throng of greedy, competing watermen. This startlingly violent image – a woman as helpless meat to be torn up by men – directly contrasts with the idealized version of the commercial city life Lucy has just described. So soon after the experience of the 'freedom and enjoyment' of consuming, Lucy sees that she could only too easily become one of the consumed.

In the business 'heart' of the city, Lucy believed she truly lived as she 'mixed with the life passing along' (p. 40), but her excitement was from mere window-shopping, not participation. She was, as before with Polly or Miss Marchmont, 'living' only vicariously through the wills of others, not acting out her own will, her 'inner self', as she called it. In reality, as one of the dispossessed, unprotected by community, kin or status, Lucy is not fit to compete with those, 'so insolent and so selfish', who live for profit. But Lucy is willing to learn how to survive among these enemies by studying them with almost anthropological zeal; the effort makes her unusually 'animated and alert', rather than frightened (p. 42).

Lucy sees, in this section of the novel, that the ethic of wilful gratification and self-interest, which forms the underpinnings of a 'male' business society, has penetrated to both genders and all classes, from the barmaid to the Lady. It is perfectly evident to all of these that Lucy herself is *not* a Lady; and she is left to marvel at the 'sagacity' of those servants who, 'in a moment's calculation', correctly estimate her worth as 'an individual of no social significance and little burdened with cash'. Thus stripped of dignity, utterly vulnerable and exposed as a commodity of 'fractional value' (p. 50), Lucy finds herself led to what is yet another Brontëan Lodging House, the boarding-school of Mme Beck.

Lucy has not escaped the threatening problem of her own and others' will by locking herself in, however. There is a wolf waiting in this refuge, disguised as 'a dumpy motherly little body, in decent shawl and the cleanest of possible nightcaps' (p. 104). Neat, efficient and orderly even in the act of rifling through Lucy's belongings, calm and even-tempered as Lucy's godmother, Mrs Bretton, Mme Beck appears quite the type of maternal femininity. She intimidates Lucy because she shows her the implications of a life based on self-will, but she also provides a model of a woman who succeeds by being, unlike Lucy, 'in nothing weak' (p. 266). It is Mme Beck, significantly, who stirs Lucy's first desires to assert her own will in the classroom.

Mme Beck is Charlotte Brontë's last and best variant of the Bitch-Rival, more complex than previous incarnations because characterized with the affection and admiration that was withheld from earlier figures such as Mlle Reuter in *The Professor* or Blanche Ingram in *Jane Eyre*. The Bitch-Rival is similar to that Victorian icon, the Lady, in that like her she calculates her own and others' desires by their usefulness to her own ends. The 'real' woman, on the other hand, is unable to suppress her feelings, though she always controls her actions.[9]

Lucy soon has the opportunity to appraise this credo when she becomes a reluctant third – once again – in two love-triangles involving the attractive Dr John, who is, as she felicitously discovers, the boy John Graham Bretton grown up. When Lucy encounters Dr

John as a man, he has already begun a flirtation with the pretty, flighty teenager, Ginevra, whom she had met on the channel crossing. Ginevra's idea of love is connected, as are all her other ideas, with her ambitious desire to become a Lady. Of dismayingly poor parentage, without talent or usefulness of any kind, Ginevra is Brontë's very type of the would-be Lady who defines herself solely through externals, i.e. her beauty, her clothes, her possessions and the social status of the men she will catch. Though she herself is without passion, sexual attraction becomes for her an important ally in the competition for these goods. It is, more precisely, the lure in the sexual variant of the game of 'robbing the robber', catching the male sexual thief before he catches you. To play well, it is necessary, not merely to hide the 'real' self, but to *have* no 'real' self, to identify body and soul with the show. As Lucy comments, 'Ginevra lived her full life in a ball-room.'

The idealization of women necessary to romantic love has the effect in a competitive society of 'hid[ing] chains with flowers' (p. 112), to borrow an apt phrase from Lucy's description of Romanism. But the connection between sexual love and acquisition also permeates the consciousness and language of the women in *Villette*. Lucy herself is indignant that Ginevra would accept presents from Dr John; as she comments caustically, 'if she cannot pay you in affection, she ought to hand out a business-like equivalent in ... gold pieces' (p. 174).

One teacher in particular, the 'Parisienne', who lives for pleasure and the acquisition of material show, disgusts Lucy with her 'frozen' eyes 'of light at once craving and ingrate' (p. 112). Yet it is this very 'craving', the slavish hunger beneath the cool exterior, which threatens Lucy's idea of herself as she is increasingly attracted to Dr John. 'Whatever could excite', she confesses, naming, as she did in her journal, a thunderstorm, 'woke the being I was always lulling, and stirred up a craving cry I could not satisfy' (p. 96). Here is our first glimpse of Lucy's possible 'real' self, constituted by a desire of such remarkable power that she must objectify it as a 'being', a tyrannical monster with a will and life of its own.

Under Lucy's humiliating consciousness of her unrewarded superiority to those women who live by and for the ethic of self-interest (not unlike Charlotte Brontë's felt superiority to her peers noted in her journal) is the terrible fear that she too shares this 'craving', if in more idealized form. For if Ginevra or the teachers come to life only under another's admiration, this is no more than what the child Polly craved, or for that matter, anyone in love. Thus the longing for romantic love poses both the greatest promise and the greatest danger to the hope of Lucy's own 'coming to life'.

Throughout *Villette* Lucy's character does, in fact, rise and fall, expand and contract, with disturbing rapidity. Until she was drawn into the flirtation between Ginevra and Dr John, Lucy lived 'in my own still, shadow world' by absolute, desperate belief in 'the whole repose of my nature' (pp. 104–5). In one of several periods of exhilarating freedom which alternate frighteningly with severe crises of repression in this novel, Mme Beck celebrates her birthday with a 'Fête', in which bonds are loosened and 'freedom the most complete seemed indeed the only order of the day' (p. 115). This licensed masking culminates in an actual show, a trivial play about a romantic flirtation. To her dismay, Lucy must perform – as usual, against her will – the part of a false and foppish lover, still one more third in a love-triangle.

Throughout *Villette*, the fluidity of gender identities marks those periods of excess freedom which threaten Lucy with loss of self-control. This gender reversal appears in her relations to Ginevra, as when Lucy finds herself drawn into 'courting' Ginevra during the play, or Ginevra is said to lean on Lucy as she would on 'a gentleman, or her lover' (p. 280).[10] But the same dissolution of gender roles affects nearly every major character in the novel at one time or other: Mme Beck, for example, is said to be man-like in her powers, as we have seen, yet not long after Lucy avers, 'Had I been a gentleman, I believe Madame would have found favour in my eyes' (p. 104). Alfred de Hamal, Ginevra's dandyish admirer, is described repeatedly as effeminate, 'pretty and smooth, and trim as a doll: so nicely dressed, so nicely curled' (p. 131). Then again, Dr John wins a lady's headdress in a lottery and is made to wear it by his mother, while sleeping, while Lucy makes a point of keeping the cigar-case she has won. Later, Dr John tells Lucy that 'if you had been a boy instead of a girl ... we should have been good friends' (p. 287), and even M. Paul jokingly suggests at one point that Lucy don his cap, 'turn garçon for the occasion' (p. 297), and go out disguised as himself!

Lucy's attraction to the male role has led to her complete absorption in play-acting the role of a sexual aggressor, 'resolute to win and conquer' (p. 125). But this experience of 'strength' and 'longing' by proxy, not unlike the experience of romantic love, proves to be a dangerous invasion of her precarious defences, and must be put by. It is as though Lucy's inner thoughts have been violated; the process of acting is like the exposure of nakedness to others in a world without trust. When she is in fact entirely alone during the long school vacation which succeeds the Fête, Lucy's negative definition of self proves insupportable; her longed-for privacy reveals itself as the other face of estrangement.

Lucy's extreme alienation of mind in this episode is embodied in the presence of a 'cretin', a 'deformed and imbecile' (p. 140) pupil also left for a time at the school, who is a dumb image of humanity separated from those traits which make it human. On the one hand, the cretin functions as a representation of social views of women and children: she only asks to be protected and cared for. Yet, without higher faculties, she is also pure will, more like 'some strange tameless animal than ... a human being' (p. 141). As the person in charge, Lucy finds herself in the controlling role of a Mme Beck: 'I could not leave her a minute alone ... an aimless malevolence made constant vigilance indispensable' (p. 141).

Thus Lucy alternates between the maintenance of the cretin's fragile humanity through severe repression of the girl's desire, and the torments of her own 'cravings'. Here we have the double message of *Villette* – indeed, of many Victorian novels: left to itself, without superimposed controls, desire must be restrained from 'aimless malevolence', yet individual self-fulfilment cannot be entirely suppressed without a comparable loss of humanity. It is a contradiction which drives Lucy half-mad.

When Lucy awakens from a swoon, she finds herself at La Terrasse, the Brettons' home in Villette, which seems to Lucy 'like a cave in the sea'. This 'submarine home' is both a womb-like psychic haven of regression and the sexual cave of subterranean female passion: 'That dark, shining glass', the mirror where Lucy saw her reflection, 'might have mirrored a mermaid' (p. 163). But though La Terrasse does not prove the home and source of sexual life it first promised to be, Mrs Bretton and her son do offer a corollary to romantic love: the opportunity for Lucy to participate in society and try on the role of a Lady. During Lucy's stay there, she is taken to a concert in a dazzling hall, 'filled with a splendid assemblage', and she passes through the 'glad, gay, and abundant ... tide of life along the broad pavement' (p. 188), as she did in London. Suddenly, she catches a glimpse of herself, dressed fashionably for the occasion, with Dr John and his mother all reflected together in a great mirror. The discrepancy between their images brings 'a jar of discord, a pang of regret' (p. 189): Lucy is not and never can be a Lady. The moment recalls the scene in *Jane Eyre* when Jane, robed in wedding garments, sees 'the image of a stranger' forebodingly in her mirror. Dressed up, Lucy is only 'a third person in a pink dress' (p. 189).

Lucy's failure to be either a Lady or the object of Dr John's romantic interest are not discrete occurrences, but inwardly connected. 'Had Lucy been intrinsically the same, but possessed the additional advantages of wealth and station, would your manner to her, your value for her, have been quite what they actually were?' Lucy later silently asks (p. 287). It is her ability to make this connection that will eventually allow Lucy to reject both these attractions as valid choices. But at this stage, Lucy feels her humiliating exclusion most deeply as an inadequacy of the sexual self. Her return to Mme Beck's school after this interval of fluctuating identity is marked by a severe repression, amounting to a rigid self-chastening, of her excited and unsatisfied cravings. It is at this point in the narrative when Lucy, feverishly agitated by the receipt of a letter from Dr John which seems her last tenuous link to affection, sees for the first time a ghost-like nun in the attic where she sought privacy to read her letter.

Lucy sees the nun at a time when her quest for a coherent selfhood seems to have resulted in a futile circling back to a deadening, enforced sacrifice of her desires.[11] At the school she is once more both radically alone and relentlessly intruded on, so that her self-sequestering in the attic represents, nun-like, both imprisonment from desire and a refuge from penetration. The apparition of the nun, inhuman behind veiled features except for eyes that are cold and grey as it emerges from a recess in the 'sepulchral garret' (p. 226), is described in terms reminiscent of the 'flat, dead, pale' (p. 182) domestic angels of the art gallery Lucy had visited. Lucy is, of course, terrified by this shadow of her human self, this image of morality achieved through an inhuman repression; but oddly, she is even more anguished by the discovery that she has lost her letter. To convey her despair, she talks of herself strangely in the third person: ' "They have taken my letter!" cried the groveling, groping monomaniac' (p. 223). It is as though the figure of herself as the slave of love is the embodiment of the most extreme alienation: the desire which is at the heart of survival bodied forth into a kind of madness.

'To keep away the nun' (p. 231), Dr John takes Lucy to a performance by Vashti, a famous, impassioned actress. Vashti vividly presents Lucy with the other extreme from the dead-hearted nun, an abandoned identification with show, a life of passion so intense it seems to Lucy 'a chaos', self-consuming. Though repelled by the furious emotion which transforms the actress's face into 'a demoniac mask' (p. 234), Lucy cannot help being drawn to the 'frenzy of energy', and strength of an 'inordinate will' unusual in a woman (pp. 235, 237).

It is while calmly rescuing Lucy – controlling and moderating the effects of the ravaging fire in the theatre – that Dr John meets the woman he will marry. This turns out to be no other than the little Polly of his childhood grown up; or rather, Paulina Mary has added appropriate age and a satisfying rank and wealth to her small self, for she is depicted as both in appearance and personality charmingly childlike.

The romantic love between Paulina and Dr John is treated with a subtly undermining irony; Lucy recognizes, for example, that Paulina is far more suited to Dr John than she could ever be merely by virtue of resembling him in his less appealing attributes. Paulina, like Dr John, gets her way through *moderated* self-interest; like Dr John also, and unlike Lucy, Paulina will succeed because she is not a slave of passion. She is destined to the peace of happiness, what Charlotte Brontë elsewhere calls 'repose', but not to the extremes of intensity in feeling. In this way, she compares to her own childhood self as the younger Catherine of *Wuthering Heights* will contrast with her passionate mother.

In loving Paulina, Dr John clearly admires the softened mirror-image of himself, his own role as 'man of the world', in other words. The quality of his admiration has a ring of rational self-interest, as in the scene of the dinner-party, where he 'surveyed both forms – studied both faces' (p. 286) of the two women, Paulina and Ginevra, whom he admires. As he silently takes their measure and judges his preference, he could be about to choose a hat or cloak from a shop. Once more the reluctant confidante of both Paulina and Dr John in their courtship, Lucy is led to see romance as a form of mutual self-love: 'There is, in lovers, a certain infatuation of egotism' (p. 387), she remarks, as both lovers in turn force her to 'witness' and reflect their happiness without once noticing the pain to herself. As Paulina muses after reading a German poem about the happiness of loving, 'Is that the summit of earthly happiness, the end of life – to love? I don't think it is.' The investment of emotion in another, she goes on reasonably, may cost great misery or prove to be great folly; therefore, she concludes, the great thing is 'to *be* loved' (p. 277).

Paulina has become, after a poignant childhood, the lap-dog to which Lucy mischievously, and startlingly, compares her (p. 379).

Lucy's attempt to enter the world of La Terrasse, outside and slightly above the mazes of the city, is now at an end. The hope of an affirmation of selfhood through the beneficence of romantic love is dead: 'I had almost worshipped my Ganges, and I grieved that the grand tide should roll estranged, should vanish like a false mirage' (p. 267). Without basis of selfhood again, once more reduced to a craving vacancy, Lucy buries the letters from Dr John which objectify her feelings on paper under the 'knotty trunk' of a giant tree which towers above the rest of the garden. Though she has come through her trial with 'sad, lonely satisfaction' (p. 269), Lucy almost at once sees the spectre-like nun again, projected likeness of the selflessness and will-lessness of Moral Femininity she cannot accept. Secluded in the 'allée défendue', a private, narrow and 'wild' path in the garden, redolent of female sexuality, she gathers the courage to ask the unknown ghost woman one question that haunts this novel: 'Who are you?' (p. 271).

It is exactly at this rare moment when Lucy has acted on her desires by refusing to be a third in Dr John's love affair that M. Paul truly enters the novel. He too has a 'mask', like Lucy, 'covering his human visage' in moments of irritability: that of 'an intelligent tiger' (p. 127), a sort of Brontëan male ideal embracing both superior culture and the masculine prerogative to act passionately and aggressively. M. Paul has the energy and freedom of action which Lucy lacks: small like her, he is 'active, alive with the energy and movement of three tall men' (p. 198).[12] Moreover, he chafes, as she does, at 'spur or curb', but where she is a secret rebel, turning anger inward to self-hatred, he is 'sure to revolt' against external authority (p. 295). M. Paul, in fact, points out that 'We are alike – there is an affinity between us. Do you see it, mademoiselle, when you look in the glass?' (p. 334). This double reflection in the glass, in which even their most opposite traits are inverted mirror-images of the same 'real' nature, recalls Jane Eyre's insistence that Rochester is 'akin' and 'assimilated' to her.

But M. Paul is no Byronic figure of wild passion and uncontrolled will, like Rochester. If he expresses the rebellious desire that is suppressed in Lucy, he also resembles her, as Rochester never did Jane Eyre, in his disciplined containment of passion and fixed self-abnegation when the impetus comes from within himself. Then too, unlike Rochester with his secret motives, M. Paul displays his emotions 'artlessly, like a child' (p. 315). Though he affects to tyrannize over Lucy, he is never the threat to the integrity of her selfhood that Rochester represented to Jane Eyre. On the contrary, he becomes at times a parody of the overblown tyrannical male who is secretly absurd because he has no real power in his bluster. In this he is the inverse of Lucy, the outwardly passive female who has hidden strength.

But M. Paul *is* like Rochester in one way: his ability to 'read' Lucy, to understand her secrets, as the other characters cannot. The 'superficiality' and falsity of social role has been made to stand for a bodily 'virginity', containing a deep, private sexual self which alone can mean and connect. At their first meeting he fixes her through his spectacles with a look that says 'he meant to see through me, and that a veil would be no veil for him' (p. 57). At a second early encounter, his eyes 'hungrily dived into me' (p. 118), recalling Jane Eyre's wonder at Rochester's ability to 'dive into my eyes' (p. 164). Rifling her desk with an intimate hand, M. Paul seems at first to Lucy still another intruder on her privacy.

However, there is also no mistaking the sexual overtones of this penetration of Lucy's disguises. In the glow of M. Paul's ever-present cigar, which he calls a 'red jealous eye' (p. 333) watching Lucy's progress, the sexual nature of their growing intimacy is slowly illuminated. At one point M. Paul makes the 'two-leaved door split' as he bursts into the room where the women sit like 'nuns in a "retreat"' (p. 299). In her turn, Lucy inadvertently shatters the eyeglasses with which M. Paul distances and intimidates everyone.

M. Paul suspects Lucy of harbouring a secret knowledge, as he insinuates she has a store of ancient languages which she is supposed 'criminally and craftily to conceal'. As mythic monkeys are 'said to have the power of speech if they would but use it, and are reported to conceal this faculty in fear of its being turned to their detriment' (p. 322), so Lucy has the faculty of strong feeling, if she would only allow it articulation. Lucy's susceptibility to emotion, her capacity and desire for sexual love, which has been her greatest source of weakness and vulnerability, is reinterpreted in a new light by M. Paul as a dangerous power. M. Paul is not merely Lucy's best 'reader' – he is also her translator.

Soon after, M. Paul undertakes to teach Lucy, becoming her 'master'. As in her novel *Shirley*, the author makes use here of a kind of sexuality of the intellect, the intimacy of mutual unmasking with words. Thus, Lucy tells us that M. Paul's mind was 'my library, and whenever it was opened to me, I entered bliss' (p. 346). Similarly, M. Paul batters, opens and penetrates Lucy with his mocking words and secret knowledge of her, the knowledge derived from spying which would be so dangerous 'if you were a wicked, designing man' (p. 333), Lucy tells him.[13]

In these scenes we are reminded once again of the closeness of anger to sexual attention in Brontë's novels. The mutual storm which this teaching situation stirs is merely the sound and fury of sexual teasing, as the would-be lovers do 'strong battle, with confused noise of demand and rejection, exaction and repulse' (p. 325). As in *Jane Eyre*, anger proves the disinterestedness of the lover's interest, his rudeness being as unlike as possible to the insincere flattery of conventional flirtations or the crafty charm of a rakish gentleman. When M. Paul is openly tender, regretting his hard words as he does on the country walk, she sheds tears; for Lucy, desire is too intense to be expressed or received directly.

The new bond between Lucy and M. Paul seems to promise what Lucy had longed for: in her words, a 'true home ... at whose feet I can willingly lay down the whole burden of human egotism' (p. 329). Yet just as Lucy's selfhood struggles into existence, the spectre-like Nun makes its third appearance. We recall that Lucy first saw the apparition in the enclosed, prison-like attic, while the second encounter took place when Lucy stood alone in the wild and untouched 'forbidden path', the garden of female eroticism. This time, while Lucy lingers in the 'forbidden path' with M. Paul in the evening, the ghostly Nun emerges as they discuss the legend of the nun who long ago was 'buried alive' (p. 334) beneath the very tree where Lucy had buried her letters from Dr John.

Like Lucy's long-buried 'real' self, the figure appears only after a strange 'rending and heaving' in the great tree, a 'travail' like that of birth. The Nun makes her last appearance to Lucy and M. Paul as a couple, just as the issue of Catholic self-denial will form a critical juncture in their relations. The problem of Moral Femininity, with its restraint of female will and sacrifice of female sexuality, has grown to outsize proportions like the Nun herself, yet it has a new significance for Lucy because, as is the Nun in this appearance, it is seen more clearly and faced as two in a loving couple.

Throughout *Villette*, episodes of freedom, of almost too fluid identity and dangerously uncontrolled will – Madame's Fête, the display of Vashti – have alternated with periods of frightening and dehumanizing repression – the Long Vacation, for example, and the sightings of the Nun. M. Paul is kept from union with Lucy by the Catholic requirement of sacrifice of will to a higher authority, in the form of a priest, Père Silas. As Lucy learns when she is sent to visit the house of Mrs Walravens, who with Père Silas and Mme Beck forms the 'secret junta' which opposes Lucy's desires, M. Paul is bound to a vow of chastity made to a 'pale dead nun' (p. 362) whom he had loved long ago. Her 'goodness' was a wholly negative one: a weak will and lack of passion which destroy selfhood in a woman. She has become a 'saint' to M. Paul, both in the Catholic sense of self-sacrifice and rigid chastity, and in the sense of romantic idol-worship, 'his angel-bride' (p. 358). She is, in fact, an extreme version of the Victorian angel of Moral Femininity, women 'most murderously sacrificed' (p. 383) for an abstract morality which disguises the self-interested motives of others.

Lucy finds the barrier of the dead nun and the challenge of M. Paul's 'heart sworn to virginity' at once 'the deepest puzzle, the strongest obstruction and the keenest stimulus I had ever felt' (p. 362). Yet her growing power in the face of the extreme subjection of will represented by Mme Beck and the spectre of the Nun is followed by the last and most nightmarish episode of extreme freedom, a *Walpurgisnacht* of a holiday in the very centre of the city.

After a sleepless night, Lucy sees herself in a mirror once more; her face 'sodden white', she is once again the inhuman, spectral shadow, the monster of selflessness that emerged in the crisis of the Long Vacation. As after her release from the near-inhuman cretin of that episode, Lucy bursts out of the school, once a refuge from the dangers of the city, now a 'jail', a 'convent' (p. 411), where the impulses that constitute what she has called the 'inner life' are betrayed and repressed.

Once in the streets, Lucy joins a Fête already in progress in Villette. Caught up in 'the strong tide, a great flow of music' (p. 411), the bonds of sexual feeling are momentarily loosened as Lucy is 'plunged amidst a gay, living, joyous crowd' (p. 412) of bodies pressed together. In the spirit of misrule that prevails, we are told that Imagination cries, 'This night I will have *my* will!' Under the spell of this heightened imaginative flow, Lucy had foreseen 'a strange vision of Villette at midnight', and most especially 'the place that could not be entered', a basin of cool water deep-set in the tree-shadows and lush greenery of the park (p. 410). By the blazing illumination of day-in-night, Lucy retraces her innermost life in a blurred, erotic flow of sexual metaphor: the locked, sentinelled park like the enclosed garden of Mme Beck's school writ large, the 'long alleys' like the 'allées défendues', forbidden paths of sensual experience, leading to thirst-quenching fountain of 'clear depth and lining', promising a paradisiacal release. Imagination, here, is represented by Brontë as a safe/wild space that contains desire as well as frees it.[14]

Lucy's relation to M. Paul, which occupies the final chapters of *Villette*, dramatizes the problem of the validity of women's sexual desire that is raised only evasively or indirectly in Charlotte Brontë's previous novels. *Villette*, like *Jane Eyre*, presents the heroine with two men, but here both are loved romantically, if differently. It is this distinction between ways of loving and their social consequences which forces us to see more clearly what is implied when Lucy builds a home in sexual love. Lucy herself makes this contrast when she encounters both Dr John and M. Paul on the night of the Fête. She is, she realizes, more jealous of M. Paul than she ever was of Dr John because she has now experienced what it is like 'to *be* loved'. The feeling associated with Dr John is 'the love born of beauty', which is shown as a form of sexual appropriation. In Lucy's relation to M. Paul, sexuality flows from intimate knowledge, rational friendship and mutual trust. It is, in Lucy's words, 'another' kind of love,

> venturing diffidently into life after long acquaintance, furnace-tried by pain, stamped by constancy, consolidated by affection's pure and durable alloy, submitted by intellect to intellect's own tests ... this Love that laughed at Passion.
>
> (p. 427)

Only in the context of such a love might one justifiably assert ownership, or as Lucy, appropriating the language of business, puts it, 'in *this* Love I have a vested interest' (p. 427). The peculiar balance of the two oddly matched lovers in *Villette* represents Brontë's effort to affix a special condition to the boundary between a valid and necessary self-interest and a morality of selflessness, between the female right to sexual love and the danger of either imitating or being subjected to the exploitation endorsed by a commercial and patriarchal society.

As the patriarchal home was ideally modelled on the fidelity of subjects to king, so the mutuality of the lovers is patterned after the 'watching over' of parental concern, as well as the protective ties of the traditional community. Whereas Ginevra could not conceive 'how any person not bolstered up by birth or wealth, not supported by some consciousness of name or connection, could maintain an attitude of reasonable integrity', for Lucy,

> it quite sufficed for my mental tranquillity that I was known where it imported that known I should be; the rest sat on me easily: pedigree, social position, and recondite intellectual acquisition, occupied about the same space and place in my interests and thoughts; they were my third-class lodgers – to whom could be assigned only the small sitting-room and the little back bedroom.
>
> (pp. 281–2)

As the metaphor implies, Lucy *is* her own Home.

But though *Villette* concludes with the creation of a new Home which is a modified version of a very old idea, it is clear, less equivocally here than at the end of *Jane Eyre*, that it is a home with a bedroom. In an outburst against her imaginary rival, the girl Justine Marie, Lucy accepts herself as 'warm and jealous'; 'I knew not til now', she says, 'that my nature had such a mood.' Sexual love is clearly not only acknowledged, but welcomed as a necessary part of the 'minds' and affections' assimilation' (p. 446) between men and women.

In the three years that follow until M. Paul's projected return home, Lucy is able to assume her place as mistress of an establishment and energetically pursue success because her selfhood is supported by her lover, who is 'the spring which moved my energies'.[15] M. Paul's love provides both the forward movement of the active will imaged in a mechanical spring, and the spring-like gush of sexual energy which is, as she calls his letters, the 'living water that refreshed' (p. 449).

Yet in the famous coda which closes *Villette*, the 'frosts appear at night' when the fulfilment of M. Paul's return impends. As he sails, the sun that warmed the blooming of Lucy's selfhood becomes 'one flame; so wild ... so bloody ...' (p. 450), as Vashti had been 'wild and intense, dangerous, sudden and flaming' (p. 236). We are reminded once again that the utter vulnerability and deep penetration of sexuality are dangerously close to annihilation; that desire, once loosened from its buried place, is primitive and insatiable, plundering like the destructive storm that 'roared frenzied' over the ocean that night.

In the final paragraphs of *Villette*, the sexual love that was delicately imaged as 'nourishment' for the human spirit, a spring of 'living water', has become, with dizzying suddenness, associated with the violent 'deeps [that] gorged their full of sustenance' (p. 451). The hunger that would have been satisfied with 'crumbs' has become predatory; the thirst for even a 'temperate draught' proves quenchless.[16] When the ocean devours its bodies, it is as though Nature herself, competitive and cruel, shares the will to consumption of selfish human beings. We have seen this sudden reversal of tone once before in this novel: when Lucy journeyed by water to Villette, she moved in one day from the heady pleasures of London, where she believed she 'taste[d] life' in an 'ecstasy of freedom and enjoyment' (pp. 39–40), to being 'served ... as a dripping roast' (p. 41) to the cheating, greedy watermen. In both instances, the skeleton shows inside the sensuous flesh.

In a bitter inversion of the conventional 'fitting' ending, in which reward is meted out to the deserving and the destructive are punished, Lucy as narrator abruptly commands us to 'pause: pause at once' (p. 451) before the question of M. Paul's survival of the shipwreck in the storm. This refusal of closure is both disturbing and brilliant, implying that there is no conciliation possible between female desire set free and the oppressions of society which inevitably shape sexual love, and therefore female identity. The experience of passion must remain a 'rumour'd heaven' only, like the Eros of Coventry Patmore's poem, if the innocence of desire is to be sustained.[17]

The very private and covert nature of this ideal love may serve to remind us that the female desire for a mutual and free sexual love, as a temporary and highly equivocal leap over the estrangement of human beings isolated from one another by a patriarchical and capitalistic system of self-interest, was not merely a 'dream to repose on', but also a subversive, even a dangerous secret. In fact, the more attractive sexual love appeared as a solution to the problem of women's desires, the more perilous a secret it became: admitting the existence of such a heaven only dramatized the emptiness of the world without it. In the novels of Charlotte Brontë, it is as dangerous for a woman to believe in it as it is impossible not to long for it.

Squeezed in this double bind, a different cultural heroine emerges. Lucy Snowe is far from a figure of Moral Femininity, rewarded for restraint by an ideal integration of sexual satisfaction and social success. Nor is she, in the end, left with the religious comforts of a heroine like Richardson's Clarissa, seeking selfhood in that ideal state of will-lessness, death. Lucy too locates her 'real' self at last, yet she remains radically alone, unable even to share a private morality in a segregated community of two, as does Jane Eyre. For Charlotte Brontë, a woman in her powerlessness is only too easily reduced to the choice of childlike, callow 'craving', or imitating the 'masculine' ethic of self-interest without the male power to pursue it.

Villette turns out to be a 'cabinet of oddities' indeed, a Victorian tale celebrating individual freedom and a radical story about the power of sexual love for women, framed in a highly orthodox criticism of modern social values. The deepest recesses of the cabinet contain the ideal of a 'real' sexuality, which is not based on gender roles, social power or acquisition, but is pure connection. This new investment of meaning in sexual love finds its narrative parallel in the 'new' method of interior writing in *Villette*, the dream-like liberation of repressed sexual feeling, a tapping of the artist's pipeline to the unconscious, seen as somehow more 'real' than the acknowledged self.[18] What we see in *Villette* in other words, is no less than the invention of a modern solution to the dilemma of the desiring female body and soul in an unjust and unequal society: the brave new sexual self, fragile yet ineluctable, as the 'real' self for women.

6
Wild Desire and Quenchless Will: *Wuthering Heights*

> No promised Heaven, these wild Desires
> Could all or half fulfil;
> No threatened Hell, with quenchless fires,
> Subdue this quenchless will!
>
> Emily Brontë, Poem No. 181

I

Perhaps one might justly say of all the Brontë sisters' heroines that they are 'quenchless' in the sense of Emily Brontë's verse above, but *Wuthering Heights* is unique even among Brontë novels as a construction of identity as a craving will which is both insatiable and unsubduable. As if they were a gloss on *Wuthering Heights*, the wonderful lines by Emily Brontë above seem to propose a Brontëan concept of self: if no Heaven could fulfil the insatiable desire of the poem's persona, neither could Hell quench the unsubduable will. Both Desire *and* the Will to act on Desire are seen here as 'quenchless', too strong to be either completed or repressed. The alliance of these two, whose strength is the hallmark of individual identity, forms an essentialist view of selfhood, in which a 'real' self, a more genuine inner core, is felt to lie buried beneath a distorting layer of social behaviour, values and roles. It would seem, in the social/historical context of Victorian England, that the unfulfilled lack in which Desire originates might easily be associated with the conventional notions of the feminine, and the self-determining practices of an indomitable Will viewed as correspondingly masculine, but this poem unites the two in one selfhood unmarked by gender.

But *Wuthering Heights* is not unmarked by gender; its sexual story

Wild Desire and Quenchless Will: Wuthering Heights

is the context for the disclosure of a crisis of female selfhood. Sexuality itself is constituted in the textual body of its two heroines, Catherine Earnshaw and her daughter, Catherine Linton. But just as the feminine is a fluid, multiple social construction, *Wuthering Heights* is a novel framed by multiple, contradictory voices, each of which subverts the authority of the others, so that no one voice is ultimately privileged, as no one view of selfhood or gender is endorsed.[1]

Catherine Earnshaw, heroine of *Wuthering Heights*, does not merely hear a *rumour* of Coventry Patmore's 'promised Heaven'; she insists on the validity and immediacy of her own heaven – which in turn is clearly not the Christian heaven about which she dreams her dream of loss and estrangement.[2] Catherine, who is not so much a 'craving vacancy' as a dynamo of the 'wild Desires' alluded to in the poem above, is Emily Brontë's most discomforting answer to the question that obsessed so many Victorians: 'What is a woman?'

Wuthering Heights is at once a continuance of the search for an answer to this problem, and an anomaly in the quest. The passivity and will-lessness of Moral Femininity, for example, do not have the same value here in as they do in Charlotte Brontë's novels. Whereas Jane Eyre typically longs to 'repose on what I trust', i.e. her lover, it is difficult to imagine Catherine Earnshaw reposing at all, even in the prison-frame of her body after death. Conversely, Catherine is much more capable of being the Lady, by birth, physical attractions and temperament than Jane Eyre or Lucy Snowe, and this possibility is more of a critical issue here than in either *Jane Eyre* or *Villette*. If sexual love promises identity to the ego-deprived heroines of Charlotte Brontë's novels, enmeshed as they are in the moral possibilities of selflessness, Catherine appears to have been born with a strong sense of selfhood, which she is only too careless about risking.[3]

Yet what she risks and what is at stake is highly problematic. As in *Jane Eyre*, the heroine is attracted to a man of implacable and relentless will, a man eager to, as Catherine says, 'seize and devour' (p. 91) a woman; yet a significant element of the story is that this same woman has, through the promise of sexual love, a certain mastery over him. If in Charlotte Brontë's novel, 'the heart' opposed the sexual outlaw, in *Wuthering Heights* the heart *is* the sexual outlaw.

As in *Clarissa*, where the problem of sexuality focused on the modern dilemma of the Christian will in a society based on self-interest, sexual love in *Wuthering Heights* has assumed a burden of so much meaning that it must either sink beneath the weight or rise above it. Thus we have the well-known tantalizing 'metaphysical' or 'spiritual' aura of *Wuthering Heights*, which is more puzzling than Richardson's resolution of sending Clarissa to Heaven. *Wuthering Heights* consigns the Christian Heaven mainly to the decent conventionalities of Nelly or the absurdly anti-human pieties of Joseph, while the chief protagonists, like the persona of the author's poem, dismiss 'promised Heaven' and 'threatened Hell' as entirely inadequate and irrelevant to the urgencies of the 'quenchless' sexual will. Instead, this novel works in terms of '*my* heaven', as Heathcliff describes his first principle (pp. 279, 283), in which sexual love forms the dangerous border crossing between individual freedom and the Hell of isolation.

Of all the many mysteries of *Wuthering Heights*, the nature of the love between Catherine and Heathcliff is the most difficult to penetrate; in a novel about the absolute commitment of the self to love, the text seems to refuse a final commitment to the judgment of love itself as a value. We know their love is 'wild' compared to the domesticated affections of the other characters', but the use of this key word (important as well to Charlotte Brontë) is itself fluid: it appears to mean, variously, inartificial as an attribute of nature, as in 'the wild green park' (p. 79); uncivilized and lawless, as when Catherine's sister-in-law warns on her return from the Lintons that 'she must . . . not grow wild again' (p. 43); or madly gay-spirited, as when Catherine is called a 'wild wicked slip' (p. 34), always singing, laughing and teasing. The multivalent significations of this word allow it at once to indicate the state of violent unruliness in Catherine's threat 'I shall get wild' (p. 99), while poetically implying the largeness of emotion that results only from the letting go of self-control, releasing a living energy that permeates a 'world awake and wild with joy' (p. 210) which is the second Catherine's idea of heaven. The result of this ambiguity of language and the famously unreliable narrative frame is a challenge laid down, not only to each of the characters, but to the reader as well, to penetrate an obscure and refractory truth. We are left, like a heroine of sensibility, to 'feel' what is right, reduced to a 'heart' in moral perplexity.

Wuthering Heights has most often been taken as romanticism at its peak, an idealization of love carried, as J. Hillis Miller says, 'as far as it can go'.[4] Yet this novel employs all the high feeling of romantic love even as it strenuously subverts it as an ideal. Throughout the novel, conventional romantic love is consistently pilloried, from the narrator Lockwood's self-styled and painfully self-conscious 'romantic' view which childishly desires only what it may not have, to the inflated and self-deceiving infatuations of Catherine for Edgar, Isabella for Heathcliff, and the second Cathy's for Linton. The idea that romantic love is noble and unselfish by nature, as Charlotte Brontë herself had tenaciously insisted, is everywhere held up to ridicule. Heathcliff himself scornfully appraises the narcissistic quality of Isabella's 'delusion', in which she pictures in him 'a hero of romance ... expecting unlimited indulgences from my chivalrous devotion' (p. 128).

Similarly, Hindley and his wife Frances, who together form a small, self-sufficient 'paradise on the hearth', in Catherine's own contemptuous words, are conventionally loving and domestic yet entirely selfish in their self-absorption. Their mutual indulgence makes them not more benevolent to others, but less so: on Sundays they 'basked downstairs before a comfortable fire', according to Cathy's journal, 'kissing and talking nonsense by the hour', while the other members of the household are banished to a conveniently distant 'congregation in the garret' (p. 16). There is not, until perhaps the final pages, a feminine angel in any house in *Wuthering Heights*, though the image of the selfless angel hovers over this novel as ceaselessly as the spectre of the nun haunted *Villette*.

In the mid-Victorian period the exact relationship of romantic love to sexual desire was so equivocal that an ideology of 'love' could be appropriated by both sides, readily identified either with conventional social striving and the selfishness of individual interests, or as a noble revolt by the individual against this social mode. This ambiguity, normally handled coyly or sentimentally in popular Victorian literature, is particularly confusing in *Wuthering Heights* because of the startling oddness of Catherine and Heathcliff's relationship.

It would seem, in order to deal with this doubleness in the novel, that we as readers are forced (not least by Cathy herself) to make distinctions between 'romantic love' and 'sexual love', or even more perplexing, between both of these and a third, vaguely metaphysical concept, 'real' love.[5] Such convenient categories, however, merely confuse the issue by begging the basic question: what is the moral status of sexual love? Is it still another form of possession in a society ever striving for more possessions? Or is it a rebellion of two against worldly values, one large and deep feeling both criticizing and substituting for the web of social relations? Is its heightened emotion an excuse for a more subtle form of exploitation, or is exploitation rather sexual possession without feeling? This, I would argue, is the pivotal issue on which *Wuthering Heights* turns, concealed by its peculiarly Victorian striving after balance and conciliation.

Early critics of the novel generally took one extreme position or other: Catherine and Heathcliff were at first seen as sexual monsters, later as idealized romantic heroes. According to the first position, Heathcliff's shocking rejection of Christian dogma, whose 'promised Heaven' and 'threatened Hell' appear in the novel as entirely inadequate to the urgencies of 'quenchless' sexuality, rendered him coherent only as a malignant dynamo of uncontrollable 'wild Desires'. The second critical perspective, beginning in the late nineteenth century, saw the fulfilment of sexual love as interchangeable with the attainment of individual freedom through the release of repressed Desire/Will, and the banishment of the Hell of the self's isolation.

In much twentieth-century criticism, however, the novel has been viewed as either a darkly sinister sexual story or else not 'really' related to sex at all, either reeking of incest and sadism or else purely spiritual-metaphysical in its concerns.[6] All of these critical perspectives tended to mystify the character of Catherine as an incoherent subject, a woman with a strong will and an unrestrained desire. The very abundance and variety of opinion on the novel is itself suggestive: when so many critics strain so hard, surely some highly disturbing (and provocative) element is present in the text itself.

It is difficult to avoid the conclusion that Brontë herself cultivated this disturbing element: from Catherine's famous confession speech to Nelly, in which she gropes for words to describe her feelings – 'I cannot express it', she tells her companion (p. 73) – and merely alludes to a dream she is not permitted to disclose, to the last intense moments of her life, Catherine never articulates the 'true' relation she desires with Heathcliff. Most confusingly, while we are taught by the text how to feel with the first Catherine, a superabundance of contradictory signs leaves us confused as to what to think of her *as a woman*. Traditionally, critics saw her as Nelly Dean speaks of her, a perpetrator of the tragedy; more recently, some have allied themselves with Catherine's own view of herself as victim.[7] In the end, the textual representation of Catherine herself proves to be the most obscurant of all barriers to the privileged story of *Wuthering Heights*, the illusory Ur-story, whose telling is always being postponed. We are offered partial truths, biased truths and a series of interconnected fragments which never complete the whole story, but direct knowledge of Catherine's inner self is withheld from us, like the dream which, if Nelly had allowed her to tell it, would 'explain my secret', or the contents of the unread books filled with Catherine's journal, mentioned – again, tantalizingly – by Lockwood.

Though Catherine is clearly spoiled, self-pitying and violent-tempered – '"I'll cry myself sick!"' she typically threatens (p. 61) – she nevertheless asserts her craving as a positive value. The dangerously wilful, self-centred but attractively passionate male hero is a well-established tradition in literature from Don Juan to Manfred, but our identification with such a heroine is radical in the British novel. It is as though Emily Brontë set out through the character of Catherine to mortify the sweetness of popular romantic love and the fragile Moral Feminine, in much the same way that Charlotte Brontë did the convention of the beautiful and dashing Lady-heroine with the plain Jane Eyre.

It has become a cliché of Brontë criticism to assert that the relation of Catherine and Heathcliff cannot survive into adulthood because it is essentially childlike, meaning, as critics have generally used the term, asexual or pre-sexual.[8] I would argue that it is doomed because it loses its unique sexual status, which was childlike in the metaphorical sense of pre-social and unselfconscious. The relation of Catherine to Heathcliff has been disturbing or exhilarating to generations of readers and critics, not merely because it is impossibly romantic and obsessive, and/or possibly supernatural – there is, after all, much literary precedent for both – but because it discloses a uniquely visionary view of female sexuality in the very midst of an otherwise expectable construction of feminine character.

II

Certainly Catherine Earnshaw is no ordinary Victorian heroine, even by the unusual standards set by the author's sister, Charlotte Brontë, whose suffering, desiring heroines – Jane Eyre, Caroline Hedstrom, Lucy Snowe – obsessively consider the moral implications of their acts. She is, of course, still less the Victorian domestic ideal (though at Heathcliff's return she confidently declares, in one of the nicest ironies of the novel, 'I'm an angel!' (p. 85). When she craves, it is not because she is a weak vessel, but from the sureness of a strong will. There is none of the sweetness or passivity of the conventional Moral Feminine about her, willingly suppressing her own sexual desire in order to uphold a social standard or a moral position.

Yet it is easier to say what Catherine Earnshaw is *not* than what she is. Though it is important in the novel that the child Catherine is a female in a motherless household (Heathcliff fills, we remember, a 'gap' left in the family by the death of a male child), yet she is neither entirely enclosed by conventional femininity, with its limited social modes and repertoires of behaviour, nor by a traditionally 'masculine' model of identity through action. While partaking on occasion of both, she does not fully live her literary life in either one.

Unlike many Victorian heroines, Catherine is represented from the moment we first encounter her in the novel as a rebel, and a comparatively successful one at that. Almost the very first words we hear from her are an unhesitating 'H. and I are going to rebel' (p. 26). Catherine recounts in her writing the story of their oppression by her tyrannical older brother Hindley as though confident that someone, somewhere, will want to redress her aggrieved sense of wrong. She projects her imaginary audience, then, out of a sense of injustice (like Jane Eyre's), directly appealing to the reader's imagined capacity for sympathy. All narrators do, of course, and both Lockwood and Nelly's accounts will vie for that sympathy, but the journal of a child has a particular narrative force in that it combines a striking conviction of the immediacy of events with artlessness, sincerity and the appeal of the vulnerable.

If the Catherine Earnshaw of this journal is more successful and less self-doubting in rebellion than the child Jane Eyre – she succeeds, for example, in escaping from the kitchen where she has been banished, unlike Jane from her temporary imprisonment – the source of this strength seems to be Catherine's double identity as an 'I' and a 'we'. So complete, in fact, is the association of wishes, fears and behaviour with Heathcliff that Catherine appears to think of her childhood self as *less* an 'I' than a 'we': '*We* took our initiatory step in rebellion'; '*we* should be ashamed' of talking such nonsense as Hindley and his wife, and so on (p. 26, my italics). Heathcliff is the gun to Cathy's 'gunpowder', her double-barrelled instrument of both aggression and later, 'wild' sexual desire, or more precisely, of that originary sexuality which becomes 'wild desire' in the context of Victorian containment.[9]

Catherine herself, in a later moment of deep mental distress, describes her girlhood as 'hardy and free'. In fact, as Catherine participates in both her own selfhood and Heathcliff's (i.e. the famous 'I *am* Heathcliff'), she seems in one sense to have escaped the constrictive social bonds and limitations of gender. Yet she is not free, as the text itself is never free, from the implications of gender: on the contrary, in another sense Catherine's self-representation as unsubduable originates in her insatiable desire to 'be' *both* sexes, to enact quenchless Desire and Will at once.

The special relation of Desire to the feminine, as feminist critics have pointed out, is that the lack on which it is based is frequently naturalized as a universal characteristic of femaleness.[10] But Catherine (unlike, for example, Jane Eyre or *Villette*'s little Polly) is not driven by desire in childhood precisely because she does not lack: indeed, she has more than enough. 'He's more myself than I am,' Catherine cries to Nelly at the moment she is about to lose her childhood tie to Heathcliff.

Catherine had already begun to fail in her early bid for our sympathy when she entered the competitive-exploitative world of ladies and gentlemen at age twelve. The crux comes, of course, when she is forced by Edgar's proposal of marriage at age fifteen to choose between 'Lady' and 'woman' for her self-identity. Like Jane Eyre, Cathy is placed between alternatively contrasting lovers in such a way that sexual choice appears inextricably involved with moral and social choice. Nelly, for one, however, is quite clear on this point: her motive is that she is 'full of ambition', not merely for wealth and social status, but also – perhaps more – for the admiration and devotion of Edgar and Isabella. These are, in Nelly's significant choice of words, 'acquisitions that flattered her from the first' (p. 56).

Dress embodies the pretension towards status through prettified surface, and Catherine assumes a 'silk dress' and hair artificially curled for the occasion of Edgar's visits. Similarly, the a priori 'we-ness' that formerly made her companionship with Heathcliff egalitarian and unselfconscious is replaced by her irritated sense that Heathcliff has little social conversation. '"You might be dumb or a baby for anything you say to amuse me, or for anything you do, either!"' she accuses him, thereby betraying the mode of unearned consumption of leisure and goods which is the hallmark of the Lady.

Then, too, romantic love in *Wuthering Heights*, associated with the world of ladies and gentlemen, involves another kind of greed, the wish to find and incorporate an ideal vision of oneself as seen through the eyes of another. We suspect that what the adolescent Catherine really loves in Edgar is the reflected image of herself as a grown-up Lady, one who is adored, petted and indulged, teasingly desirable yet eminently respectable. Ladyhood, the only allowably 'feminine' way to be wilful, is the social structure of legitimate female power to which all around her urge Catherine. By contrast, as Catherine describes her feelings, she does not need to attach herself to Heathcliff's qualities because she *is* Heathcliff, preternaturally resembling him.

The impassioned force of Cathy's speeches about her two loves tends to overshadow the striking oddity of the terms in which she couches her decision to marry Edgar. After stating clearly that she would have married Heathcliff had not her brother degraded him into a brute socially and intellectually, that their physical and emotional separation is 'impracticable', she posits a future relationship between them after her marriage to Edgar which will be an extension into adulthood of their childhood 'we-ness', which she sees as pre-sexual. 'He'll be as much to me as he has been all his lifetime,' she answers indignantly to Nelly's query as to how Heathcliff will bear her desertion (p. 69).

Her proposal is that they will inhabit the physical world together, necessarily connected in all ways but the sexual, just as they shared one bed as innocent children. Catherine thus treats her own sexuality, not as a necessary part of her selfhood – which is, as she herself has defined it, her relation to Heathcliff – but as a commodity to be dangled or concealed, used or denied to obtain social ends when most convenient.

Moreover, Catherine believes that this denial of the sexual aspect of her love for Heathcliff is justified by that sympathy which she is able to feel for him alone. In her own view, Cathy sees herself as the Lady who will 'aid Heathcliff to rise' (p. 69) both materially and from his ignorant brutality, with her husband's money and status. The pose that Catherine would assume is, in fact, based on the sentiment of Moral Femininity: that by withholding or denying her sexuality, the woman-as-angel can influence the recalcitrant male and 'help' him to rise above his own brutality.

In deciding to marry Edgar, Catherine insists she is going to balance both relations, binding Heathcliff to her while keeping his sexuality at a distance. But Heathcliff *is* sexuality, or rather he is a figure for sexuality as the essential kernel of her own selfhood, and he therefore must be, at least temporarily, entirely absent to Catherine if she rejects him. Whereas the requirements of a culturally constructed femininity call for the repression of wild, disruptive Desire, the text of *Wuthering Heights* simply will not allow for mediation between essential identity and femininity, just as conventional romantic love will not accommodate the expression of female sexuality in this part of the novel. When Heathcliff returns after her marriage, Catherine is said to laugh 'like one beside herself' (p. 85), as she later is beside herself with madness: the 'real' self of Catherine – her secret sexual self, in other words – has returned to haunt her.

Trapped between an essentialist definition of female selfhood, constituted by Desire separated from the Will to act on it, and a social definition of femininity, which requires its repression, Catherine can neither bear nor resolve the call to profound sexual experience which her love for Heathcliff implies. Later, self-exiled in her room, we see manifested in Catherine's delirium a frightening separation of self from self, which Dr Kenneth later calls 'the danger . . . [of] permanent alienation of intellect' (p. 112). In a grotesque parody of the Lady's manipulative pout, Catherine's 'frenzy' usurps its part, and she becomes frozen in the role she has acted. Now, both physically and metaphorically, Catherine seems 'beside herself': 'Does [Edgar] know how I'm altered?' she cries, staring at her mirrored reflection opposite, 'Is that Catherine Linton?' (p. 104).

Just as she had confessed to Nelly in her adolescence the recurrent dream that has 'gone through and through me, like wine through water, and altered the colour of my mind' (p. 72), her dream of being flung out of Heaven onto the top of Wuthering Heights, Catherine now relates to Nelly a vision, 'what has kept recurring and recurring till I feared for my reason' (p. 107). It is the vivid delusion that she is enclosed in her oak-panelled bed at Wuthering Heights, her heart aching with 'a great grief': 'I was a child; my father was just buried, and my misery arose from the separation that Hindley had just ordered between me and Heathcliff – I was laid alone, for the first time . . .' She then speaks agonizingly of her wrenching conversion 'at a stroke' into 'Mrs. Linton, the lady of Thrushcross Grange' (p. 107).

Catherine's new negative definition of her present self, Mrs Linton, as 'the wife of a stranger; exile and outcast' (p. 107), derives from the loss of her positive definition of female selfhood in her former relation with Heathcliff. But the choice of her moment of childhood separation from Heathcliff as the emotional turning point of her life seems strangely puzzling in the midst of her crisis of decision between two lovers. Why not remember as the greatest grief, for example, the traumatic scene of Heathcliff's departure from Wuthering Heights at her decision to marry Edgar?

It is here, on the meaning of childhood to Catherine and Heathcliff's relationship, that so many critical opinions have diverged. It is surely this scene, above all others, of which V.S. Pritchett, for example, was thinking when he wrote that 'the love of Catherine and Heathcliff is not one of the great love affairs [because] it is an attempt to get back to their childhood and its sexless companionship.'[11] One would readily expect to identify Catherine's poignant memory of childhood loss with a wish to return to childhood's 'innocence', meaning, as most critics have used it, asexuality, but it is worth remembering that the precise scene which recurs to Catherine as her greatest grief is being 'laid alone', i.e. Heathcliff's expulsion from her bed, just as she is about to enter adolescence. I would argue that the emphasis of this scene is not on the negative value of sexuality in favour of an asexual 'innocence', but rather on the positive value of sexuality, a visionary sexuality which has its origins in childhood and is a natural extension of Catherine and Heathcliff's undifferentiated and unselfconscious childhood 'weness'.

While Catherine described her attraction to Edgar as *another kind* of romantic love in the confession scene to Nelly, it is also clearly placed by her in a constellation of social values associated with courtship. The formula for feminine success of a certain kind is a familiar one to any reader of nineteenth-century novels: access to money, respectability and the status of membership in a valued social class, at the price of the moderation of desire. But Brontë has Nelly, with a shrewd irony lost on a Catherine absorbed in feeling, question the univocal simplicity of this definition of heroineship from the bourgeois novel:

> Well, that settles it – if you have only to do with the present, marry Mr. Linton.... You will escape from a disorderly, comfortless home into a wealthy respectable one; and you love Edgar, and Edgar loves you. All seems smooth and easy – where is the obstacle?

(p. 67)

Wild Desire and Quenchless Will: Wuthering Heights

The 'obstacle' is a 'secret' which Catherine, in the same scene, promises to explain, only to qualify her promise by adding, 'I can't do it distinctly – but I'll give you a feeling of how I feel' (p. 67). She then refers to a dream, somehow meant to be explanatory, which Nelly refuses to permit her to tell – 'I won't hear it, I won't hear it!' she cries – and the reader never does hear either that dream or the explanation.

What we are given 'instead' is Catherine's metaphorically significant dream of her discovery that heaven is not her true home, but even this is very much a displacement rather than a direct articulation of her meaning; we are given no indication that either Nelly nor Catherine herself can make it out as a disclosure of Catherine's selfhood. Catherine's dream of being expelled from Heaven thematically fits the frames surrounding the novel – Christian and irreligious, realist and supernatural, masculine and feminine – without being clarified by them. It is the untellable which must constitute the essential for Catherine, as both language and social practices constrain her, proving inadequate to identity.

In *Wuthering Heights* the untellable is an unspeakable sexuality. Catherine's feelings for Heathcliff are impossible to convey through the medium of language, because they are as complex and contradictory as sexuality itself. It is not so much that such a love is possible only in childhood, before the development of adult sexuality, as several critics have suggested,[12] as that the childhood intimacy shared by the two is itself a metaphorical representation of the Brontëan idea of a sexuality which is 'unselfconscious' in the literal way of having no consciousness of boundaries between selves, or (what amounts to the same thing) of having no vocabulary to talk about the separation of selves.[13]

When Catherine cries in anguish, 'Oh, if I were but in my bed in the old house!' (p. 106) the recurrent image of that bed, pervading the novel from the scene of Lockwood's dream to its close in Heathcliff's deliberate choice of it as his death-place, unites the themes of childhood, sexuality and death in one densely wrought symbol.[14] The old-fashioned, oak-panelled bed shares in the gathering emotional force of Wuthering Heights itself as a sacred place. As an enclosed space at the far end of a bedroom located deep in the interior of the house, it appears to be its inmost sanctuary. Carefully described as bordered by sliding panels on one side and a window on the other, it is clearly associated with the sympathetic intimacy of Catherine and Heathcliff's childhood bond, before the adult sensibility separated the two into selves, but it is also something more. A boxlike structure, it is like a coffin with exits for a kind of movable death, the sort that will allow Catherine's ghost to attempt to enter the bedchamber window, or her remains to dissolve with Heathcliff's after he has 'struck one side of the coffin loose' (p. 228). And last, this dark rectangular enclosure with one window-opening to the outside world is emblematic of the deepest secret of all: the longed-for yet fearful site of female sexuality, of 'wild Desire'. Like a woman's desire, it is simultaneously prison-house and place of freedom.

Immediately following Cathy's recounting her memory, she wishes aloud that she were 'a girl again, half savage and hardy, and free', and, sure that she should 'be myself were I once among the heather on those hills', she urges Nelly to 'Open the window again, fasten it open!' Nelly refuses, saying, 'I won't give you your death of cold'; to which Catherine swiftly returns, 'You won't give me a chance of life, you mean' (p. 107). Like the incursion of sexuality, the opening out of the window to the world of childhood implies both death and the chance of life at once. Though Catherine has now located her lost 'real' self in the authenticity of childhood, she cannot see how to unite that selfhood, which is contained in her relation to Heathcliff, with the body of the Lady which is no longer 'herself'. It seems that the only recourse is to renounce that physical shell along with the role she rejects.

Now slipping into delirium, she speaks aloud to Heathcliff, as she dares him to defy their separation by a union in death, the road home to a perpetual childhood which will evade her present problem: 'But Heathcliff, if I dare you now, will you venture? If you do, I'll keep you. I'll not lie there by myself: they may bury me twelve feet deep and throw the church down over me; but I won't rest till you are with me ... I never will!' Though Catherine now recognizes the 'impracticability' of their separation, the necessity of some undefined quality of selfhood which Heathcliff brings to her, she envisages a 'spiritual' joining, literally a union of ghostly spirits, much as at her decision to marry Edgar she had planned on a purely social relation between them. Like the spiritual adulterers of medieval courtly love, she now believes she and Heathcliff will enter a space 'beyond' sexuality.

When we next see Catherine it is two months later. We now learn for the first time that Cathy is and has been pregnant; moreover, she is recovering from 'what was denominated a brain fever' (p. 114).

Wild Desire and Quenchless Will: Wuthering Heights

Just before her last, climactic meeting with Heathcliff, Catherine's unearthly beauty is described minutely as she sits near the open window, 'in a loose white dress', with her hair 'simply combed in its natural tresses over her temples and neck'.

Ethereal, pale, angelically white-robed, her appearance stripped of Lady-like artificiality, curls or ornament, she could almost be the quintessential Moral Feminine renouncing bodily pleasure and earthly self-will for something 'beyond and above us all' (p. 137), as she herself will say. As Nelly describes her:

> The flash of her eyes had been succeeded by a dreamy and melancholy softness: they no longer gave the impression of looking at the objects around her; they appeared always to gaze beyond, and far beyond – you would have said out of this world.
>
> (p. 133)

To recall the literary convention that is being invoked, we have only to compare this with Richardson's description of Clarissa as Belford finds her awaiting her death:

> We beheld the lady in a charming attitude. Dressed, as I told you before, in her virgin white, she was sitting in her elbow-chair.... One faded cheek rested upon the good woman's bosom, the kindly warmth of which had overspread it with a faint but charming flush; the other paler and hollow, as if already iced over by death. Her hands, white as the lily, with her meandering veins more transparently blue than ever I had seen even hers ... her aspect was sweetly calm and serene.
>
> (IV, p. 332)

Yet it should be clear by this time that it is Emily Brontë's method to prime us for a conventional expectation, only to demolish it to better effect. For in the scene that follows, it is Cathy's very state of extremity, the madness, pregnancy and nearness to death – all invitations to sentimental writing about female fragility and/or passivity – which induces a defiant atmosphere of lawlessness in which she can make her final leap into a state which Brontë allows for only at the very point of death.

At the very end of Catherine Earnshaw's life, the consciousness of Desire, her sexual love for Heathcliff, is stained with a heightened vulnerability to death, like wine through water. The scene of

Catherine's last reunion with Heathcliff is a melodramatic but carefully orchestrated dialogic struggle between the conflicting views of the two lovers on the validity of sexual love in shaping selfhood. Who has killed Catherine? Catherine herself suggests at first that it was Edgar, by refusing to allow her to choose both Ladyhood and her sexual self at once. Or was it Heathcliff, who would not permit the repression of her sexuality? No, says Heathcliff, '*You*, of your own will, did it' (p. 137).

We have been prepared for this all-important struggle by being left deliberately unprepared. As the intensity of the conflict between Cathy and Heathcliff began to mount, we have hardly noticed the absence of any articulation of Cathy's feelings for him. Heathcliff is given the scene with Nelly immediately after his marriage in which he describes his intentions and justifies them by calling Cathy an 'oak in a flower-pot' (p. 131) but all we have from Catherine is her joy at his return and her desire for some kind of possession. Between these there are no enlightening words to a confidante comparable to her early confession scene, no journal entries, no aid to inform us of Cathy's self-knowledge or her state of mind. Catherine's sexual response to Heathcliff is a gap in the text, a mystery that has been deliberately cultivated.

Before Heathcliff's last visit, Catherine has been silent and passive in the extreme, as becomes dying femininity. She does not speak as she sits dreamily by the window; she seems unable to read Heathcliff's letter asking for an interview by herself, or even to reply: 'She merely pointed to the name, and gazed at me with mournful and questioning eagerness' (p. 134), as Nelly says. Heathcliff enters the room and kneels down on one knee to hold her in the traditional stance of courtly adoration, much as Clarissa's long-awaited cousin Morden 'folded the angel in his arms as she sat, dropping down on one knee' (IV, p. 335). His first words, 'Oh, Cathy! Oh my life! how can I bear it' (p. 135), echoing Lovelace's 'An eternal separation! O God! O God! How can I bear that thought?' (IV, p. 342) should appropriately evoke an answering speech of physical renunciation; Clarissa's 'He will not let me die decently', or 'God's will be done' (IV, pp. 305, 308), will do for a model.

Yet in an abrupt and shocking reversal, the moment Heathcliff has her grasped in his arms, Catherine resumes her former mastery, berating him cruelly as though his mere touch is enough to bring to life the impetuous strong will she showed formerly. So far from acting the withdrawing angel, the resistant maiden or well-bred

Lady, Nelly tells us plainly that 'my mistress had kissed him *first*' (p. 135, my italics). Though she is the aggressor in this agonized interchange – she keeps Heathcliff in a stance of submission momentarily by 'seizing his hair' – she is in fact surrendering to his demand for sexual love.

When she cannot control him, Catherine retreats into her former longing for death. Her body, she muses, is a 'shattered prison', from which she is 'wearying to escape into that glorious world, and to be always there...' As pure spirit, Catherine will not only be forever 'beyond and above us all', but out of the reach of the vicissitudes of her human sexual nature. She would be, in other words, a Clarissa, who affirmed that 'she should be a happy creature as soon as she could be divested of these *rags of mortality*' (IV, p. 305).

In the delirium of her mad episode, Catherine showed her knowledge that Heathcliff would 'rather I'd come to him', i.e. embody their 'we-ness' in the leap to a human sexual relation, rather than in death, the way through the kirkyard. Now, as tension between them mounts to fearful climax, 'An instant they held asunder; and then how they met I hardly saw, but Catherine made a spring, and he caught her, and they were locked in an embrace from which I thought my mistress would never be released alive.' The sexual feelings released in this spring seem strong enough to shatter Catherine's mental frame: 'To my eyes,' says Nelly, 'she seemed directly insensible' (p. 37). This 'spring' is the inverse of that 'spring from the window' with which Catherine had threatened Edgar if he mentioned Heathcliff's name; it is not an attempt to bridge over 'the abyss where I grovelled', Catherine's consciousness of the empty universe and the vacancy of her selfhood, by an avoidance of irresolvable conflict. It is a daring – and literally dangerous – leap *into* the unknown, a momentary immersion in sexual experience which is, too late, her 'chance of life'.

Desire and Will unite at last in Catherine's last gesture, made with 'mad resolution' in the anarchic name of love: her refusal to allow Heathcliff to leave on Edgar's arrival, though Nelly pleads 'for Heaven's sake' (p. 135). In *Wuthering Heights* we are never allowed to forget that the energy generated by the spring into full female sexuality is not a warm glow, but a self-consuming inferno. Catherine never regains consciousness from the swoon that follows their last embrace, and her life ends that night. One might say that Catherine dies both *from* sexual desire and in order to forestall its physical consummation, leaving the reader suspended at that heightened climactic moment in which both the joyous Heaven of fulfilled Desire and the Hell of subsequent deprivation are always deferred.

Catherine died, Nelly tells Heathcliff, 'like a child reviving' (p. 142), immersed in the 'glorious world' of eternal childhood, which Nelly pictures as unending prelapsarian innocence. Once again we are returned to the image of Catherine as the womanly angel in Nelly's observation of her death as 'perfect peace': 'Her brow smooth, her lids closed, her lips wearing the expression of a smile. No angel in heaven could be more beautiful than she appeared' (p. 140). We need only turn to Richardson's description of Clarissa at the point of expiring to see the very type of will-less feminine passivity that is being invoked:

> 'Bless – bless – bless you all . . .' And with these words, the last but half-pronounced, expired: such a smile, such a charming serenity overspreading her sweet face at the instant, as seemed to manifest her eternal happiness already begun.
>
> (IV, p. 347)

Yet as we know, in death Catherine is neither silenced nor subdued: if anything, she is more quenchless than ever, seeking to exercise her power over Heathcliff as she dominates the text – through her absence. Withholding her presence from Heathcliff, as she drove him wild in life by withholding her sexuality, she continues to haunt this novel as a desirous spirit, a figment or fragment of her self – that is, of her embodied self. We are left at the end with a paradox: the spirit Catherine may have achieved selfhood without social or gender boundaries, the perfect state of being as a 'we', by subsuming Heathcliff into her own state of ghostliness, but she is once again lacking, since she is no longer a living woman when she achieves this consummation.

Like Heathcliff wanting to catch one more glimpse, readers and critics continually resurrect her by recasting her conceptually, recreating her for themselves. In attempting to 'understand' and place her in a larger context than her own story, we are teased, again like Heathcliff, by the partial satisfaction of our expectations in the process of reading the text of *Wuthering Heights*. Thus the visionary possibilities of the (possibly) supernatural realm textually undermine the realism of Nelly's domestic pieties and ethical certainties even in the second half of the novel, in which the narrative of another Catherine and her two loves seems to reduce the original story of sexual love to a project of revision rather than vision.

Most of all, the literary convention that traditionally enclosed the heroine in a certain kind of sexual narrative – one with an ending that transformed sexuality into the story of courtship and marriage – is found wanting here, and literally burst apart, splitting the story in two. The second half of the novel, depicting Catherine's daughter and her courtships, does satisfy this particular literary expectation, as we all know, but because the first Catherine has passed beyond the social/physical world, *this* story is too late for her, as well as besides the point in the timeless world she is said to inhabit.

The structure of the second half of the novel, in which the relationships of the younger generation parallel the first on a smaller and less intensely emotional plane which at times approaches caricature, is too well known to require detailed repetition here. When we have been taxed and drained by outrageous reversals of expectation, and while our own emotional involvement with the proponents of sexual love is at its height, the novel suddenly draws a breath and begins again. In doing so, it slowly rights itself back to the convention that was earlier stood on its head, until the rebels are rebelled against, and the values of the questioners questioned.

Whereas the elder Catherine began in passion and rebellion, but was attracted in the sexual crisis of adolescence to the rewards of Ladyhood, young Cathy is born the 'little lady', with the 'petted will' of one indulged and protected, yet she is increasingly attracted to the risky possibilities of experience. In an early exchange with Nelly, Cathy wishes repeatedly to visit the 'golden rocks' of Penistone Craggs, 'high and steep', which Nelly tells her she is not old enough to climb. These 'bare masses of stone', as Nelly calls them in the same conversation, the Penis-Stone, in effect, represent a romanticized view of male sexuality – or, to put it another way, Penistone Craggs are a representation of male sexuality enhanced by adolescent romanticization. Young Cathy is equally drawn towards an exploration of her own female sexuality, as embodied in the image of the cave near the crag, an analogue in nature of her mother's enclosed bed:

> One of the maids mentioning the Fairy cave, quite turned her head with a desire to fulfil this project; she teased Mr. Linton about it; and he promised she should have the journey when she got older.
> (p. 162)

Young Cathy is inevitably drawn back by her restless, as yet unnamed longings to Wuthering Heights, to which she naughtily runs away as a child, as her mother had run away at the age of twelve *from* nature to Thrushcross Grange. Desire has been awakened by a perceived lack, and we are, narratively speaking, on an odd backward journey towards the original Will and Desire located in the text at the site of Wuthering Heights.

At the Heights, Cathy meets Hareton for the first time, a gentleman's son in the guise of a servant (as Heathcliff is the former servant of the family now in the guise of a gentleman). Hareton, at Cathy's request, 'opened the mysteries of the Fairy cave' (p. 168). By the close of the novel, Hareton will 'show her the way', as she asks him at one point, to the evocative meanings of the Cave and the Crag, those sexual constructions which are visited in tandem.

But Cathy is not yet ready for this climb, as Hareton is not ready for her: thus, she refuses to acknowledge her blood relation to him at this first meeting. In the term 'blood relation' – they are first cousins – we may see again the multivalent meanings that attached to the 'incestuous' relation of the first Catherine and Heathcliff. Cathy's distressed assertion of her superiority of rank and 'culture' at this encounter is an inverted parallel to Catherine's painful rejection of Heathcliff's dirtiness after her visit to Thrushcross Grange. Significantly, this conversation between Cathy and Hareton is in the same tone of comic misunderstanding with which the novel began. Most importantly, the focus here is on the absurdity of the second Cathy's desires, which need correction and moderation, rather than on the tragic pain inherent in the oppressive contradictions of female sexuality itself.

The same broad touch of caricature marks the character of Linton, the son of Heathcliff and Isabella, whom Cathy begins to visit at Wuthering Heights when she is sixteen, just as her mother was visited there by Edgar in *her* adolescence. Linton, 'more of a lass than a lad' (p. 188), as is intimated several times, is a parody, not only obviously of Edgar's own effeteness, but of the stereotypical passivity and manoeuvres of the Lady. Linton 'giggles', 'titters', weeps, sulks, pouts, worries endlessly about his food and his comforts, and finally fades in a decline as delicate as that of any fragile Lady. Cathy's relation to him is what Heathcliff and Catherine's is often said to be: truly asexual. Though she fancies herself in love, her affection never extends much beyond 'stroking his curls, and kissing his cheek, and offering him tea in her saucer, like a baby' (p. 171), or later, 'wish[ing] you were my brother' (p. 202).

Entirely self-absorbed, Linton sees Cathy as the Lady sees a potential husband, the source of amusements, material comforts and protection, physical and economic, from the world's abuse and hardships. In our last glimpse of him before death he is stretched on the settle, 'sole tenant, sucking a sugar-candy, and pursuing [Nelly's] movements with apathetic eyes' (p. 236); he could be the childish and spoiled young lady in any number of Victorian novels, including the self-indulgent, weak and useless Georgiana, asleep on a sofa in *Jane Eyre*. It is as though Cathy were set to grotesquely expiating in her 'love' for Linton both her mother's ambition to profess the role of Lady and the false asexuality of her desired relation to Heathcliff. Fittingly, Linton dies before the marriage with Cathy is consummated; indeed, one feels that it never could have been consummated. Like any conventional romance, it is a relation in name only, and incapable of providing a true Home.

But Cathy, unlike her mother, is allowed to marry *twice*; that is, she is proven educable, transformable from an essential identity into a feminine self. As Heathcliff had predicted, on forcing her back to Wuthering Heights after her father's death, 'You shall be sorry to be yourself presently' (p. 228). The implication of her malleability is that Cathy must face the death of her girlhood self before assuming full life as a woman who is also a Lady – a good Lady, which is to say, an exemplar of 'real' femininity, in the way Victorian society fashioned that paradigm.

Nevertheless, a vivid note is struck by Brontë even here, where so many critics, feminist and otherwise, have expressed disappointment in the novel: Cathy and Hareton, bent together over a book, are said to be 'animated with the eager interest of children; for though he was twenty-three and she eighteen' – she is the same age, one notes, as her mother when the latter renounced her childhood love in marrying Edgar – 'each had so much of novelty to feel and learn, that neither experienced, nor evinced the sentiments of sober disenchanted maturity' (p. 254). The two lovers are, in other words, recapturing the state of 'eager children' lost by the two who began the story.

When, having offended Hareton, Cathy kisses him first, her 'gentle kiss' (p. 248) is a naively childlike expression of her sexual will, contrasting sharply with Catherine and Heathcliff's tumultuous last reunion, when she (the first Catherine) also was said to have 'kissed him first' (p. 132). The intimate relation Cathy and Hareton achieve, that of 'sworn allies' (p. 249), seems intended as a triumphant recapturing of the 'we-ness' forged in rebellion by Catherine and

Heathcliff, an absorption of both childhood *and* sexuality within the conventional vocabulary of romantic love. It is difficult, in this second half of the novel, but not entirely impossible, to be a childlike adult, i.e. to grow up by journeying backwards into a mode of sexuality that does not entirely abrogate an essential, desiring female self.

But *Wuthering Heights*, we remember, does not end with a scene of domestic happiness, nor can it, as a text, be enclosed by a single voice or frame. As Heathcliff becomes more and more conscious of Catherine's spiritual presence after Cathy and Hareton's rapprochement, the sexual tension in the novel builds once more to nearly its former state. Heathcliff is described as shivering 'as a tight-stretched cord vibrates', with 'a strong thrilling'. To Nelly, his joy is 'unnatural' (p. 278) as he rushes towards death and a kind of sexual consummation which requires his anguished renunciation of the will to live. In a most evocative image, Heathcliff himself declares that living in such a state is 'like bending back a stiff spring'; the more that this spring, the mechanism of his desire, is bent or warped or forced back, the greater the force with which it will fly to his 'one universal idea' (p. 275), the return to a state of 'we-ness' with Catherine. Heathcliff is about to spring towards union, a kind of metaphor combining death and sexuality, to surrender, as Catherine did, to being 'devoured' by a stronger will: 'I am swallowed', he says, 'in the anticipation of its fulfilment' (p. 276).

The famous ending is the suggestion of a haunting, not a union of two bodies. Like the interiority of the Fairy cave fascinating to both Catherines, the lure of Catherine's and Heathcliff's spirits, last seen 'under t' Nab' (p. 286), which haunts the novel's conclusion, invokes the unresolved nature of sexuality, with its uneasy relation between a 'quenchless', irreducible Will and the necessity of submitting Desire to social convention. Though in *Wuthering Heights* the code of identity is inscribed onto a revisionary story of sexual love, the refusal of closure is the novel's resistance to *dis*closure of the female self. Panelled bed, coffin, cave or fiery Hell are the signs of female sexuality as a dark space, enclosed as an untellable secret shut off and shut up by social, religious or bodily limitations. Both definition and articulation disrupt the unspeakable force of Desire which is the seed of a Brontëan female identity, and at the close of the novel the first Catherine continues to resist this process as much as the second submits to transformation.

Thus *Wuthering Heights* is emphatically about both Catherines, Catherine younger and older, Catherine as body and spirit, Catherine as natural and as socially mediated figure, Catherine herself and Catherine through Heathcliff, Catherine speakable and Catherine unspeakable: a seemingly endless multiplicity of Catherines. It is also about Woman by herself and at one with man, gendered and double-gendered, its text containing a single, essential definition of femaleness and yet also withstanding containment in its plural, relativistic tellings. Similarly, though *Wuthering Heights* appears in our hands as a whole text, it remains open to us in one sense as a series of fragmented, singular and contradictory stories, never satisfying our thirst for narrative completion. An entirely unquenchable author herself, Emily Brontë explored the quenchless force of female sexuality in a form that defied convention and enclosure: the tragic space of Desire, Will and death, never rendered fully 'understandable' to the reader – nor to the novel's narrators, who seem to silence the 'real' story, as convention suppresses the female sexual self.

7
George Eliot and the 'Hidden Wound'

> Certainly a marvelous *mind* throbs in every page of *Middlemarch*. . . . We know all about the female heart; but apparently there is a female brain, too.
>
> Henry James, *Letters*

> It is a help to read such a life as Margaret Fuller's. How inexpressibly touching that passage from her journal – 'I shall always reign through the intellect, but the life! the life! O my God! shall that never be sweet?'
>
> George Eliot, *Letters*

If the Brontës brought the living spring of female passion to the British novel, it cannot be said that the waters merged smoothly into that wider, calmer stream. No one was better suited to this latter task, however, by the intelligence and care of her method, by her deep attraction to the subject, and by the respect and popular enthusiasm accorded her on all sides, than George Eliot.

The theme of sexual love as a tidal pull on the firm anchors of selfhood is an important one for George Eliot, yet it is her ability to predict and control the tides which is central to her successful assimilation of this theme into the form of the traditional British novel. It is characteristic of this author that she always attempts to be at her most consciously intellectual about the irrational. Thus, though the experience of passion for the heroine in a George Eliot novel is like navigating a river on which she is borne helplessly and ceaselessly onward, the experience of reading the novel is like looking downward into a pond, with its well-defined borders and apparently smooth surface. The water seems clear, but it is full of life; bits of emotional matter swim furiously in it, only to be quickly ingested by a much larger narrating intelligence, which seems to dominate the whole. Only now and again do we see that under the deceptive transparency, the harmonious mingling of drops, there is a flood.

While the very power of sexual love as a theme in the British novel derived from its subversive presence as an irresistible undercurrent, George Eliot could only come to terms with it by channelling its formidable energies into the mainstream. No one was more interested than George Eliot in the problem of sexual love for women in a self-interested society; like Richardson and the Brontës, she is concerned to oppose and weigh the legitimate claims of female selfhood against the power of renunciation, representing both the social costs of individual acts of self-interest as well as the private price of social repression.

Yet at first glance it seems difficult to reconcile the passionate revelations of Richardson and the Brontës to the novels of George Eliot, with their narrators who stand back like so many professors lecturing on the fine points of the human heart. After a reading of these authors, it is not difficult to concur with Henry James in his observation that 'there is ... but little genuine passion in George Eliot's men and women' – however surprising this remark is from such a source.[1]

The critic Q.D. Leavis, however, in a rare compliment, once praised Eliot for the contrast between her narrative method and that of the 'typical' Victorian novelist in treating strong emotion, and in this distinction particularly likened her to Emily Brontë; both, she believed, are linked by a return to what she calls 'the eighteenth-century code', a rational code of feeling which allows the novelist to preserve a certain distance from romantic expectation.[2] Emily Brontë achieves this distance by putting a frame around her story, as Leavis pointed out, but she does not add that the frequent use of first-person narration within that frame allows Emily Brontë to plunge into as well as ironically detach herself from the tale. In an entirely different manner, George Eliot in her finest work found a way to accomplish simultaneously a new depth of entry into her narrative through internal dialogue of self with self and the distancing of the sexual passion she treated by a new – even extreme – extension of the omniscient, omnipresent author's voice. The demands of this disparate tugging on the reader are similar to those created by the warring between the Nellie point of view and the speaking desires of *Wuthering Heights*.

At its best, a George Eliot novel is fuelled by the tension between the immediacy of internal dialogue, in which the passion and will essential to subjectivity are invoked as we see *with* the character, and the distance of the narrator's authoritative voice, which sees *through* the character and thus coolly undercuts the power of that subjectivity. Again and again, from *Scenes of Clerical Life* to *Daniel Deronda*, we see the illusion constructed in a character's mind that meaning is discernible in human passion; whereupon this illusion of value is then shattered by the authorial voice. This rhetorical act, in turn, creates a higher meaning, that of the novel as a whole, a monument to our common need to generate meanings, and our common ability to master that need.

George Eliot accomplishes this feat through her narrative technique, in which the narrator continually draws attention to herself creating, and to the reader in the act of observing and judging that creation, as equal in importance with what is being observed.[3] The result is that her novels read at times more like recipe-books for God-making than as the secular Bibles they are sometimes taken to be. In the beginning of Book Four of *The Mill on the Floss* the author quietly spreads her skirts and sits down with us to discuss this very question, and her suggestion that she is a sort of natural scientist, possessed of a 'mind that has a large vision of relations, and to which every single object suggests a vast sum of conditions'[4] is an apt one. It is as God of her little world that she creates for us the Mystery of the 'free' human will and its moral significance; it is in her role of Scientist that she dispels it. Yet as the student of natural science – and the metaphor recurs throughout her fiction – she also links all together in a new order, a Unity that both intellectually binds yet has its own peculiar sanctity. In her fiction, we may drink from the sacred fount and measure its precise depths at one and the same time.

George Eliot, then, took the secret of female sexuality left as an inheritance, so to speak, by the Brontës to the Victorian novel, and put its existence to the test by the most rigorous form of research available to her. The secret of sexual love as the source of a 'necessary' female selfhood was secured to the Victorian novel partly by the very air of scientific detachment that Eliot conveys, and partly by its return to the safer context of larger social weavings. We might say that whereas *Jane Eyre* seduces the reader into sympathy with the passion of the protagonist, and *Wuthering Heights* has something of a violent quality to its affair with the reader, in the novels of George Eliot we are persuaded that what we are conspiring in is a sort of marriage of social meanings and individual passion.

In addition, time is on George Eliot's side; or rather, she uses historicity to allay the anxiety of such a reading with great adroitness.

The setting of the novels in the historical past at once assures the reader that the drama, safely behind us, is subject to being gathered together and sorted out as an entity distinct from the flux of experience, and yet one with the present in a universal and timeless truth of imaginative feeling. It is in this context – and perhaps it was the only one possible – that female passion could be returned to the 'great tradition' of the Victorian novel. The reader (no less than the author herself, we may speculate) is continually reassured about the control Eliot has over the uncontrollable Will by three fictive devices: the perspective of an explicable Past, the rational narrative voice that will explain all irrational urges, and the weaving of antisocial act into a web of social connections which give it the shaping force of origin and consequence.[5] In the novels of George Eliot unquenchable sexual will *is* quenched in the end, either by domesticity, sudden death, the mere passage of time, or the sheer brilliance (or tedium) of the narrator's explanation.

In *Clarissa* and *Jane Eyre* we knew where heaven lay, though it seemed impossible for Jane to reach it, as Clarissa did; in *Wuthering Heights*, heaven and hell were turned upside down; but in the world of a George Eliot novel, both have fallen away. Though we are presented with the seemingly smooth surface of a microcosmic Time Past, the portrait of a once-unified society, through the fine cracks in the antiquated painting we can glimpse the modern chaos, in which human desire is all there is. 'When we are just liberated from the wretched giants' bed of dogmas,' wrote Mary Ann Evans to a friend in 1843, just a year after her conversion from Evangelicalism, '... speculative truth begins to appear but a shadow of individual minds, agreement between intellects seems unattainable, and we turn to the *truth of feeling* as the only universal bond of union.'[6] Oddly, in her fiction George Eliot seems often to elevate the 'truth of feeling' the better to attack it. The 'feeling heart' may be the only criterion left to us on which to base action in a society whose chief credo is self-interest, but in what then do we trust when the workings of the heart itself come into the writer's focus? If Truth is assumed to spring from natural feeling, the formula becomes far more problematic when sexual passion is given its due as one of the most powerful of 'natural feelings': for it is another of Eliot's credos that where passion rules, Truth is inevitably blurred.

Thus, while the author's mind explores the heart of experience, and the heart illuminates 'truth of feeling' to the reader's mind, the Heart itself is shown to be one with the human mind in obeying the laws of organisms as a whole. 'Our thoughts are often worse than we are, just as they are often better than we are,' says Maynard in 'Mr. Gilfil's Love Story', as though there is a 'we', a whole or 'real' self, separate from these thoughts, 'And God sees us as we are altogether, not in separate feelings or actions, as our fellow-men see us. ... We don't see each other's whole nature.'[7] Yes, but *we* – i.e. not humanity as a whole, but the implied readers of the text – *do* see that nature in its wholeness, the thoughts as well as the feelings and actions, with the help of the godlike narrator who sees all. 'We' alone are allowed to see, for example, as the ordinary folk of the *Scenes of Clerical Life* are not, that the actions (or in Milly Barton's case, inaction) we judge are tempered by the extreme 'susceptibility' of the heroines. Different as they are in character and circumstance, Milly, Tina and Janet all have in common what is called in 'Mr. Gilfil's Love Story' a 'loving susceptible nature ... too likely ... to have its susceptibility heightened into unfitness for an encounter with any harder experience' (p. 110).

This is not to say that all three are equal in their sufferings or tell the same story: the last two women are craving, passionate, even voracious, whereas the first, Milly Barton, seems purposefully will-less by contrast, an archetypal example of the Moral Feminine gone somehow askew, whose quiet, 'ordinary', continual self-sacrifice is relieved rather than rewarded by death. It is true that she dies at the end of 'Amos Barton' 'very happy' by her own admission, while the two wilful heroines of the last two Scenes watch the lover and husband who have cruelly used and thwarted them die painfully; yet Caterina also dies a premature death, 'deeply bruised', and Janet survives to watch the early death of the one man on whom she could have reposed. It is to these latter heroines, who suffer from throwing themselves on the pyre of the craving will, that we will now turn.

'Mr. Gilfil's Love Story' is George Eliot's first depiction of sexual love as a problem for women. Caterina is, on the one hand, a 'little monkey', as her guardian calls her, which seems to imply that she is both too sensual to be humanized and too common to attain the status of Ladyhood. On the other hand, however, she is also a 'little singing-bird', as the characters and narrator repeatedly term her, possessed of a capacity for Art which allows her to float above her own grosser nature as well as her more vulgar rival, Miss Asscher. Tina is one of those female birds who seeks a nest and finds a cage.

Like Richardson's Pamela, Caterina does not aspire to Ladyhood for its own sake, yet must suffer for being excluded from that status. She is also more vulnerable to her lover's will for being in an inferior position to him; like Jane Eyre (and altogether unlike Pamela) she has a highly ambiguous position in her household, all the more tormenting because she is 'regarded as one of the family', yet is not and never could be one of them. She is both superior to the rest because of her artistic sensibilities, and inferior, lacking even any 'particular promise of cleverness or beauty' (p. 113). She cannot, therefore, like the heroines of *Pamela* and *Jane Eyre*, or Lucy in *Villette*, or Janet Dempster in the tale that follows, rise above, draw back or master the situation by either a superior consciousness or a consciousness of her own superiority. She is purely a victim, not only of her lover's falseness, but more importantly, of her own uncontrolled desire. The inescapable conclusion of the first two Scenes is that women who exert little will, like Milly, are weak and need protection, while women who have too much will, like Tina, are weak because they are incapable of controlling it. Either case leads to tragic suffering or disaster. It is no wonder that John Blackwell, George Eliot's publisher, with one eye to the public, looked askance on her 'Thackerayan view of human nature', and advised her anxiously to '*soften* your picture'.[8]

What is remarkable about *Scenes of Clerical Life*, however, is the firm grip the author already has in this first work on her method of exposition. The reader is challenged, mocked, even tricked from the first page. In 'Mr. Gilfil's Love Story', great pains are taken to establish that Maynard Gilfil is no romantic hero, while we are slowly drawn back into his history, so that after all the joke will be on us; it is our own prejudices, blindness and capacity for sympathy which will be tested in the end. In retrospect – and with George Eliot as our guide, there is always a retrospect – this purposeful ordinariness is seen as a clue we ought to be able to read, if only between the lines. 'Mr. Gilfil's bachelorhood is the conclusion to which you would probably have come if you had entered his sitting room', says the narrator, laughing up her sleeve, and describes for us a 'bare and cheerless' setting, which is then tantalizingly contrasted to a 'locked-up chamber in Mr. Gilfil's house: a sort of visible symbol of the secret chamber of his heart' (pp. 84–5). Leave it all to me, the author seems to be saying, as she impresses us with her own absolutely thorough knowledge of her characters and their setting, her cool summaries of their natures ('Lady Cheverel, though not very tender-hearted, still less sentimental, was essentially kind' (p. 102)), and her willingness to serve up to us her symbols on a convenient platter. It all seems a far cry from the romantic metaphors of the Brontës (is it possible to imagine Charlotte Brontë writing, as Eliot does, 'The moon, a sort of visible symbol of the romantic imagination...'?), or from the unreliable hearts and narrators we have seen. We feel – because we are openly invited to feel, we are *made* to feel – that we can lean on this author intellectually if we can lean on anyone at all, and we are likewise imbued with the necessity of leaning on *something* in the bewilderingly complex world she creates, so like reality in its palpable deceptions.

'It is a wonderful moment, the first time we... witness the fresh birth of consciousness' in someone who has temporarily lost it, the narrator assures us just after Caterina has fainted, and then dwells on the process of coming to consciousness which clearly holds a larger significance for her:

> A slight shudder, and the frost-bound eyes recover their liquid light; for an instant they show the inward semi-consciousness of an infant's; then, with a little start, they open wider and begin to *look*; the present is visible, but only as a strange writing, and the interpreter Memory is not yet there.
>
> (p. 162)

Just as Tina needs her wiser interpreter, Maynard, to decode experience, we are taken in hand by the Writer, who is also our Reader of invisible signs, 'that terrible handwriting of human destiny', that 'strange show', as it is called in 'Amos Barton' (p. 69). The painstakingly created consciousness of the Narrator is like another character, the most important of all, one who is dispassionate about passion, but also passionate in her insistence on the importance and complexity of human drama, continually demanding the reader's involvement with the wilful heart.

A passage such as the following from 'Mr. Gilfil's Love Story' illustrates the double effect of the narrator's gradual distancing of the subject, and the ironic emphasis on the high drama of 'life in the water-drop':

> While this poor little heart was being bruised with a weight too heavy for it, Nature was holding on her calm inexorable way, in unmoved and terrible beauty. The stars were rushing in their eternal courses.... The stream of human thought and deed was

hurrying and broadening onward.... What were our little Tina and her trouble in this mighty torrent...? Lighter than the smallest centre of quivering life in the water-drop, hidden and uncared for as the pulse of anguish in the breast of the tiniest bird that has fluttered down to its nest with the long-sought food, and has found the nest torn and empty.

(p. 127)

It is true that a life like Tina's is small and insignificant, the author is assuring us, but only if you have no heart. In this scheme of things it is the Narrator, at once intelligent and broad enough to point out the figure in the carpet, enabling her to rise above rigorous systems of belief, yet sympathetic enough to believe in the inherent 'truth of feeling', who comes off best.

Again and again, beginning with the *Scenes*, we, the implied readers, are lectured and mocked, appealed to and remonstrated with, as though our implicit argument with the Narrator is the dialectic of the fiction itself. And in this argument, *we* haven't a chance against *her*: if we take the wide view, encouraged to do so by the largeness of the social setting, we are at once cajoled by a voice that passionately reminds us of the life in the water-drop; if we identify and sympathize, she is there also, blowing herself up suddenly like a genie released from a bottle and coolly surveying us all, characters and readers alike, from what Blackwell called the 'Thackerayan point of view'. Passion is created, let loose and contained all in the same textual space through its relation to a 'truth' which is seen as the product of objective situation.

When George Eliot wrote the third Scene, 'Janet's Repentance', she had found a subject that would engage her to the end: the woman of large capacities whose position in life allows her no true outlet for her strong desires, and who therefore must feed on herself or go hungry all her life. The existence of this craving self is the Secret in which reader, narrator and character jointly share; in later works the secret is of a sexual nature, but in 'Janet's Repentance' the thirst is for literal drink. Even Eliot's by now loyal publisher John Blackwell was a little shaken by this 'bold choice of plot', and spoke with cautious anxiety of 'the unpoetic nature of her weakness and temptation'.[9] He was reassured by the finished whole, however, as we are meant to be by the narrative devices through which we are manipulated into sympathy.

The first of these is the care with which we approach the heroine, circling her first, as if some secret wildness were lurking there. We start with a broad, superficial glance at Milby, therefore, taking in the ordinariness, the 'dismal mixture of griping worldliness, vanity, ostrich feathers, and the fumes of brandy', and then in a startling reversal we are castigated by the narrator in Chapter Two for not 'looking closer', for assuming that Milby was 'nothing but dreary prose' (p. 202).[10] In this new view its very commonness constitutes its profound interest; moreover, the town, like the heroine of the story, is capable of being transformed in its ugliness by 'sweet Spring', with its 'strange transfiguring beauty', an image embodying both themes of religious renewal and love/fertility. The narrator, at least, has found out the renewing fount of secret poetry in the 'dreary prose' that is Milby, and implies that, upon looking closer, we will too.

The second device by which we are led to accept the possibly unacceptable is the fiction that though we need to be taught in our ignorance by the narrator, we are at least eminently teachable. There is in this Scene, as in 'Amos Barton', a good deal of ironic smiling – one is tempted to call it flirtation – between the knowledgeable narrator and her presumably understanding reader, as Eliot speaks of good Mrs Jerome's 'deep sense of injury' or of 'poor Miss Eliza' with her large cannon curls. We are assumed to be fond of these rural characters, as George Eliot herself is, but also, like her, modern, urban, sophisticated even to hardness in our own sensibilities about sexuality and love; in fact, we may be all the more fond of them because we are decidedly *not* one of 'them'.

Taken from this point of view, the story of the relations between the increasingly alcoholic housewife Janet Dempster and the pious evangelistic minister Mr Tryan may look as 'disagreeable' as it did to one Rev. G.C. Swayne, a contemporary of Eliot's, who Haight tells us, was indignant at a tale in which 'an evangelical parson contracts at the end a passion for the reformed gin-drinker, the explosion of which in scandal is happily prevented by his *timely* death'.[11] The Rev. Swayne had his sensitive points, but the ordinary reader is not permitted to take such a view: no sooner are we caught laughing along with the narrator than we are pinned to the wall for our lack of human feeling towards those who transgress. At a crucial moment, for example, the narrator freely admits that Mr Tryan is not one of those ideal heroes who 'believes nothing but what is true, feels nothing but what is exalted, and does nothing but what is graceful'. He is instead one of the 'real heroes', who blends prejudice with sympathy, just as we might be hoped to do in reading fiction.

Whereas the local critic will sneer at 'the habits of his species' – the *reader* in the role of natural scientist is quite another thing – the narrator, for one, is 'not poised at that lofty height. I am on the level and in the press with him' (p. 256). By contrasting very carefully the feeling and non-feeling views of her hero and admitting to the sum of his 'faults' at once, all criticism is forestalled. The reader has been, in effect, pulled up short: we thought we knew all about these characters, yet the 'only true knowledge of our fellow-man', we are told here, 'is that which enables us to feel with him'. We are now prepared, after the salutary icy bath, to be warmed at last by opening our hearts to what Eliot calls 'the essential truth'. We will now hear – we may say we are engaged to hear, in more senses than one – the 'real' story.

This story, however, which we have been promised as the final, the naked truth, however, contains a secret also; that is, there is a story within the story, for which we are *not* overtly prepared. The nature of this story, its very seed, is found in Mr and Mrs Jerome's meticulously described garden, a locus which is not at all essential to the narrative events of the tale. It is, the narrator tells us, 'one of those old-fashioned paradises which hardly exist any longer except as memories of our childhood', and in which the owners take an 'innocent pride'. The latter little phrase is particularly telling, for this is a tale of innocence lost and regained, of false pride contending with that germ of proud selfhood which is necessary for healthy survival. What makes this particular garden unusual is that it is a blend of flower and kitchen garden, 'a charming paradisiacal [note the repetition of this word] mingling of all that was pleasant to the eyes and good for food' (p. 238). In Eliot's version of the first paradise, women united innocent beauty and earthy fertility in a mode of sexuality now lost to us except in small walled corners of fictional worlds.

By contrast we have a heroine, Janet Dempster, who is beautiful but ravaged by her husband's brutality;[12] who is childless and thus deprived of the occasion of nourishing another from her body; and who nourishes herself with drink, thus eating herself up out of a larger hunger. She will be transformed by her encounter with the Rev. Tryan, whose large heart and gentle soul would nourish all who need him, but whose own weakness is his sensibility, his 'dependence on sympathy' (p. 246). This need for purely human love is a handicap in a man's world. Mr Tryan also has his secret, much like Janet's in a literally different cloth: it is that he too is afraid of life's brutalities. Like her, he is one of those who needs love too much, and who has sinned also; his 'sensitive failing body' (p. 256) is the corporeal symbol of that emotional vulnerability which in a man is defined as cowardice.

The stage is set for a love story, yet we are not given one: the two protagonists never exchange vows or even declarations, and the only touch is a chaste kiss on pale lips before death. What is presented instead is a tale of repentance and redemption, in which the strong craving will of the woman is curbed by the gentle example of the hero, and the self-sacrificing hero in some mysterious way seems to give up his life so that the heroine may grow healthy and strong in her own particular walled garden.[13] It is absolutely essential to this story, it should be noted, that Janet is curbed two ways, first by a monster and then by a minister.

The means by which the latter accomplishes his mission is that the two, Janet and Mr Tryan, give up their secrets to one another. In the pivotal confession scene that opens the door to her redemption, Janet seeks to do what the author herself has engaged to do for her characters: to 'unlock all the chambers of her soul' (p. 282). The key which unlocks these chambers, however, is left deliberately vague; we are, in fact, chastised by the narrator for wanting to know its nature: the 'blessed influence of one true loving human soul on another' is, says the narrator, 'not calculable by algebra, not deducible by logic, but mysterious, effectual, mighty as the hidden process by which the tiny seed is quickened, and bursts forth' (p. 294). This is, after all, a religious story – or rather a story about religious values – and all rational questions are therefore subsumed in the workings of faith. It is clearly not intended for a sexual or even romantic tale at all: though the sympathy which transforms both Janet and Mr Tryan is a kind of 'passionate egoism' (p. 256), an appeal to our own narcissism by identification with another, it is the best that frail humans can do. By revealing their inmost selves, their most 'real' selves, to one another, the protagonists come closest to the purity of that first garden, where man and woman lived in harmony, naked yet innocent of desire.

Yet 'Janet's Repentance' achieves this effect by making use of the conventions of that sexual love which it pointedly disavows. Its essential relation to a romantic love story is unmistakable: there are, for example, the heroine's unusual beauty and passionate, unfulfilled nature; the hero's attractiveness (all unthinking, of course) to women, his ineffable magnetism and charm; there is the convenient death of Janet's husband when the intimacy grows; and especially, there is the death of the hero himself at the precise moment before consummation is possible and seems likely by virtue of a now permitted intimacy, which brings to mind instantly the ending of *Villette*, as well as the premature death of Catherine in *Wuthering Heights* just at the point when her desire is recognized at last.

Most significantly, perhaps, there is the starting point of their relations in what we may call The Look: that moment when the heroine of a romance is surprised into forgetting herself and stares into the meeting eyes of the hero, often, as here, as he appears framed in a doorway. The portentousness of this look is frequently, in romance, as it is here also, itself framed by forming the end of a chapter, though not often given added impetus by such a narrator as Eliot provides, who tells us all about the 'power in the direct glance of a sincere and loving human soul' (p. 265). It is of particular significance that during this look Janet stands with 'an entire absence of self-consciousness', because this signals that in her self-forgetting, her 'real' self will emerge; it *can* emerge only for him, and this too we may compare with the ability of the Brontë hero to penetrate to the 'real' self of the Brontë heroine.

Later, during the confession scene, it is iterated that Mr Tryan sees Janet's face 'uncontrolled by self-consciousness', and that in seeing this, one feels 'waked into the real world' (p. 287).[14] In both religious and romantic redemption, the key to unlocking souls is to penetrate the 'screen' which Janet tells us is always before faces (p. 295). The very act of being *seen*, and seen naked, whether literally or metaphorically, and still being loved and understood, reveals a 'real' self in this mythos.

By the time Mr Tryan dies his gentle death – it is remarkably like that of Milly in 'Amos Barton'[15] – Janet is so nourished by his 'words', which 'come to me like rain on the parched ground' (p. 295), that she is able, like Lucy Snowe, to be stronger for having been understood, though deprived forever of the one who understands her. Her wild hungry desire, which had begun to turn destructively on herself, is placed and controlled to a 'deep stillness', until at last she 'thirsted for no pleasure; craved no worldly good' (p. 335). Appropriately, she ends by cultivating her own garden in the form of an adopted child.

'Janet's Repentance', then, is at its core an inversion of a passionate love story. In place of a female angel who teaches moral restraint by the example of self-sacrifice to a threatening, wilful, sexually voracious male, we have a male who is a ministering angel – and of course, it is particularly fitting that he should be a minister, that traditional restrainer of passions in the lower classes and the worldly – who transforms the voracious female will into self-forgetting restraint. It is fitting too that he should die himself in the process, quite spent, so to speak. In *Wuthering Heights*, sexuality was so intense it became transcendental; in 'Janet's Repentance', the transcendent is animated by unspoken sexual intensity.

We have seen that 'Janet's Repentance' approaches the problem of the craving female through the distancing device of a narrative by whose means the author can fit on a higher meaning or reveal secret depths at will. In *Adam Bede* she began to use to her own purposes the human ability to synthesize disparate elements of experience into logical sequences in order to make the unacceptable both plausible and valid – which we have learned to call, in a post-Freudian age, rationalization.

But if feelings are not mysteries, as we saw in 'Janet's Repentance', this emphasis on the human tendency to fictionalize reality, to make the world into a novel with oneself as hero, serves to keep before our eyes the dismaying unreliability of feeling, the difficulty of trusting to its 'truths' at all. It is not only the weak-minded and selfish who are seen rationalizing: nearly every character in *Adam Bede*, with one significant omission, is overheard in the process.

Adam Bede himself, when faced with evidence of Hetty's romantic involvement with Arthur – her discomfiture when he finds a locket – turns this into 'a proof' of what he wishes to see, that she cares about his opinions.[16] The Truth is therefore impossible even for the best and wisest to know, clouded as the clearest eye is by the blinding screen of self-interest, the inevitable impulsions of Desire. Therefore the 'heart' on which we are forced to rely in a self-interested society, i.e. the 'real' self, is discovered to be ultimately unreliable. Even in *Villette* the inner self was discernible, if buried and ghostlike; here the mind is seen as impossible to pin down.

This weaving of what Eliot herself called an 'ingenious web of probabilities' by which the fiction-making minds of men and women screen themselves from harsh truths, however, is also theoretically the novelist's device for revealing Truth. George Eliot, in particular, to a degree that reflects her debt to the broad landscaping of Scott, weaves a web so intricate in its mingled filaments, so finely detailed in its realism, that we are seduced temporarily into forgetting that the tension that electrifies its linking bonds are those of Romance.

Though Adam Bede is the nominal hero of this novel named for him, the dramatic centre of the story rests on the contrast between its heroines, Hetty and Dinah, just as its source was an anecdote involving two comparable real-life women.[17] Between the two poles marked out by Hetty, the 'pleasure-craving' farmer's niece (p. 379) and her cousin Dinah, the idealistic and idealized preacher, is the answer to 'What is a woman?', that question which gained new significance in the nineteenth century, merged with its corollary, 'What could a woman be?' We know all along in this novel what a man is: it is Adam, first and last, manly even in error, whereas the relation between Hetty and Dinah is the more complex difference between mere femininity, the social behaviours of women, and true womanliness, as George Eliot saw it.

The two, Hetty and Dinah, are of course extreme in their different representations of womanhood, but they are enough alike so that we are constantly invited to compare them. They are, for instance, in the same social stratum, and in fact are blood relations; they are both young, attractive and marriageable; they even have simultaneous, if contrasting, fantasies on either side of a thin wall. At different points in the narrative each is an outsider to the community, though Hetty ends as a stranger to it after wanting only too eagerly to enter the hierarchy at the wrong point, while Dinah is integrated fully into it only when she accepts a conventional female role. Whereas Dinah's is a whole being, Hetty is what Leo Bersani calls a 'hole in being' which 'can be filled up only if other being is poured into it'.[18] Hetty is incomplete, eternally desirous of more: 'Such lovely things without souls', says the narrator about Hetty, 'have these little round holes in their ears by nature, ready to hang jewels in' (p. 295). Her tragedy as a craving vacancy is inevitable once she opens to allow sexual suffering to pour in; but Dinah's soul is a full, rounded, closed system, impervious to harm.

Romantic love for Hetty is self-worship transposed; this is not an adult sexual love, and it is not meant to appeal to us with the same force as the love affair in *The Mill on the Floss*, for example. When Arthur and Hetty meet in the wood, a sexual relation between them seems almost inappropriate. A longing for paradisiacal childhood is expressed by the narrator just before sex is about to rear its tragic head: if these two had been 'in that golden age of childhood' when love is a 'butterfly kiss' only, they both could have gone home to their beds innocent, and 'would have slept without dreams' (pp. 175–6). Instead they go to bed together, poisoned by the very sweetness of the romantic dream.

When the novel pursues the romantic, fiction-making thoughts and acts of Hetty and Arthur, then, it is anti-romantic in both purpose and method; even Adam is not spared the fine blade of the author's irony, when she notes the egotism and blindness in a man who could see 'something quite charming in Hetty's pettishness' (p. 308), so that he is unable to understand the real problems she faces. The workings of romantic love are exactly like those of rationalization: we see what we want to see, self-indulgently projecting our own wishes, so that even a man like Adam 'creates the mind he believed in out of his own' (p. 400).

Adam Bede begins with a depiction of Seth's love for Dinah and closes with Adam's marriage to her; both of these are romantic solutions to the disturbing problem of sexual love. Once again, it is the ambiguous relation of romantic love to sexuality that allows for this romanticism. Seth himself, though 'in love', is as asexual as possible: whenever a man's eyes are described as 'confiding and benignant' (p. 52) in a Victorian novel, we can be sure he is not a sexually magnetic figure.[19] Seth seems selfless next to manly Adam, and also quite improbable in his utter lack of jealousy, personal needs or passions. He *must* be selfless in order to make his love 'hardly distinguishable from religious feeling' – that is, what Eliot calls 'real' religious feeling, which is itself inextricable from a generalized sense of 'love and beauty' (p. 81).

At the end of the novel Eliot makes a match between womanly Dinah, with her glorious dream life, and Adam, with his 'real', pragmatic manliness. Yet Dinah's character has stood throughout the novel for values in opposition to the self-interest of sexual love. Given Eliot's assumptions about the selfish nature of love, Dinah must be shown as somehow justified in her individual craving rather than hypocritical, lest, like Pamela, she seems to be rewarded with the very thing she had all along denied. In the closing chapters, therefore, Dinah explains that she will have all the more strength for doing God's work because she is filled with Adam's love; and besides, 'it is the divine Will' (p. 576).

This slip in the all-encompassing consciousness of the author has to do with a secret and self-contradictory version of the romantic, which in effect makes the narrator of the novel as unreliable as the minds she so acutely probes. Adam's explanation for sexual passion, that 'it's a mystery we can give no account of' (p. 168), seems at odds with a narrator who explains everything to us. Her choice of subject, setting and narrative method frequently reflect this need to impose order while at the same time convey the unpredictability of feeling, her urge to accept the inexplicable in tension with her insistence on man's free will, her desire to court our trust as a teacher of Truths, yet warn us that the first truth is the untrustworthiness of mind.

This same deep ambiguity became a favourite metaphor recurrent throughout George Eliot's fiction: 'Nature has her language, and she is not unveracious; but we don't know all the intricacies of her syntax just yet, and in a hasty reading we may happen to extract the very opposite of her real meaning' (*Adam Bede*, p. 198). If we try to 'read' Nature as we read novels, in order to make the mystery intelligible, we find ourselves reading our own lips in a mirror. Yet again, the true significance of this passage is the sense that there *is* a 'real meaning' to be extracted, an invisible truth like a kind of language, made legible at times by sudden intuitions of feeling on experience.

It is not so much a question of the truth of feeling, therefore, which is not in the end to be completely trusted, but of feeling our way half-blindly to the truth. When Adam sees Arthur and Hetty kiss in the wood, he suddenly connects the pattern in the little bits of evidence available to him, and 'a terrible scorching light showed him the hidden letters that changed the meaning of the past' (p. 342). It is in this epistemological context that we must judge the problem of the hungry sexual self: if all knowledge is encompassed and limited by the demands of each single narcissistic self, what can it then mean to act at any particular moment?

George Eliot, in *Adam Bede*, sees the tenuousness of our grounds for moral knowledge, yet is unwilling to let go entirely into meaninglessness. The firm construction of this novel in particular, with its illusion of roundness and wholeness of being, is her attempt to find a way between the blurred obscurity of that hieroglyphic alphabet of truths and the yearning for what she had called 'real meaning'. To put it differently, we might say that in *Adam Bede* the author still maintained a holding position, rowing against an inundation of sexual love on the sturdy craft of her text.

Eliot's metaphor of meaning as a kind of language read by the human mind – and recorded by the author – reappears with new significance in her next novel, *The Mill on the Floss*. It occurs near the beginning as a reference to the unreflective experiences of childhood which are 'the mother tongue of our imagination, the language that is laden with all the subtle inextricable associations . . . of our childhood' (p. 94); it recurs, as we shall see, in the sexual crisis of womanhood at its end.

In *The Mill on the Floss*, George Eliot lets out a secret of her own: she confesses, as though she were one of her characters looking for that all-important sympathy, that the depth of longing for meaning on the part of those with an 'imaginative and passionate nature' (p. 367), i.e. the 'deep hearts' of Richardson and the Brontës, are matched only by the meaninglessness of 'human life – very much of it'. This meaninglessness is in reality not simply that of modern life, as *Adam Bede* would imply, but of life itself, that 'narrow, ugly, grovelling existence, which even calamity does not elevate, but rather tends to exhibit in all its bare vulgarity of conception' (p. 362). If God were a novelist, He would be a poor one indeed.

In this important transitional chapter, which prepares us for the failure of the community to prevent the Tullivers' downfall and tragedy, the godlike narrator pauses to reflect that though romance fascinates her by raising up the 'vision of an epoch', she must impart her 'cruel conviction' that all life is 'part of a gross sum of obscure vitality, that will be swept into the same obscurity with the generations of ants and beavers' (p. 362). The passionate needs in Maggie that find their expression in sexual love – the desire for personal meaning – emerge in the frame that this 'cruel conviction' puts around the novel.

The Mill on the Floss is unique among Victorian novels in opening the gates to waters that threaten to swallow one up if not safely dammed. It is also unique to Eliot's fiction in its concentration on the central consciousness of its desiring heroine, Maggie.[20] This concentration gives the novel a full measure of the passion Henry James insisted was missing in Eliot's work. As a character, only Janet Dempster comes close to Maggie in her great capacity for larger life and her great need of being loved (Caterina possessed the latter without the former; Dinah, the former without the latter). And like Janet, Maggie has an addiction, which Eliot calls her 'opium' (p. 102): her fancy, the habit of 'refashioning her little world into just what she should like it to be' (p. 101).

This 'faculty', as Charlotte Brontë would have called it, this 'wide hopeless yearning' for significance, comes directly from Maggie's impulse to passion, from having 'larger wants than others seemed to feel' (p. 381). She is clearly 'not one of them', like Jane Eyre, and in fact she could be Jane's spiritual daughter: the angry, passionate, rebellious will fuelled by unsatisfied longings without direction, her need for a true home in which she is valued, and the fascination she develops with scenes of her own humiliation connect her directly to that heroine in *her* childhood. When Jane stands on the battlements at Thornfield and wishes for a new 'power of vision', an experience of the larger world, or a more 'vivid kind of goodness', she might almost be calling to young Maggie sitting within

> the dull walls of this sad chamber which was the centre of her world ... full of eager, passionate longings for all that was beautiful and glad; thirsty for all knowledge; with a blind, unconscious yearning for something that would ... give her soul a sense of home in it.
>
> (p. 320)

Like the small, soft rabbits she allows to starve, Maggie is at once an intensely animal nature and a creature of anomaly, a 'thing out o' natur' which can 'niver thrive' (p. 82). Those eyes 'full of unsatisfied intelligence and unsatisfied, beseeching affection' (p. 253) mark her as one of those unable to thrive in a society which rewards only those who desire narrower satisfactions. As in 'Janet's Repentance', life for such a woman will be insupportable.

When little Maggie, her brother Tom and her cousin Lucy are instructed to build card-houses to keep them quiet, Lucy proves she knows how to act with a male: she 'moved gently' and 'asked [Tom] to teach her' (p. 146). Lucy is 'kitten'-like, as was Hetty, but in a more pleasant way, as dear little grown-up Paulina Mary in *Villette* is likened to a lap-dog. Maggie, on the other hand, is both competitive with Tom and awkward in her movements, a combination which gains her neither achievement nor male support. As Maggie's houses 'would never bear the laying on of the roof', she is destined never to be complete, nor find a home as large-souled Dinah does, because she has no solid self. She is, to put it another way, still another craving vacancy, waiting to be filled. 'Communion of spirit', wrote George Eliot in a letter when she was only 23 years old, 'is the drop of nectar in the cup of mortals ... the mind that feels its value will get large draughts from some source if denied it in the most commonly chosen way.'[21] The seeds for a sexual crisis are being sown as early as this in *The Mill on the Floss*:

the female child deprived of 'sympathy' is made ready for a consuming passion.

Though a longing for love is acceptably 'feminine' in Maggie's society, the sheer strength of impulse in Maggie, her lack of self-control and desire for power and recognition, are repulsed and punished by everyone around her because they are inappropriate, 'out o' natur'. Life in St Ogg offers no more to young girls than loving and being loved, but a strong craving for any one thing in a woman, even for love, is like those forces in a plant-seed 'which will make a way for themselves, often in a shattering, violent manner' (p. 320). It is no wonder that Maggie's eyes remind Philip, Maggie's childhood friend, of 'stories about princesses being turned into animals' (p. 253), or that Maggie herself fears 'that it was not difficult for her to become a demon' (p. 380). This early addiction to 'waking dreams' (p. 366), this vulnerability to the hungers of the soul, foretell an ominous susceptibility in adulthood to the animal hungers of the body: Maggie is a potentially dangerous creature, to herself as well as others.

But this is only part of the story. If women are assumed at a disadvantage in life because their softer emotions do not suit them for a selfish world, it is this same susceptibility to feeling which supposedly preserves them from the merely animal, as humankind is 'gifted with that superior power of misery which distinguishes the human being' (p. 100). Maggie's imagination allows her, not only to rush to passionate deeds which she later regrets, but also to see all their consequences. Impulse, passion and imagination are thus subtly allied to selflessness and moral discernment, and this is one of the important ways in which the question of Maggie's later guilt, when put to the sexual test, is qualified.

The test of innocence is prefigured in one of those small significant incidents that illuminate this novel, this one near the very beginning of the tale: Maggie as a small girl is questioned by her father and his friend, in an idle sort of way, about a picture in her book of a woman given the water-test of drowning to decide if she is a witch. Maggie, ingenuously eager to please and impress the males of her world, observes that the poor woman loses either way, for if she is not proved evil, presumably with disastrous consequences, she must drown. The men avoid this basic problem, so like the one facing Maggie at the end; Mr Tulliver is ignorantly concerned only with the binding of the book, as he thinks more of Maggie's gender than her nature, while his friend recommends a 'prettier book' (p. 67) as suitable for a little girl.[22]

This shaping force of gender is unquestionably another important qualification to the problem of Maggie's desire. Because of her sex, Maggie's capacity for yearning, her craving to be of 'consequence' and well-thought of in the male world of father and brother, is denied her in the 'commonly chosen way' of personal achievement. This is the story of how plant seeds shoot up in different gardens, which culture carefully labels 'boy' and 'girl' (the title of the first book in *The Mill on the Floss* is 'Boy and Girl') and cultivates in different ways. Since the sexual temptation and choice are dwelt on only at the very last, rather than occupying the first half, as in *Adam Bede*, we are led to concentrate instead on its roots in the grounds of socially defined masculinity and femininity. In this way the novel is about sexuality in its broadest sense.

Jane Eyre was oppressed and Lucy Snowe repressed, but Maggie seems more completely smothered by the expectations of femininity itself. Maggie is not so much saddened or silenced or timid or trodden on as 'checked', as so many Victorian heroines are, not held down like Jane or held in like Lucy, but held back like some rearing animal.[23] If we place the brother and sister in *The Mill on the Floss* beside the almost sibling pair in *Wuthering Heights*, Cathy and Heathcliff seem androgynous and equal by comparison. Tom sees himself in the way Maggie and his mother see him, as rather godlike, the stern and unswerving God of the Old Testament, perhaps: 'He would punish everybody who deserved it: why, he wouldn't have minded being punished himself if he deserved it, but then he never *did* deserve it' (p. 91). Tom is a 'practical person' (p. 90), which means that he is not handicapped by the keen moral sensibilities or romantic longings of his sister. His childhood speculation on Maggie's future is a hilarious summing up of the Victorian view of women as helpless, selfless, domestic and weakly childish: 'He was very fond of his sister, and meant always to take care of her, make her his housekeeper, and punish her when she did wrong' (p. 92).

In Tom we see a half-humorously sympathetic, half-scathing portrait of the male being groomed for success, for whom there is no need of rationalization because he was never taught to justify or doubt. His strongest feeling after a crisis, we are told, is usually, 'I'd do just the same again' (p. 107). Learning not to feel, making oneself one's own God, is the surest route to survival in a male-dominated and essentially godless society, and Tom should be one of the novel's pre-eminent survivors, in spite of his humiliations.

Yet while Maggie dreams of being queen of the gypsies, Tom is inevitably attracted to the sword of a former soldier, by which he wounds himself. The sword of masculinity can be as self-destructive, as laming, as the unfulfilled dreams of femininity which handicap Maggie; the desire to achieve, and the dictum to suppress feeling in order to do so, is in a different way a burden to Tom, as Maggie's desire to love and be loved is to her.

But if this book is about how Tom is taught to be a sword and Maggie a vessel, it is also about the ways in which Tom is an empty-souled, empty-headed vessel and Maggie a true sword. When Maggie, whose brain is stuffed with 'wild romances', envisages rescue from the dreariness of life after the Tullivers' downfall, her father's complaints interrupt her, '[piercing] through Maggie like a sword: there was another sadness besides her own, and she had been thinking of turning her back on it' (p. 381). Later, during her 'great temptation', Maggie will learn to wield as her own weapon the very selflessness that now cuts her in two.

The crisis of sexuality in *The Mill on the Floss*, like that of *Wuthering Heights*, which was also a choice between two very different lovers, is heralded by the death of the heroine's father and the consequent breaking-up of the small cohesive household in which she has lived. When we take into account the orphaned heroines of the Brontës, it is remarkable how many fathers are missing from these novels of sexual choice. Aside from the need to replace the father as an 'idol' – Eliot's word – and perhaps the implicit permission his absence gives to sexual fulfilment, the death of the paternal figure also signifies a wider breakdown of traditional support and authority. Similarly, the 'myth' of the river Floss flooding angrily when the mill changes hands romantically expresses how self-interest breaks the bonds of the traditional community. The worldly ruin of the father in *The Mill on the Floss* precedes the near-fall of the daughter from innocence, that 'promise made in Eden ... when the starry blossoms grew side by side with the ripening peach – impossible to be fulfilled when the golden gates had been passed' (p. 263). As Maggie passes from Book Five, which ends with the death of her father, she stands ripe for temptation at the threshold of the gates of female sexuality – the subject of Book Six, whose title is 'The Great Temptation'.

Maggie's parents have been failures in more than the business sense: they have failed their young children, not in spite of but because both have done their best to fulfil their prescribed sexual roles. Mrs Tulliver is hyper-'feminine' in the nineteenth-century sense: fluttering, anxious, protective – and entirely ineffectual. Mr Tulliver, by taking his business failure and his subjection to his enemy Wakem as a personal slight, a measure of his worth in the world, is led to behave with masculine decisiveness in angrily beating Wakem, and this 'violent passion' of masculinity actually brings on his final attack of illness. Between these two, Maggie always chooses her father as the object of her sympathies. And before she must make her decision between lovers, representing the indulgence or suppression of her sexuality, she has to decide between a related pair: her professed lover Philip Wakem and her brother Tom. It is really a choice of brothers, one ineffectual but mothering and one sternly fatherlike, that she faces.

Even as a man Philip has a 'pale small-featured boy's face'; he is removed from the patriarchal world also in his sensibilities and capacity for devotion: 'Kept aloof from all practical life as Philip had been, and by nature half-feminine in sensitiveness, he had some of the woman's intolerant repulsion towards worldliness and the deliberate pursuit of sensual enjoyment' (p. 431). Always palely loitering about, like Keats's knight-at-arms, he is peculiarly vulnerable to the attractions of his own Belle Dame. In sum, he is a non-threatening but also non-attractive lover, the perfect recipient of the 'butterfly kiss' mentioned in *Adam Bede*, who has, in addition to these other obstacles to social and sexual success, a physical deformity – a sort of visible symbol of his emotional impotence with Maggie.

In her early attraction to Philip, Maggie is given the opportunity to recognize, to care for and help to adulthood, one side of herself – the 'deformed' feminine side which she has never valued and which has been denigrated by Tom. Oddly enough, in some ways the young Philip is like the boy Heathcliff to Cathy, the *alter ego* to the strong-willed young heroine, a youth who suffers from his strangeness, his exclusion from society, his secret sensitivity to slights as a child. And like Heathcliff, one of his most important functions is to present to the heroine the value of her own will, of 'reviving into your real self' (p. 435), as Philip explicitly says, instead of choosing the socially acceptable course of self-suppression.

We know that Heathcliff changed considerably as he grew to adulthood and chose the masculine courses of violence, worldly success and sensual enjoyment himself, and that we are meant to value him differently as he grows. But Philip does not change; as his adult features are said to be 'wonderfully little altered . . . only a larger, more manly copy' of his boyhood self, so Philip as a man is just more of the same, which is both his value and his undoing. 'What a dear, good brother you would have been, Philip,' remarks Maggie (p. 427), just when Philip is hoping for a good deal more.

Yet as an adult, Philip is more an Edgar Linton figure in Maggie's life: both Edgar and Philip have as potential husbands a handicap impossible to overcome: their 'niceness', their more than usual goodness, which is inextricably bound up with their lack of sexual energy and attractiveness.[24] Their inner softness, one might say, *is* their lack of virility. It is doubly ironic, then, that it is Philip who delivers what seems today a textbook modern argument against renunciation and the sacrifice of the 'real' self in favour of self-fulfilment: 'You will be thrown into the world some day, and then every rational satisfaction *of your nature* that you deny now, will assault you like a savage appetite' (p. 429, my emphasis). Maggie fears being 'in love with this world again' (p. 402), as if the first taste of affection, the first acknowledgement of hunger, would lead to 'the seductive guidance of illimitable wants' (p. 424). Satisfy one need and female desire becomes insatiable: even her simple delight in Philip's 'affectionate admiring looks', in the knowledge that her appearance is praised and her speech valued, paves the way for the misery of illimitable longing.

In George Eliot's version of the sexual choice, we have still another turn of the screw on the story of the good man versus the sexual tempter. Like Edgar in *Wuthering Heights*, the rejected lover is 'feminine' and 'cultured', yet Stephen Guest, the sexual tempter, is very far from being Heathcliff: in his conventionality, privileged social standing and worldly acquirements, he is also like Edgar, and this constitutes part of his desirability for Maggie. It is extremely important that between Jane Eyre's sacrifice and Maggie's is a deterioration of the sexual object from fascinating Byronic Rochester to rather ordinary Stephen Guest. Rochester offered Jane a true Home; in Stephen's house, we might say, Maggie would only be a Guest.

Stephen's is a purely physical, worldly attractiveness, without much disguise: he is a *little* clever, but nothing like M. Paul in *Villette*; a *little* witty, but certainly no Lovelace; he can also be a little daring and wicked, though not nearly a Heathcliff, or a little good-hearted and generous, but not quite so much as Rochester or even Philip himself. The character of Stephen, who caused considerable discussion in Eliot's time as well as our own as unworthy of noble Maggie, disproves Maggie's childhood text (and Emily Brontë's) that 'the devil takes the shape of wicked men' (p. 67); sometimes the devil is in mediocrity itself.[25]

When we first see Stephen, in fact, the author is at pains to present him as somewhat foppish, a 'fine young man' (p. 469) wielding a scissors, more than a little narcissistic, and entirely guided by self-interest in his choice of a bride. His glance is said to be '*half*-ardent, *half*-sarcastic' (p. 470, my italics) and he superciliously claims to 'know *half* the names and faces in the neighbourhood in that detached, disjointed way' (p. 471, my italics). He is also half-engaged, which would seem to make him only half as guilty in later betraying Lucy. His knowledge of women too is by halves, detached and disjointed, and Stephen is meant to be enlarged by learning the answer to that significant question, What is a woman? In Maggie his preference for women who are 'insipid' – Lucy's accusation – and ignorant, his mistaking silliness for charm, will be punished as well as corrected.

Just as Maggie was not satisfied until she could manage both oars of the rowing boat and row both Stephen and Lucy, she wishes as deeply for competence and power as for narcissistic gratification.[26] These desires, moreover, are fully appreciated by the author, and represented with sympathy, though the heroine's feet slip in leaving the boat because she has chosen an 'inopportune moment' (p. 492) in her life to row. But Maggie is also attracted to what is variously called in this novel 'the firm grasp' (p. 492) or the 'firm arm' (p. 521) of Stephen Guest, the desire to 'be taken care of . . . by someone taller and stronger than oneself' (p. 492): 'There is something strangely winning to most women in that offer of a firm arm', the narrator tells us after Maggie has been 'ambitious' in learning to row, '. . . the presence of strength that is outside them and yet theirs, meets a continual want of the imagination' (p. 521). Clearly, one can put a straightforwardly sexual interpretation on this symbolic arm, but the sexual potency itself seems itself to represent a great deal more in the way of strength and worldly competence than physical sexuality alone.[27]

It is one of the most basic contradictions of sexual love for the Victorian heroine that she is attracted to the male for strength and power she lacks, yet in yielding herself to him, she forfeits her own. Stephen's look – it is *The* Look – is so 'strangely powerful' that 'it *made* Maggie's face turn towards it and look upwards at it' (p. 560, my italics).

The immersion in the sexual dream is like an addiction to opium, an image Eliot uses in this novel to signify both Maggie's love of the imagination and her love for Stephen (p. 550): it seems to bring with it a 'new consciousness' (p. 561), yet in reality it dulls our perceptions. It makes us both strong and weak, 'strong for all enjoyment, weak for all resistance' (p. 532); it drowns out the 'chill eating thoughts of past and future' (p. 520) which haunt Maggie, yet we are liable to drown in it ourselves. For women in particular sexual love is the dream that by submitting to another one can enlarge an inadequate self, augmenting it with the 'added self which comes with the sudden exalting influence of a strong tonic' (p. 589). But the danger lies in never waking from that perpetual dream, so that it becomes a kind of death.

Because Maggie likes being rowed, the time comes when she is asked to '[sell] her soul to that ghostly boatman who haunts the Floss – only for the sake of being drifted in a boat forever' (p. 584). Stephen is only taking his position to its logical conclusion when he uses an opportunity to impose his will on hers. He does not imprison or rape his lover, like Richardson's heroes; he merely takes the oars and rows her beyond the reach of home. In other words, he forces her hand by giving her exactly what she liked in him all along, the playing-out of a sexuality marked as male and a show of the strength to which she was attracted.

At first this sensation of being borne along 'without any act of her own will' (p. 588) seems 'a natural joy' (p. 589); it is easy to believe that 'the tide was doing it all' (p. 590). And Stephen claims her with the argument that falls so familiarly on twentieth-century ears: those social bonds not based on the gratification of feeling are 'unnatural', and since our feelings for ourselves are most natural of all, we owe our first duty to ourselves. 'Strong feeling', says Stephen, is a *'natural law* [that] surmounts every other' (p. 601, my italics). It is surely not coincidental that the language of seduction in the novels we have been examining is so often the language of interest and property, the very terms used in a lawsuit over ownership of private rights such as Tulliver versus Wakem: claim, possession, debt. Maggie counters at once with the larger claims of social indebtedness: 'Remember', she tells Stephen in the same terminology, 'that we owed ourselves to others and must conquer every inclination which could make us false to that debt' (p. 601). Maggie's chastity, her withholding of sexual love from Stephen, is for her, as it was to her literary sisters, an assertion of her own will against those males who control her, who would say with Stephen that 'you are mine, now' (p. 605).

The scene in which Maggie and Stephen argue over the validity of personal happiness as a moral guide or 'natural law' is, in fact, remarkably similar to the confrontation between Jane Eyre and Rochester just before she leaves him. Stephen even employs the same tactics: alternating personal appeals with threats of misery, madness and future wickedness, trying out the seductiveness of a kiss. And in spite of George Eliot's caveat about *Jane Eyre* in her letter, the heroine's answer is essentially the same: there would be a warrant for all selfish behaviour if we allow this one instance as morally valid.

Like Rochester with Jane Eyre, Stephen appeals to Maggie's 'real' self, the primal store of passion that women 'can't help'. But Philip, in his letter to Maggie after her return, implies that the real self whose cause he had been the first to urge to Maggie is not necessarily the best self he had known: 'The strong attraction which drew you together proceeded only from one side of your characters ... I have felt the vibration of chords in your nature that I have continually felt the want of in his' (p. 633). It is easier now to see why Stephen cannot be a Rochester: there must be this separation of the best self from the real self, because the religious ground on which Jane Eyre made her moral stand has all but disappeared here. Rochester could be granted all the appeal of Byronic fantasy, noble culture and charismatic sexuality and still not stand up to God, but Stephen must be less than either Maggie or Philip, lest his own reasoning have too much weight of sympathy behind it. The craving vacancy that is Maggie is not nearly as empty as the Universe containing her, in which all that connects human experience in a web of meaning is a moral pattern of our own making.

On waking from her opium dream, in the chapter called 'Waking', Maggie feels she has 'let go the clue of life' (p. 597), those barely legible scratchings we interpret as we will in guiding our behaviour, as if it were a matter of holding onto them. Yet the author comments through the sympathetic Dr Kenn that the right judgment of Maggie's case is 'hidden in ... darkness', while the passage that follows might have been written in answer to *Jane Eyre*. 'The mysterious complexity of our life is not to be embraced by maxims', the narrator reminds us, and again, 'we have no masterkey that will fit all cases' (p. 628).[28] Speech itself, that continuing metaphor of implicit meaning in this novel, is nothing if not deeply ambiguous, 'at once sincere and deceptive' (p. 437). All we have in the end is the cultivation of 'fellow-feeling' – but feeling itself has been established as a blind guide to truth.

'Conclusions are the weak point of most authors,' George Eliot had observed to her publisher in 1857, 'but some of the fault lies in the very nature of a conclusion, which is at best a negation.'[29] At the conclusion of *The Mill on the Floss* the tragedy of Maggie's death has the unfortunate effect of making Stephen's arguments seem more true by Maggie's own standards even while they have been proved unworthy: all who suffered from Maggie's elopement, after all, suffer no less from her renunciation. Maggie is not allowed to be swept away by sexuality, but she *is* swept away by a cataclysm; she takes control only to be a senseless victim, once again damned if she does act and damned if she doesn't. Try for a drop of the nectar of sympathy and you will get a flood; keep the cup from your lips and you will die of thirst in the wilderness.[30] We are supposed to feel that she is going down in the triumph of self-sacrifice, as Clarissa rose up heavenward in the triumph of hers, but the result is that she seems to be taking all the punishment onto herself, as Caterina did, for having craved at all.

The reason for this cataclysm is surely a desire to reconnect Maggie to her brother Tom, a thinly disguised wish to return to childhood, with its untrammelled golden gates and butterfly kisses.[31] 'O God, where am I? Which is the way home?' she cries before seizing her oar with the great strength of extremity, just as all the heroines we have seen from Clarissa onward searched for that lost home in the last hour. Maggie's search ends where Clarissa's did, in the asexuality of childhood; she seems to journey backwards as she passes in the rowboat the scenes of her childhood, one by one, until she reaches the Mill.

When Maggie goes down she is imprisoned but also freed of all longing in the arms of her now ideal brother, who has had at last his long-awaited 'revelation' of 'awe and humiliation' toward Maggie (p. 654). If the ending of the novel signifies that Maggie has been flooded by sexuality, as Bertha in *Jane Eyre* was consumed by fire, it is also the negation of sexuality, as Clarissa's death negated her bodily self in sainthood.

In a way the medieval test of innocence has been applied to Maggie: she drowns, therefore she was innocent. Yet she remains, on a deeper level, also demonic, the cause, however innocently, of misery to all who loved her, as Cathy Earnshaw was, and the agent of her brother's 'humiliation' – and death.[32] Maggie cannot win the test of sexual innocence – perhaps no woman can – but by dying as she does, Maggie not only chooses the 'masculine' side of herself represented by Tom, but also removes herself from his and Stephen's clutches, all at the same time.

Daniel Deronda, Eliot's final work of fiction, presents a different perspective on the problem of women and sexuality: Gwendolen Harleth, the novel's heroine, functions by *not* desiring, thus protecting herself from the vulnerability of not being loved in return. The narrative logic of her emotional life is that when men use female sexual desire to advance their own power over women, the safest sexual strategy is to empty oneself entirely of desire. 'The life of passion had begun negatively in her', comments the narrator.[33] So far from repressing desire in the name of self-sacrifice, in accordance with the model of Moral Femininity, or else seeking equality of desire, as would the romantic heroine, Gwendolen coolly assesses her social milieu and makes her choice. In her judgment that all relations are unreliable, that one cannot trust and survive, Gwendolen takes a defensive posture against an oppressive social practice to its logical conclusion in personal life.

In a way, Gwendolen is an inversion of the Jane Eyre type: Charlotte Brontë's novel presents a heroine whose 'plain' or common exterior is a negative sign of her inward exceptionality. By contrast, Gwendolen's exceptionality is all outward; it is her inner self which is diminished. When Gwendolen 'inwardly excuses herself on the ground of a peculiar sensitiveness which was a mark of her general superiority' (p. 53) for an act of self-will, we might hear a parodic echo of the sensitive Jane Eyre. But Jane, in her position as narrator and moral authority of her text, knew what the universe *was*, while Gwendolen is a 'soul burning with a sense of what the universe is *not* . . . [yet is] held captive by the ordinary wirework of social forms [and so] does nothing in particular' (p. 83, my italics). Spiritual as well as sexual absence is at the very centre of Gwendolen's subjective experience.[34]

The critic Barbara Hardy, with specific reference to Eliot's *Middlemarch*, long ago pointed to the appeal of another 'patriarchal script', the literary convention she calls the 'rescue into love', in which a heroine is unlocked from her self-imposed captivity by a young, virile man.[35] Romantic love, in this conceptualization, fills the intolerable gap between an affirmative but self-aggrandizing sexuality and the absolute self-sacrifice demanded of Moral Femininity by transforming sexual desire into a benign presence, a spiritualized sexuality without self-seeking.

According to the usual pattern, Gwendolen Harleth should also be rescued by romantic love; in fact, she seems almost entitled to it as a heroine. In Gwendolen, after all, we see heroine-like qualities; in spite of her defects, she clearly displays intelligence, wit and sudden flashes of guilt or sympathy, as for example, that other petty, pretty narcissist, Rosamund Vincy of *Middlemarch*, does not. Most importantly, Gwendolen's narrowness is expandable by suffering, so that her failings of character at the beginning of the novel could easily be taken by the reader as a sign of the conventional resolution to come, in which a long-delayed fulfilment of desire has the force of moral reward for spiritual conversion. Already a self-defined 'princess in exile' when we meet her, as Esther Lyon in *Felix Holt*, also rescued from narcissism by love, was an unrecognized Lady, Gwendolen is a perfect candidate for narrative resolution by 'marrying up', or romantic rescue, or both.

This pattern, however, George Eliot subverts by two narrative strategies, one of which allowed her to pursue a new vantage point on the problem of women's desire, and the other of which made use of a conventional model in disguise.[36] The first is that the romantic paradigm is reversed: Gwendolen's downfall *begins* when she chooses to 'marry up', and she is punished by achieving the very state of Ladyhood she wanted.

Gwendolen's nemesis is Grandcourt, the wealthy English gentleman who will be the instrument of her ascent into Ladyhood. As passionless as she herself is, as unwilling as she to touch or be touched emotionally, he is born to 'torture' her – it is Eliot's own word – by enacting a 'masculine', as well as radically perverse, version of her selfhood. Like Gwendolen herself, Grandcourt never 'lets go' into desire:

> The correct English gentleman, drawing himself up from his bow into rigidity ... suggests a suppressed vivacity, and may be suspected of letting go with some violence when he is released from parade; but Grandcourt's bearing had no rigidity, it inclined rather to the flaccid.
>
> (p. 145)

He is also akin to her in that he is serpent-like, frequently described as a 'lizard'. This 'flaccidness' of Grandcourt's is, of course, emblematic of his lack of passion, yet he is not asexual: snake-like, he can stiffen to strike at any moment. In fact Grandcourt's sexual power is particularly dangerous because it does not spring from sexual desire for Gwendolen, and therefore he uses his sexual dominion over her body as a kind of menace against her.

Gwendolen's early conception of marriage, that it will enable her to 'mount the chariot and drive the plunging horses herself' (p. 173), is precisely that of her more powerful husband, who is until his final days 'perfectly satisfied that he held his wife with bit and bridle' (p. 744). The terms of sexual relations in this novel are that one must wound or be wounded, ride or be ridden, master or be mastered by another.

All that we observe of Grandcourt being bored, being commanding, sneering at others, depending on the admiration of those he sneers at, or eschewing all passion for the purpose of self-interest, may also be said of Gwendolen Harleth herself. Grandcourt, then, is one side of Gwendolen allowed to act out, to the destruction of others – and ultimately to self-destruction. The embodiment of both the sexual poison of the snake and the state of 'flaccidness', or lack of true desire, he is therefore the part of her that must be murdered if she is to live humanly at all.

Gwendolen, without the life-blood of human passion, needs a rescuer, according to the traditional script, one who is not so much her 'real' self as an idealized image of what she might be – someone outside both herself and the society which has bred her to the false solution of 'marrying up'. In the strategy of romance, a substitute will is frequently conferred on the will-less, selfless heroine in the form of a lover. Instead, Gwendolen is given Daniel Deronda, the occasion for Eliot's second subversion of the rescue into romantic love.

Daniel Deronda is tailor-made (or author-crafted) for the business of filling up the narrative gap in the failed romantic rescue that is occasioned by Gwendolen's lack of desire. The text charts the contrasts of their character and progress as though the two were competing for the reader's sympathies: if Gwendolen acts wrongly because she is too narrow, Daniel can find no outlet for action because his sympathies are too wide; where Gwendolen grasps eagerly at her chance to enter society, Daniel slowly drifts out of it, into Otherness. Gwendolen has no true father; Daniel, on the other hand, has more than enough. In addition, Daniel's ego boundaries are remarkably permeable without being at all fragile, the very reverse of Gwendolen, whose ego is fragile yet initially impervious to influence. As Heathcliff assumed the burden of selfish sexual passion for *Wuthering Heights*, Daniel Deronda takes this novel's burden of *unselfish* love on his extremely capable shoulders.

But though a sexual relationship between Gwendolen and Daniel is suspected and discussed by nearly everyone else – Grandcourt, Mirah, Sir Hugo and Hans, to name a few – it is eternally frustrated, kept before our eyes and negated all at once. The result is somewhat similar to the triangle in Eliot's own early story, 'Janet's Repentance': once again a spiritual man (in contrast to a selfishly cruel husband) ministers to the woman who has a soul-sickness upon her. Replacing the woman as a Victorian sign of conscience, this saviour is the male version of Moral Femininity, and in fact Daniel is variously called Gwendolen's 'priest' (p. 485), her 'conscience' (p. 468) and a 'terrible-browed angel' (p. 737). Like other exemplars of Moral Femininity, Daniel admirably restrains his own as well as others' impulses, and is curiously passive, will-less and self-less. In other words, Daniel here enacts the part of idealized Woman, teaching one who is represented as lacking in essential femininity how to be healed by imitating him.[37]

But Daniel does not want to play Mr Tryan to Gwendolen's Janet: he has better things to do. Instead, the usual pattern is purposefully transformed here, and the sexual choice displaced onto the male rescuer. In place of the passionate, wilful but highly moral heroine poised between two representatively different lovers, then, we have Daniel Deronda tossed between two women, one of whom, for most of the novel, is married and unavailable to him. As if in some European novel of adultery, the pair are always coming together to have snatched moments of low-spoken conversation before being parted by her husband or the crowd; at one point Gwendolen is jealous of a young lady to whom Daniel devotes himself in order to keep out of Gwendolen's way, occasioning a rather sophisticated play on words about the double heat of the kitchen they are touring, a place 'of shadow in the niches of the stoned walls and groined vault' (p. 471).

Yet during most of the novel, we find Gwendolen, increasingly a sympathetic character, pursuing Daniel, while the latter retreats like a nervous virgin before her. The situation is odd to say the least: Daniel cannot even be excused, like Mr Tryan, as mistaking it for something else. When Daniel denies to his foster-father, Sir Hugo, that he has been 'playing with fire' in his intimacy with Gwendolen, the older man remarks that 'there may be some hidden gunpowder' in the situation (p. 510). Sir Hugo's hints are later said to have made Daniel 'alive to dangers' (p. 625); later still, Daniel himself acknowledges a 'nervous consciousness' of a 'something', which he then identifies as a possibility of 'some ruinous inroad' from which he must shrink. Daniel is said to be sorry for Gwendolen's growing need for him, but he is nevertheless made to '[watch] her drowning while his limbs were bound' (p. 509).

Why does George Eliot bind her hero's limbs? In the tradition of the romantic rescue, the self-seeking desire associated with masculinity must be restrained by the selfless heroine. But here the impulse behind the separation of hero and heroine seems less to keep Gwendolen from sexual fulfilment with the Dark Other than to keep Daniel from Gwendolen's influence. In the end the double bind of Daniel Deronda is not Gwendolen versus Mirah at all, but the metaphysicality that Mordecai offers versus the dangerous lure of 'this fair creature [Gwendolen] . . . with her *hidden wound*' (p. 625, my italics): in other words, of the power and threat of female sexuality itself. Mirah is merely thrown in as a consolation prize, since Mordecai himself (like Mr Tryan) is too spiritual to survive on this earth.

To balance Daniel's attraction to the female 'hidden wound', the real investment of intense passion in this novel is in the father–son relationship, the 'spiritual perpetuation in another' (p. 553). The vocabulary of sexual love and religious transformation are conflated in describing this ecstatic relation:

> In ten minutes the two men, with as intense a consciousness as if they had been two undeclared lovers, felt themselves alone in the small gas-lit bookshop and turned face to face . . ,
>
> (p. 552)

Evoked in Mordecai's description of their spiritual coming together is the look of understanding that conventionally takes place between those who recognize one another in a relation of romantic love:

> Our souls knew each other. They gazed in silence as those who have long been parted and meet again . . . and all their speech is understanding.
>
> (pp. 633–4)

Mordecai penetrates Daniel's vague opacity with his spiritual breath: 'What is needed', the older man declares, 'is the seed of fire' (p. 596).[38] Daniel in relation to Mordecai is vulnerable, teachable, desirous yet selfless, i.e. all that Gwendolen is not before her marriage to Grandcourt. The transformative power of the rescue into sexual love is reclaimed by the religious/moral experience, and reserved for a male, not a female subject: Gwendolen herself will neither fulfil a sexual passion nor undergo a religious journey. By the time of Mordecai's entrance into the text of *Daniel Deronda*, the narrative interest has shifted away from an exploration of a female crisis of desire in Gwendolen and towards the task of constructing the ideal Feminine in the character of Daniel.

We may glimpse why George Eliot draws the reader towards yet withholds a sexually fulfilling love affair between Gwendolen and Daniel by contrasting Daniel's ideal partner, Mirah, and his rejecting mother, both of whom we are invited to compare with Gwendolen. The two former women are both Jewesses who have attempted careers in singing, but Mirah, a Victorian little woman, 'small of face', delicate, as refined as a lady, has acted on the stage only *against her will*. A perfect exemplar of Moral Femininity, Mirah does not act in any sense, even to the point of not committing suicide when she has intended to. Similarly, she expresses an aesthetic which is appropriately 'womanly' when she plays her calm, soothing music. Metaphorically, as well as literally, she is always giving lessons: the lesson of female passivity.

In marrying Mirah, Daniel recuperates all that his mother should have been and defiantly was not: he rewrites, in short, the brief, strange episode of his meeting with this previously absent and unknown woman. In the hierarchy of Daniel's values, the Princess Halm-Eberstein is an absolute negative of Mirah. Everything about her is Moral Femininity's nightmare: Daniel's mother has rejected her home and religion, flouted her father, denied maternal love or even responsibility, put her career as a singer before all other interests – and remarkably, she is not the least bit sorry. God and George Eliot will strike her down for this – she will 'very likely not live another year' (p. 691) – but in the meantime she is one of the very few who have had, in her words, 'desire . . . will . . . choice' (p. 693) as the measure of their lives.

The Princess Halm-Eberstein does everything wrong and still emerges as a sympathetic character. Needless to say, this woman can act, unlike Mirah: 'All feeling . . . immediately became matter of conscious representation: experience immediately passed into drama, and she acted her own emotions'; she has the 'double consciousness' of the true artist (p. 691). The dramatic and highly combustible mixture of attraction and repugnance with which the author paints this improbable but fascinating character is reminiscent of no one so much as Charlotte Brontë's portrayal of Vashti, that other quintessential female artist, whose fiery will and uncontrolled emotion set the theatre on fire in *Villette*.

When we see the many parallels between Gwendolen and Daniel's mother, who really is a princess in exile – the initial rejection of their families, their common desire to be singers, a strong need to be independent, and not least important, the wish to 'rule' and 'never willingly [be] subject to any man' (p. 730), as the Princess says – we can also see that Daniel must be lured by the attraction of the sexual mother in order to reject her in favour of the asexual idealized mother, represented by little childlike Mirah. Daniel, in other words, can approach the 'hidden wound' that is Gwendolen's subversive self – her secret sexual self – only to heal it.

The Princess had lived by the very principle of 'self-assertion' that Daniel succeeds in breaking down in Gwendolen: that is, in her own way she is an exaggeration of the ethos of Gwendolen, who has become in turn for Daniel an 'image of what was amiss in the world' (p. 685). Yet in another way, the life of the Princess is in George Eliot's own terms a noble one, based on the very quest for self-definition that moves Daniel himself, and therein lies both her sympathetic attractiveness as a character and the ambiguous sense of danger that is associated with her. Her cry, 'I had a right to be free. I had a right to seek my freedom from a bondage that I hated' (p. 689), is the secret subtext of the novel itself, though perhaps only a character who is a 'real' artist could be allowed to get away with the unchristian trinity of Desire–Will–Choice for so long.[39]

The same covert and ambiguous admiration is accorded Mrs Glasher, Grandcourt's mistress: her fate encodes a warning to those who act impulsively on the priniciple of sexual love, but she also speaks to Gwendolen as the 'unwomanly woman', commanding her respect for the fierce energy of her self-protectiveness, the strength and righteousness of her desire to live out the bitter consequences of her actions and still endure.

At the close of the novel Grandcourt is dead, Gwendolen has learned something of the social and moral costs of sexuality through meeting Mrs Glasher, and Daniel and Gwendolen have moved apart again, after their near coming together. When Daniel discovers felicitously that he is a Jew and therefore deserves Mirah, it is in much the same way that heroines in popular romantic novels of the day used to discover they were 'really' born ladies and deserved their landed gentlemen. While Daniel's story concludes on a note of dream-making, however, Gwendolen's final moments are among the most painful of Eliot's novels: having ascended the social ladder to become an actual Lady, she must remain spiritually 'in exile' and sexually in stasis as she discovers her true value on the chain of being.[40]

Daniel's place, on the other hand, is so far above Gwendolen's that he seems to disappear from the novel into some divine afflatus at its end. Just as division is the social and moral theme of this novel, it is also its ultimate form. In keeping Gwendolen from Daniel, George Eliot separated elements that were a dangerous mix: the air which is the pure breath of souls, the fire of the body's passion, the drowning waters of the heart's too-ready impulses. Yet when Daniel ascends his spiritual ladder at last, we are left with the unresolved problem of female sexuality in Gwendolen below, remaining as she does, in those still uncharted nether regions of body and soul.

There seems nothing, finally, for Gwendolen between the two extreme possibilities of her own character that Grandcourt and Deronda represent. There has been Grandcourt, who is flaccid and lifeless (literally, at the end) but who could penetrate cruelly like a steely weapon when he chose, and there is Daniel, who seems to have achieved spiritual perfection at the cost of being not quite whole sexually.

Once Daniel has renounced his role as Gwendolen's potential lover and mounted his holy hillside instead, we can see that for George Eliot there *can* be no such thing as a 'real' English gentleman whose sexual desire would not wound vulnerable womanhood cruelly. Daniel, in other words, can approach the 'hidden wound' that is Gwendolen's deepest self – her secret sexual self – only to heal it. Imaginatively, this is another way of saying that this novel will admit of no true conciliation between the potential force of female sexuality and the morality of a modern society driven by an ethos of self-interest.

Gwendolen's selfhood has been tied to the system of terms around which the text has been structured: the opposition of being wounded versus being whole. To be sexual *is* to be wounded; to be spiritually whole, one must be sexually lacking. Gwendolen's womanhood, then, is a wound that must remain hidden, yet self-restraint, the ethos of Moral Femininity, is found to be irreconcilable with the strength of desire necessary for a heroine to resist being subsumed by male domination. As attracted as she was to the moral power of the ideal of Moral Femininity, Eliot rejects this possibility as a viable alternative for her heroine in *Daniel Deronda*: for women, it is not enough to follow the paradigm which transforms desire into a domesticated version of the sexual, thus reconciling self-interest and morality. As long as women represent the 'heart', they are vulnerable to the power of the knife.

In *Daniel Deronda*, George Eliot coveted a double role as creator of fictions: no less than to bring to the problem of representing female sexuality a clarifying honesty about romantic solutions, without renouncing entirely the warm glow of Moral Femininity. To do so, she had to undermine the convention of the rescue into romantic love for her heroine, while presenting a subject who is a figure of moral restraint for the self-aggrandizing will, the male Victorian angel, Daniel Deronda. The result was a wounded heroine, and an oddly ambiguous plot.

There is, consequently, a double gap in the narrative of *Daniel Deronda*: the evasion of adultery, and the representation of female sexuality as a secret impairment, a 'hidden wound'. Both may perhaps be seen as providing the author with a 'safe' textual space in which to explore new possibilities of dealing with the impossible subject of sexuality. In Gwendolen's pathology, Eliot found a modern version of an old sexual story: the way in which female sexual desire stands in inverse relation to the spiritual needs of men, and how the absence of sexual feeling can ally itself with self-interested as well as self-sacrificing values. Probing the hidden wound of womanhood in *Daniel Deronda* was a way of revealing other hidden wounds in the life of modern society, as the narrative itself was an attempt to heal them.

Conclusion

I began this study by invoking the mighty blasts of wind which Charlotte Brontë recorded in her journal before she began a career as a novelist. That storm aroused what she called a 'craving vacancy', a desire and an awareness of absence which could then only be 'filled a little' by her waking dreams. The image of the wild storm reappears at the conclusion of her final work, *Villette*, rising, swelling, 'shriek[ing] out long' (p. 450). This time, however, that blast cannot be 'lulled' – only ignored by a 'sunny imagination'. The 'dream' of her adolescent journal had become a novel which gives a voice to desire in its multiple forms, but particularly that desire which emerges as a dream of sexual love.

I began also by calling attention to perceived oppositions which frequently underwrite a subject as highly charged as sexual love: disjunctions such as those between rational and irrational, between order and disorder, human and inhuman, the realms of ordinary and extraordinary or public and private experience. Two other ways of considering sexual love intersect with these categories: the relation of sexuality to gender, and the organization of experience we know as narrative.

In any given novel, a character of either sex may possess an exhilarating power over the beloved or else be helplessly in the power of the beloved. Yet a feminist consciousness tells us that a woman's desire for a man who already possesses power over her by virtue of his gender (and usually in nineteenth-century novels by virtue also of age, class or occupation) inevitably skews this relation toward *her* submission, *her* dependence, her experience of incompleteness and lack of control. The concept of perfectly mutual sexual love, in which each one's equal power over the other elides this imbalance, only serves to remind us of the desperate craving which gives rise to this idealization. The narrative's progression towards such a 'solution', in other words, at once endorses sexual love as a panacea for the problem of women's place in society, and highlights the subject as the sort of problem absolutely requiring imaginary resolutions.

Similarly, the narrative act both creates a boundary between public and private which seeks to fix sexual love firmly in the social order, and at the same time breaches that boundary by creating a reading audience in the public domain which participates vicariously in the intensely private feelings, thoughts and acts of its characters. Rather than accept the received categories of self versus society or male versus female as givens, I have attempted to see the values of sexuality and gender as historically malleable. It has been my assumption that all ideals and practices which are the site of conflict in a society can be utilized by either side in that conflict. Thus, depending on context, women can be represented as both 'sweet' and 'good', centres of moral authority, yet also irrational, consuming demons; their presumed emotionality can 'prove' them either weak *or* entitled to greater influence; romantic love can be represented as a value beyond market considerations *and* yet somehow also available to the public as readily as (what it often in fact is) a mass-produced commodity.

In these novels, as in Victoriana in general, romantic love continually shifts in significance as it is framed by social considerations and their effects: while it asserts the values of individualism and the dignity of free choice in personal relations associated with modern capitalist society, it also proclaims itself as transcending the self-interested ethos that is this society's foundational cornerstone. This contradiction is further complicated by the ambiguous relation of love to women's sexuality. The fulfilment of romantic love was one of the attractive new freedoms for women in the burgeoning middle-class individualism of the nineteenth century. But female sexual desire may be a forceful sign of female agency: once desire for sexual love is acknowledged, it gestures to and permits the power of other desires – for power, wealth, status or knowledge.

For this reason, the narrative engines of the novels of the Brontës are fuelled by the authors' need to distinguish between the positive, self-sustaining, independent desire of their heroines and a generally destructive ethic of self-interest; thus Caroline Helstone in Charlotte Brontë's *Shirley* sharply and pointedly differentiates between 'love', for which 'no purest angel need blush', and 'forwardness', which implies the female pursuit of sexual desire, just as Charlotte Brontë herself was to reject Harriet Martineau's version of her characters' craving on the grounds that Martineau did not know 'what love is'.

In the rather lengthy time since I began this study, my own view of 'what love is', and more specifically the relation of women to sexual love in the novel, has undergone a change. The Brontës, I began by thinking, heard a particular bedtime story from their cultural antecedents: that suppression in and by the virginal heroine ensures the perpetuation of society as we know it – or knew it, or rather wish to know it. This story seemed uniquely suited to the social and moral exigencies of the hundred-year period following the publication of Richardson's *Pamela* and *Clarissa*.

But the conventional paradigm of Moral Femininity, I would argue, has a surprisingly disruptive subtext, the empowering myth that women possess a moral energy drawn from the sealing off of their sexual longings into a sacred space. This space requires a female character both like and unlike the traditional male hero. She is not simply the female counterpart of the knight who sublimates the sexual into religious energy in heroic texts, because sexuality is very much present as the subject and the problem. She does engage in stages of psychic 'experience' which are not unlike traditional successive tests of worthiness; however, the goal is to gain entry to a kind of secular religious mystery which is written into the story of sexual love. At one and the same time, the pleasure and the sacrifice of the heroine's sexuality are *of* the body while representation is denied *to* the body; from this mutual resistance of activity and passivity, of body and psyche, of representation and denial, emerges the power and force and intensity of a Brontë novel.

Later, during the course of writing this book, I came to see the heroines of the Brontë novels as rebels against the solutions of Moral Femininity to the dilemma of female selfhood, that of living out a double bind, being a woman in an aggressively acquisitive *and* oppressively patriarchal society. Here intertextuality does not imply a smooth transmission of ideology, but rather a historically situated attempt to receive, make sense of and transform that ideology. In the Brontës' work there is a new concern with the 'real', suppressed selfhood of a heroine whose emotional and sexual craving is as much a part of her humanity as her moral self. It was the Brontës' mission to attempt a reconciliation between the contradictory Victorian messages of self-restraint by women (which I have here called Moral Femininity) and the heaven of sexual gratification, requiring the liberation of a 'real' self experienced as suppressed or oppressed. The modern heroine, with all her strengths and dilemmas, emerges from the struggle of these and other nineteenth-century woman authors with contemporary paradigms of significant female sexuality.

For both Charlotte and Emily Brontë, romantic love encompassed both sides of the question of the validity of self-interested desire in a capitalist society because it was, particularly at this time in Victorian England, a straddler of the fence on this slippery issue. In the role of the Moral Feminine, to whom self-denial is peace and peace is all, the woman-in-love can appear as the very type of modern nobility, a poignantly fragile bulwark against encroaching materialism and crass selfishness. As such, the meaning of romantic love was directly connected to the mystification of the family and home in Victorian society.

But as we have seen in, for example, Harriet Martineau's exchange with Charlotte Brontë, the craving for romantic love also mirrors a rebellious celebration of the individual freedom with which it has long been associated in Western tradition. From this perspective, a reversal as abrupt as any in *Wuthering Heights*, the 'selfish will' and self-absorption of such love reflects, if not incites, the larger covetousness and exploitation that rules modern society. It is as though, in this double point of view, sexual love speaks in two different languages, as Charlotte Brontë implied when she wrote to Miss Martineau: 'I know what *love is as I understand it*.' One is the language of sexuality, which, in this letter at least, Charlotte Brontë chose not to 'understand'; the other is a language from which sexuality is markedly absent from the abstract category called 'love'. It is particularly appropriate, and not at all coincidental, that this double discourse is paralleled in the diametrically opposed critical judgments about *Wuthering Heights*, which can appear to critics either supercharged with *or* entirely devoid of sex.

It is no wonder, then, that in her Editor's Preface to the 1850 edition of *Wuthering Heights*, Charlotte Brontë wrote, in defence of her sister, that 'having formed these beings, she did not know what she had done', and made anxious reference to a 'creative gift' which 'at times strangely wills and works for itself' (p. xxviii). One is reminded immediately of the child Jane Eyre's reckless cry of rebellion which issued from her 'without her will consenting' (p. 60), or perhaps Jane's later compulsion to love Rochester 'with little sanction of free will' (p. 279). The very idea of writing – or loving – either 'against one's will', or without the knowledge of the will, implies a separation of one Self from another, i.e. an ethical, controlling will locked in battle with a primal, stronger self. The consequence of this splitting is to confound the issue of which of these truly represents the construct of the 'real' self. Its downfall as well as advantage as a solution to Victorian contradictions of sex and gender is the abdication of agency and therefore of responsibility for one's own feelings and even actions, since it is not the 'real' – or at least the whole – 'I' who feels or acts. In its construction it is similar to those pre-Richardsonian amatory novels in which the heroine was allowed to succumb to sexual temptation 'without knowing that she did'.

While Charlotte and Emily Brontë partake in a mutual ambivalence about the legitimacy of an uncontrollable sexual love and the meaning of either sexuality or romantic love to women, *Wuthering Heights* must have especially threatened Charlotte's point of view by taking one side, Catherine and Heathcliff's, to its extreme. Thus an entire page in the Editor's Preface, which is filled with awe at Emily's power, is devoted to convincing us that it may not have been 'right or advisable' even to imagine a character like Heathcliff because his passion is 'inhuman' (p. xxviii), as though the very *naming* of the possibility is enough to incite the human heart to wildness. The same 'love' that Charlotte was prepared to admire wholeheartedly in its noble or unselfish incarnation implied possibilities which were to her dangerous in their social consequences.

There is a constant sense in reading Charlotte's Preface to *Wuthering Heights* that Emily has naively exposed what should better have remained a secret. Charlotte herself in fact used the word 'secret' twice in describing her sister both in this Preface and in the 'Biographical Notice of Ellis and Acton Bell', which accompanied it in the 1850 edition of *Wuthering Heights*. In the 'Biographical Notice', she referred to the '*secret* power and fire' that lay under Emily's deceptively simple exterior (p. xxii); again in the Preface, she stated that Emily's sources were 'those tragic and terrible traits [related in] the *secret* annals of every rude vicinage' (p. xxvii, emphasis mine). Emily's compulsion to read aloud those 'secret annals', to explore the female cave with that 'secret fire', was quite another thing from Charlotte's conception of the purpose of art.

On reading Harriet Martineau's newly published *Letters on the Nature and Development of Man* (1851), Charlotte wrote in distress to her editor about her friend's disbelief in God and the afterlife: 'Sincerely, for my own part, do I wish to find and know the Truth; but if this be Truth, well may she guard herself with mysteries, and cover herself with a veil.'[1] In a similar vein, after reading a lecture by Thackeray on Fielding which treated lightly the latter's 'vices' and 'wild ways', implying sexual licence, she indignantly observed in a letter that a great artist like Thackeray 'ought to devote his vigour to guard and protect' if he be 'the true lover of his race'.[2]

The secret that must be veiled in mystery, therefore, from which the author must protect not only us but herself, is more than simply a knowledge of sexuality that has been repressed. It is the terrible, agonizing 'Truth' at the heart of the sexual dream, that the final authority for the condition society calls Woman cannot be found external to the self, and more, that the ethic of self-denial does not confer the promised Kingdom of Heaven, spiritually or emotionally, to those women who uphold it. Except perhaps in *Villette*, Charlotte Brontë stood guard over this unbearable suspicion by veiling it in the mystery of Romance, in which love *can* be at once the deepest individual gratification and the highest expression of human nobility, where blind trust *does* reward those of special 'faculties' at the last, in which Dreaming provides a place to 'repose on what I trust'. Emily Brontë, tough in the very places where Charlotte was most unsure, exposes the egoism of romance in *Wuthering Heights* and insists stubbornly on the complexity of sexual love; yet she also implies the vastness of loss as women pay the gigantic price for either self-abnegating 'peace' *or* absolute authority of selfhood divorced from social power.

Charlotte Brontë's 'instinctive horror' of Harriet Martineau's materialism and atheism, which Charlotte called 'this hopeless blank ... this bitter bereavement ... this unutterable desolation', was of a piece with her dismayed awareness of a social ethic based on self-interest and the acquisitive will of the individual in modern society.[3] But though she writes that she cannot welcome this separation from traditional spiritual values as 'a state of pleasant freedom', both she and Emily were, as their novels show, in fact deeply attracted to the very freedoms for women which this 'state' implied. Indeed, the more the suspicion of a growing spiritual alienation and social oppressiveness, the more necessary it seemed to arm oneself *as a woman* with *both* a strong desire and the haven of romantic love as a means of sheer survival.

As the 'Truth' of the modern limits to female selfhood mounted in intensity in the mid-nineteenth century, the contradictions of romantic and sexual love reached their highest peak. The Brontës trace the outlines of an idyllic sexual love, constituting the focal centre of a construct I have called the 'real' female self. This heaven, whether underlying or supplanting the traditional Christian heaven, is no longer the 'rumour'd heaven' identified by Coventry Patmore; it is, increasingly, an open secret, sounding especially clearly in the outrageously passionate tones of *Wuthering Heights*.

'My mind', says Casaubon early in *Middlemarch*,

> 'is something like the ghost of an ancient, wandering about the world and trying mentally to construct it as it used to be, in spite of ruin and confusing changes. But I find it necessary to use the utmost caution about my eyesight.'[4]

As our own lampholder, whose self-professed objective as an artist in *Theophrastus Such* was to '[bring] into new light the less obvious relation of human existence', George Eliot wished to teach us to trust in human relations; yet her greatest gift as a novelist was her willingness to distrust, to be cautious about all eyesight.[5] She memorably admits in *The Spanish Gypsy*, her long poem of 1868, that 'Speech is but broken light upon the depth of the unspoken', while in *Middlemarch* the observation is made that in our inmost thoughts we can never be wholly truthful: 'Who can represent himself just as he is, even in his own reflections?' (p. 763).[6] Speech itself, that 'alphabet of knowledge', as well as the self as a concept, is always being called into question, even as it is being minutely recalled.

This fundamental problem, and the various ways in which the author dealt with it, are of course not static throughout the body of her work: one might trace a movement, for example, from wisdom as an invisible but present alphabet in *Adam Bede* to a more problematic view in *The Mill on the Floss* and *Middlemarch*, in which self-knowledge is questioned, to an attempt to 'let in the light' in *Felix Holt* and *Daniel Deronda*.[7] But in the end, though a wish for belief in a 'real' female self confirmed by passion continues, this self is composed of so many threads that it seems a thing hardly knowable at all, by another as little as ourselves. It is difficult, because of this ambiguity, to imagine a character in a George Eliot novel saying with conviction, 'I *am* Heathcliff', much less, 'He is more myself than I am.' In the most passionate love affair of her fiction, that in *The Mill on the Floss*, it is questionable whether Stephen ever knows or understands the whole Maggie, the 'real' Maggie, or even the 'best' Maggie, or whether anyone, including author or reader, can. Gender is problematic and gender identity cannot be sought or affirmed through the medium of sexual love because there is no longer possible a reliable 'I am'.

The metaphor of woman as a craving vacancy could not be understood in the same way after the advent of the New Woman in the decades following George Eliot's death. The absence that defined Woman – sexually, socially and economically – and made her a perfect trope for the radical gap between individual self-interest and the more stable patterns of moral and cultural coherence that had dominated traditional society had to change when women developed more of an economic and social presence at the end of the Victorian age.

The dual moral nature of romantic love in nineteenth-century thinking had conventionally conferred meaning on this image of vacancy, either fulfilling the craving for significance through emotional and sexual gratification, or else sanctifying its lack through the spiritual significance of moral superiority. This latter alternative was seen as far less viable after this period, when women were no longer – to use Charlotte Brontë's phrase – quite so 'kept down'. Women still lacked, socially and economically, but the metaphorical meaning of this absence in literature was not as tied to sexual self-suppression as it had once been.

Whether or not the heroine of the twentieth-century novel is a literal virgin, or lacking in sexual experience, she is, more importantly, no longer the paradigmatic Virgin, whose transformation of sexual temptation into courtship best defines her own strong will, as well as contains that of her wild lover. *That* particular paradigm still exists, but it has gone, not quite underground, but into wide distribution as a form of popular culture, where it has been so visible and pervasive for years that it has only recently begun to be studied as a scholarly tradition: I refer, of course, to the multi-million dollar industry of mass-produced romantic novels and movies.

I suggested early on in this study that the social ideals of both Moral Femininity and the Lady, while particularly characteristic of Victorian culture, may also be seen as directly impinging on a larger question: how we may view women as creators of their own representations, rather than, as some theorists would imply, simply rendering them as passive victims of the dominant masculinist social order. If the self-suppressing values of Moral Femininity are so distasteful to feminists today that it is discomforting to imagine women choosing this ideal, we should remind ourselves that some form of essentialism has constituted (and still does) an important part of a complex feminist discourse. The emotional and spiritual dichotomies of gender as seen by Moral Femininity are not so far removed from the views of such contemporary moral dualists as the philosopher Sara Ruddick after all.

In literary culture, the celebration of sexual love, the subversive theme of the Victorian novel, has been for a long time now neither a secret nor even a 'rumour'd heaven'; it is an explored space that many a writer has travelled to and returned from, disillusioned, to report about in exhaustive detail. A great deal has been said and printed since the nineteenth century on the subjects of sexuality, romantic love and women's rights, and yet somehow, in the spiritual vacancies of our own time, the problems that absorbed the literary energies of Charlotte and Emily Brontë remain: how to reconcile female self-interest with the quest for a more just society, how women might act on love and desire in private life within a public space which does not recognize Woman as an authentic subject, how to shape a female craving for meaning and definition into a new concept of female sexuality.

The works of the authors in this study are certainly part of the traditional canon, but as such they form their own unique site for a subtle resistance to social power: by interrogating as well as underwriting convention and ideology, they inject an established field of meaning, the domain of sexual love, with a new vigour. I have said earlier that questions of gender roles and personal identity may be most in flux when they appear most firmly circumscribed and rigid. We may, therefore, see these texts in their time as disturbing an apparently stable and fixed field of values surrounding women, sexuality and romance, charging future generations of readers to ask different questions of a very old story: the narrative of the triangular relation among women, their desire and the men they love.

Notes

PREFACE: A 'CRAVING VACANCY'

1. Charlotte Brontë's journal, actually a small collection of fragments, is reproduced in part in Fannie Ratchford's *The Brontës' Web of Childhood* (New York: Russell & Russell, 1964). It remains unpublished to date, the originals being in the Bonnell Collection of the Brontë Parsonage Museum. Winifred Gerin, *Charlotte Brontë: Evolution of a Genius* (Oxford: Clarendon Press, 1967) also contains excerpts from the diaries, but there are some discrepancies between the two versions. Additional fragments appear also in T. Wise and J.A. Symington, eds., *Miscellaneous and Unpublished Works of Charlotte and Patrick Branwell Brontë* (Oxford: Shakespeare Head Press, 1934). See the information in Christine Alexander's *The Early Writings of Charlotte Brontë* (Oxford: Blackwell, 1983), especially Chapter 19, 'The Roe Head Journal'.
    The quotation above is from Gerin, p. 103, emphasis added. Ratchford, p. 108, reads 'do' for Gerin's 'to'.
2. Sandra Gilbert and Susan Gubar, *Madwoman in the Attic: The Woman Writer and the Nineteenth Century Literary Imagination* (New Haven: Yale University Press, 1979), extensively analyse the metaphor of starvation, which is obviously connected to the meaning of 'craving', though I emphasize the sexual connotation of the word. Barbara Rigney discusses fire, hunger and madness as multiple symbols of psychological fragmentation in *Madness and Sexual Politics in the Feminist Novel* (Madison: University of Wisconsin Press, 1978).
3. See Dianne Sadoff, *Monsters of Affection: Dickens, Eliot and Brontë on Fatherhood* (Baltimore: Johns Hopkins Press, 1982), chapter on 'Language and Desire', for a discussion of the 'trance-like' nature of Charlotte Brontë's 'dream'.
4. The body is the subject of a good deal of recent study. See, for example, Catherine Gallagher and Thomas Laqueur's *The Making of the Modern Body: Sexuality and Society in the Nineteenth Century* (Berkeley: University of California Press, 1987).

CHAPTER I SEXUAL POSSIBILITIES AND IMPOSSIBILITIES

1. The ambiguous, uncharted and shifting nature of sexuality has made it a special point of controversy to feminists, who are concerned with the political relation of women to their sexuality. See, for example, Carol Vance, 'Pleasure and Danger: Toward a Politics of Sexuality': 'Sexuality is simultaneously a domain of restriction, repression and danger as well as a domain of exploration, pleasure and agency', in *Pleasure and Danger: Exploring Female Sexuality* (Boston: Routledge &

Kegan Paul, 1984), ed. Carol Vance, p. 1; and Catharine R. Stimpson and Ethel Spector Person, eds., *Women: Sex and Sexuality* (Chicago: University of Chicago Press, 1980). The literature on sexuality as the intersection between gender and society has become increasingly interdisciplinary in recent decades; some examples are Susan Rubin Suleiman, ed., *The Female Body in Western Culture: Contemporary Perspectives* (Cambridge, Mass.: Harvard University Press, 1986); Nancy Armstrong and Leonard Tennenhouse, eds., *The Ideology of Conduct: Essays in Literature and the History of Sexuality* (New York and London: Methuen, 1987); Pat Caplan, ed., *The Cultural Construction of Sexuality* (London: Tavistock Press, 1987); Catherine Gallagher and Thomas Laqueur, eds., *The Making of the Modern Body* (Berkeley: University of California Press, 1987); Kathy Peiss and Christina Simmons, eds., *Passion and Power: Sexuality in History* (Philadelphia: Temple University Press, 1988); Lynn Hunt, ed., *Eroticism and the Body Politic* (Baltimore: Johns Hopkins Press, 1990).

For the construction of women, culture and nature, see Michele Rosaldo and Louise Lamphere, eds., *Woman, Culture and Society* (Stanford: Stanford University Press, 1974); and Sherry Ortner and H. Whitehead, eds., *Sexual Meanings: The Cultural Construction of Gender and Sexuality* (Cambridge: Cambridge University Press, 1981). One should note, however, that there is a range of views on the construction of gender identity among feminists of various disciplines; for an informative discussion of the implications of these perspectives, see Martha Vicinus, 'Sexuality and Power: A Review of Current Work in the History of Sexuality', *Feminist Studies* 8 (1982): 133–56; Sue Cartledge and Joanna Ryan, eds., *Sex and Love: New Thoughts on Old Contradictions* (London: The Women's Press, 1983), especially Wendy Hollway, 'Heterosexual Sex: Power and Desire for the Other'; Joan Cocks, *The Oppositional Imagination: Feminism, Critique and Political Theory* (London and New York: Routledge, 1989); Janet Holland et al., 'Power and Desire: The Embodiment of Female Sexuality', *Feminist Review* 46 (1994): 21–38.

2. Ellen Ross and Rayna Rapp, 'Sex and Society: A Research Note from Social History and Anthropology', in *The Powers of Desire: The Politics of Sexuality*, ed. Ann Snitow, Christine Stansell and Sharon Thompson (New York: Monthly Review, 1983), p. 51. For a survey of changing theories of sexuality, see Don Milligan, *Sex-life: A Critical Commentary on the History of Sexuality* (London: Pluto Press, 1993).

3. See Arnold I. Davidson, 'Sex and the Emergence of Sexuality', *Critical Inquiry* 14 (1987): 16–48; the idea of sexuality as a category in history is explored by David M. Halperin, 'Is There a History of Sexuality?', *History and Theory* 28 (1989): 257–74; Jeffrey Weeks, *Sex, Politics and Society: The Regulation of Sexuality since 1800* (London: Longman, 1989) and many others. See Peter Laipson, 'From Boudoir to Bookstore: Writing the History of Sexuality', *Comparative Studies in Society and History* 34 (1992): 636–44.

4. Michel Foucault, Preface to *The History of Sexuality*, Vol. II, in Paul Rabinow, ed., *The Foucault Reader* (New York: Pantheon, 1984), p. 338.

5. J. Michelet, 'On Love', reproduced in Susan Bell and Karen Offen, eds., *Women, Family and Freedom*, Vol. I: *The Debate in Documents, 1750–1880* (Stanford: Stanford University Press, 1983).
6. Roland Barthes, *Mythologies* (New York: Hill & Wang, 1972), p. 143.
7. *Ibid.*, p. 142.
8. Nina Auerbach, *Woman and the Demon: The Life of a Victorian Myth* (Cambridge, Mass.: Harvard University Press, 1982); Nancy Armstrong, *Desire and Domestic Fiction: A Political History of the Novel* (New York: Oxford University Press, 1987); Mary Poovey, *Uneven Developments: The Ideological Work of Gender in Mid-Victorian England* (Chicago: University of Chicago Press, 1988).
9. Judith L. Newton and Deborah Rosenfelt, eds., *Feminist Criticism and Social Change* (New York and London: Methuen, 1985), p. xxi. See also Newton's *Women, Power and Subversion* (Athens, Ga: University of Georgia Press, 1981), which redefines power to show how women were able to conceptualize their own 'influence' as a form of power. For a useful study of the relation of 'femininity' to power, see Sandra Bartky's *Femininity and Domination: Studies in the Phenomenology of Oppression* (London and New York: Routledge, 1990).
10. *Ibid.*, p. xix.
11. For a complex and subtle consideration of female desire, especially as it appears in the law, see Tracy Higgins, 'Reconsidering Sexuality in Feminist Theory', unpublished paper delivered at Conference on 'The Centrality of Sexuality in the Shaping of Feminist Legal Theory', Columbia University Law School, 1994.
12. 'Introduction: Coming and Going in Victorian Literature', *Sex and Death in Victorian Literature*, ed. Regina Barreca (Bloomington: Indiana University Press, 1990), p. 4. Nancy Miller, 'Emphasis Added: Plots and Plausibilities in Women's Fiction', *PMLA* 96 (1981) seems to have been the first to make this latter point.
13. Lawrence Senelick, 'Ladykillers and Lady Killers: Recent Popular Victoriana', *Victorian Studies*, 21 (1978): 494.
14. Michel Foucault, *The History of Sexuality*, Vol. I: *An Introduction*, trans. Robert Hurley (New York: Random House, 1980), p. 69.
15. Anonymous, 'Chastity: Its Development and Maintenance', *Westminster Review*, 114 (1880): 421. The author's quotation is from the Rev. Ralph Wardlaw, 'Lectures on Magdalenism', 1842.
16. Some of the best-known studies of Victorian sexuality have been Gordon Haight, 'Male Chastity in the Nineteenth Century', *Contemporary Review*, 219 (1971), pp. 252–62, and Keith Thomas, 'Double Standard', *Journal of the History of Ideas* 20 (1959): 195–216 on chastity; Peter Cominos, who related the ideal of chastity to the accumulation of wealth under capitalism in 'Late Victorian Sexual Respectability and the Social System', *International Review of Social History*, 8 (1963): 18, 33–4. Steven Marcus, *The Other Victorians* (New York: Basic Books, 1966), p. 2, who pioneered the idea that the Victorian sensibility was 'problematic'; Ben Barker-Benfield, 'Spermatic Economy: A Nineteenth Century View of Sexuality', *Feminist Studies*, 1 (1972): 45–66, reiterated the metaphor of the Victorian male body as an economic system:

Michel Foucault criticized this hypothesis to great effect in *The History of Sexuality*, Vol. I (New York: Pantheon, 1978), pp. 5–6. See Sarah J. Stage, 'Out of the Attic: Studies of Victorian Sexuality', *American Quarterly*, 27 (1975); and F. Barry Smith, 'Sexuality in Britain, 1800–1900: Some Suggested Revisions', in *A Widening Sphere: Changing Roles of Victorian Women*, ed. Martha Vicinus (Bloomington: Indiana University Press, 1977) for the burgeoning social history of the 1970s. Peter Gay, *The Bourgeois Experience: Victoria to Freud*, Vol. I of *Education of the Senses* (New York: Oxford University Press, 1984); Jeffrey Weeks, *Sex, Politics and Society*; and Françoise Barret-Ducrocq, *Love in the Time of Victoria: Sexuality, Class and Gender in Nineteenth Century London* (London: Verso, 1991) are representative of more recent work in the field. *Sexuality and Victorian Literature*, ed. Don R. Cox (Knoxville: University of Tennessee Press, 1984), pp. 264–5; and *Sexuality and Subordination: Interdisciplinary Studies of Gender in the Nineteenth Century*, ed. Susan Mendus and Jane Rendall (London and New York: Routledge, 1989) are collections on sexual themes in literature and culture; Lynda Nead's *Myths of Sexuality: Representations of Women in Victorian Britain* (Oxford: Basil Blackwell, 1988) examines sexuality in the visual arts of the period.

For other works on sexuality in nineteenth-century America, see Linda Gordon, *Woman's Body, Woman's Right: A Social History of Birth Control in America* (Harmondsworth: Penguin, 1976); Daniel Scott-Smith, 'Family Limitation, Sexual Control and Domestic Feminism in Victorian America', *Feminist Studies*, 1 (1973): 40–57; Nancy Cott, 'Passionlessness: An Interpretation of Victorian Sexual Ideology, 1790–1850', *Signs*, 4 (1978): 229–33.

17. The best-known formulation of this dilemma is, of course, Freud's *Civilization and its Discontents*. See also 'The Most Prevalent Form of Degradation in Erotic Life', in *Collected Papers*, III, ed. E. Jones (New York: Basic Books, 1959): 'Altogether it is not possible for the claims of sexual restraint to be reconciled with the demands of culture. The irreconcilable antagonisms between the demands of the two restraints – the sexual and the egoistic – have made man capable of even greater achievement, though ... under the continual menace of danger', p. 216.

18. See A. Schopenhauer, *The World as Will and Idea*, III, for a nineteenth-century view of the relations between sexuality and the problematic human will. John Reed's *Victorian Will* (Athens: Ohio University Press, 1989) is a rich source for the consideration of the role played by the construct called 'the will' in Victorian culture. See also John H. Smith's interesting work on 'Abulia: Sexuality and Diseases of the Will in the Late Nineteenth Century', *Genders* 6 (1989): 102–24, which explores 'abulia', the clinical term for diseases of the will and a male counterpart of hysteria. 'Weakness of the will' in males was seen as an alternative state to 'increase of the will, inordinate desire'.

19. 'Chastity', p. 421.

20. There has been a considerable feminist reliance on Foucauldian theory, as well as a reconsideration and critique of his conception of power,

too numerous to mention here, as in Biddy Martin, 'Feminism, Criticism and Foucault', *New German Critique* 27 (1982): 3–30; Jana Sawicki, *Disciplining Foucault: Feminism, Power and the Body* (London and New York: Routledge, 1991); and Nancy Hartsock, 'Foucault on Power: A Theory for Women?', in Linda Nicholson, ed., *Feminism/Postmodernism* (New York and London: Routledge, 1990). See the exchange between Isaac Balbus and Jana Sawicki in *After Foucault: Humanistic Knowledge, Postmodern Challenges*, ed. Jonathan Arac (New Brunswick: Rutgers University Press, 1988).

21. Nead, *Myths of Sexuality*, p. 5; see also Sally Shuttleworth, 'Empowering Fictions: The History of Sexuality and the Novel', *Eighteenth Century: Theory and Interpretation* 30 (1989): 51–61, for contradictory versions of womanhood: 'From the late 18th century onwards, women were figured both as angelic creatures in full possession of an interiorized selfhood and as biological organisms whose primary function was to subordinate subjectivity to the material process of social reproduction' (p. 58).

22. 'Chastity', p. 422.

23. *Webster's New World Dictionary* defines the medical term 'stricture' as 'an abnormal narrowing of a passage in the body'. One might apply here the anthropologist Mary Douglas's discussion of 'a kind of sex pollution which expresses the desire to keep the body (physical and social) intact. Its rules are phrased to control entrances and exits', in *Purity and Danger: An Analysis of the Concepts of Pollution and Taboo* (Harmondsworth: Penguin, 1966), p. 166.

24. Karl Marx, *Economic and Philosophic Manuscripts of 1844*, trans. Martin Milligan (New York: International Publishing Co., 1961), p. 101.

25. Nancy Armstrong's *Desire and Domestic Fiction* is particularly helpful in tracing the complex relations of desire, textual structure and political ideology in the history of the novel. See also Linda Hunt, *A Woman's Portion: Ideology, Culture, and the British Female Novel Tradition* (New York: Garland Press, 1988).

26. Martha Vicinus, 'Sexuality and Power: A Review of Current Work in the History of Sexuality', *Feminist Studies* 8 (1982): 133–56. See also Barbara Harlow, *Resistance Literature* (New York: Methuen, 1987); and Newton, *Woman, Power and Subversion*.

27. Vicinus, 'Sexuality and Power', p. 136.

28. Elizabeth Hardwick, *Seduction and Betrayal* (New York: Random House, 1972); Patricia Meyer Spacks, *The Female Imagination* (New York: Knopf, 1975); Ellen Moers, *Literary Women* (New York: Doubleday and Co., 1976); Elaine Showalter, *A Literature of their Own: British Women Novelists from Brontë to Lessing* (Princeton, NJ: Princeton University Press, 1977); and Nancy K. Miller, 'Emphasis Added', among others, have all discussed the prominence in nineteenth-century literature of the heroine who sacrifices herself or is sacrificed. A somewhat different view which emphasizes the importance of self-denial to women's own interests can be found in Kathleen Blake, *Love and the Woman Question in Victorian Literature: The Art of Self-Postponement* (Totowa, NJ: Barnes and Noble Books, 1983).

29. John Kucich in *Repression in Victorian Fiction: Charlotte Brontë, George Eliot and Charles Dickens* (Berkeley: University of California Press, 1987) interestingly reworks the traditional psychological notion of 'repression' to look at the ways that desire and the repression of desire together constitute an interlocking organization of selfhood in Victorian fiction.
30. See Lloyd Davis, ed., *Virginal Sexuality and Textuality in Victorian Literature* (Albany, NY: SUNY Press, 1993).

CHAPTER 2 CHASTITY AND 'RUMOUR'D HEAVEN': WOMAN AND THE DOUBLE MESSAGE OF SEXUAL LOVE

1. Simone de Beauvoir, *The Second Sex* (New York: Vintage, 1952), p. xvii.
2. Janet Holland, Caroline Ramazanoglu, Sue Sharpe and Rachel Thompson argue against the 'conceptual dualism' between essentialism and poststructuralist views of female sexuality, 'Power and Desire: The Embodiments of Female Sexuality', *Feminist Review* 46 (Spring 1994): 21–2.
3. Important work has been done on the Romance Plot and the heroine's marriage/death alternative as closure by Nancy K. Miller, *The Heroine's Text: Readings in the French and English Novel, 1722–1782* (New York: Columbia University Press, 1980); Nina Auerbach, *Woman and the Demon*; Rachel Brownstein, *Becoming a Heroine: Reading about Women in Novels* (New York: Viking Press, 1982); Rachel Blau du Plessis, *Writing Beyond the Ending: Narrative Strategies of Twentieth Century Woman Writers* (Bloomington: Indiana University Press, 1985); and Leslie Rabine, *Reading the Romantic Heroine: Text, History, Ideology* (Ann Arbor: University of Michigan Press, 1985). The uniquely English articulation of the courtship plot is the subject of Ruth Bernard Yeazell's *Fictions of Modesty: Women and Courtship in the English Novel* (Chicago: University of Chicago, 1991).
4. Joseph Allen Boone, *Tradition Counter Tradition: Love and the Form of Fiction* (Chicago: University of Chicago Press, 1987); Laurie Langbauer, *Women and Romance: The Consolations of Gender in the English Novel* (Ithaca, NY: Cornell University Press, 1990), and Robert Polhemus, *Erotic Faith: Being in Love from Jane Austen to D.H. Lawrence* (Chicago: University of Chicago Press, 1990) consider the relation of romantic love as ideology to romance as traditional genre in the British novel.
5. Some contributions are Patricia Branca, *Silent Sisterhood: Middle Class Women in the Victorian Home* (Pittsburgh: Carnegie-Mellon University Press, 1975); Carol Dyhouse, *Girls Growing Up in Late Victorian and Edwardian England* (London: Routledge, 1981); Eric Sigsworth, ed., *In Search of Victorian Values: Aspects of Nineteenth-Century Thought and Society* (Manchester: Manchester University Press, 1988).

   For nineteenth-century America, see Nancy Cott, *Bonds of Womanhood: 'Woman's Sphere' in New England, 1780–1835* (New Haven, CT: Yale University Press, 1977), Frances Cogan, *All-American Girl: The Ideal of Real Womanhood in Mid-Nineteenth Century America* (Athens:

University of Georgia Press, 1989); and Gillian Brown, *Domestic Individualism: Imagining a Self in Nineteenth-Century America* (Berkeley: University of California Press, 1991), which in turn build on the work of Barbara Welter, Carroll Smith-Rosenberg and Mary Ryan. Carol Groneman's essay, 'Nymphomania: The Historical Construction of Female Sexuality', *Signs* 19 (1994): 337–67, reviews the history of theories of female sexuality from the Enlightenment through the Victorian era.

6. See particularly Newton, *Women, Power and Subversion*, Poovey, *Uneven Developments*, and Armstrong and Tennenhouse, *The Ideology of Conduct*; sources range from Catherine Hall, 'The Early Formation of Victorian Domestic Ideology', in *Fit Work for Women*, ed. Sandra Burman (New York: St Martin's Press, 1979), to a recent assessment in Elizabeth Langland's 'Nobody's Angels: Domestic Ideology and Middle-Class Women in the Victorian Novel', *PMLA* (107) 1992: 290–304; their work investigates an area that is essential to my own view but has an entirely different centre of interest. Kate Ferguson Ellis, *The Contested Castle: Gothic Novels and the Subversion of Domestic Ideology* is an important model for analysing the complexity of literary reactions to official ideologies. A recent, provocative analysis of Victorian domestic ideology which is rooted in cultural history is Anita Levy's *Other Women: The Writing of Class, Race, and Gender, 1832–1898* (Princeton, NJ: Princeton University Press, 1991).

7. Compare John Maynard's formulation of Patmore's 'erotic consciousness' in 'Victorian Discourses on Sexuality and Religion', *Studies in Literature* 19 (1987): 61–9.

8. Julian Pitt-Rivers, 'Honor and Social Status', in *Honor and Shame: The Value of Mediterranean Society*, ed. J.G. Peristiany (Chicago: University of Chicago Press, 1966), p. 72.

9. Some historical studies of sexuality and family relations are Edward Shorter, *Making of the Modern Family* (New York: Basic Books, 1975); Peter Laslett, *Family Life and Illicit Love in Earlier Generations* (Cambridge: Cambridge University Press, 1977); Randolph Trumbach, *Rise of the Egalitarian Family* (New York: Academic Press, 1978); Lawrence Stone, *The Family, Sex and Marriage in England, 1500–1800* (New York: Harper & Row, 1977), J.-H. Flandrin, *Families in Former Times: Kinship, Household and Sexuality* (Cambridge: Cambridge University Press, 1979); Paul-Gabriel Bouce, ed., *Sexuality in Eighteenth Century Britain* (Manchester: B & N Imports, 1982); Alan Macfarlane, *Marriage and Love in England: Modes of Reproduction 1300–1840* (Oxford: Blackwell, 1986); G.J. Barker-Benfield, *The Culture of Sensibility: Sex and Society in Eighteenth-Century Britain* (Chicago: University of Chicago Press, 1992); Peter Gay, *The Bourgeois Experience: Victoria to Freud*, Vol. II: *The Tender Passion*.

Some sources which trace the growth in importance of Western romantic love in the nineteenth century and beyond are Steven Seidman, *Romantic Longings: Love in America, 1830–1980* (New York: Routledge, 1991); Elaine Hoffman Baruch, *Women, Love and Power: Literary and Psychoanalytic Perspectives* (New York: New York Univer-

10. Here I disagree with Nancy Armstrong, who sees 'love' more monolithically as middle-class political ideology disseminated through the medium of the domestic novel. See Sally Shuttleworth's critique of Armstrong in 'Empowering Fictions'.
11. Anne Carson, *Eros the Bittersweet: An Essay* (Princeton, NJ: Princeton University Press, 1986), p. 10. See also Roland Barthes, *A Lover's Discourse*, trans. R. Howard (New York: Hill and Wang, 1978).
12. *Westminster Review*, 35 (1841): 122. For a consideration of popular journalism in assessing women's relation to romantic love and sexuality, see Sally Mitchell, *The Fallen Angel: Chastity, Class and Women's Reading, 1835–1880* (Bowling Green, Ohio: Bowling Green University Popular Press, 1981); Judith Newton, 'Engendering History for the Middle Class', in *Gender and Discourse in Victorian Literature and Art*, ed. Antony Harrison and Beverly Taylor (DeKalb: Northern Illinois University Press, 1992), discusses the ideological stance of male essays on women in nineteenth-century journals.
13. Vol. 27, p. 274.
14. 'Loops and Parentheses', *Temple Bar*, 6 (1862): 56.
15. Mary Poovey's *The Proper Lady* is the best study of the concept of Ladyhood and its effect on literature, but her view differs from mine in that she does not separate the idea of Moral Femininity from the social ideal of the Proper Lady. See also Martha Vicinus, 'The Perfect Victorian Lady', in *Suffer and Be Still*, ed. M. Vicinus (Bloomington: University of Indiana Press, 1972); Ann Douglas, *The Feminization of American Culture* (New York: Knopf, 1978); Leonore Davidoff and Catherine Hall, *The Best Circles: Women and Society in Victorian England* (Totowa, NJ: Rowman and Littlefield, 1973); and M. Jeanne Peterson, *Family, Love and Work in the Lives of Victorian Gentlewomen* (Bloomington: Indiana University Press, 1989).
16. I do not wish to overstate the difference between these social ideals and set up a new binary opposition to replace good/bad women; rather, I would like to emphasize here that these are, I believe, useful but artificial constructs with a good deal of overlap between them, especially, as I have said, in the matter of sexual *conduct* permissible to women. I employ the distinction between these categories in the spirit of correcting what I see as a glossing over of the complex subtleties of Victorian social forms in much critical literature.
17. 'Women vs. Ladies', *Athenaeum* (1847): 1128; 'What Constitutes a Lady?', *Ladies' Wreath*, 1 (1846): 33.
18. *Bow Bells* 3 (1865): 571.
19. *The Girl of the Period and Other Essays*, reprinted from a series originally published in the 1860s (Leipzig: B. Tauchnitz, 1884), pp. 9–12.
20. 'Modern Mothers', in *The Girl of the Period*, p. 17. See also, 'The Modern Revolt', *Macmillan Magazine*, 23 (1870): 143: 'The reaction against maternity is spreading rapidly.'

21. Quoted in Banks, *Feminism*, pp. 68–71.
22. *Ladies' Wreath*, 1 (1847): 184.
23. 'Breakfast in Bed', *Temple Bar*, 6 (1862): 498.
24. Mrs S.T. Martyn, 'The Social Position of Women', *Ladies' Wreath* 1 (1847): 76.
25. Mrs S.T. Martyn, 'What Constitutes a Lady?', *Ladies' Wreath* 1 (1846): 1.
26. See Janet Wolff, 'The Culture of Separate Spheres: The Role of Culture in 19th c. Public and Private Life', in *The Culture of Capital: Art, Power and the Nineteenth Century Middle Class*, ed. J. Wolff and J. Seed (New York: St Martin's Press, 1988); see also Linda Hunt, *A Woman's Portion*, for the complex interaction of ideology and literature in women's lives.
27. 'Womanliness', *Sharpe's London Magazine* (1866): 152.
28. See Armstrong, *Desire and Domestic Fiction*.
29. Carlyle, *Past and Present*, Book III, Ch. 2, in *Prose of the Victorian Period*, ed. William Buckler (Boston: Houghton Mifflin, 1958), p. 136.
30. *Monthly Religious Magazine*, 27 (1862): 205–6.
31. Havelock Ellis, *Man and Woman: A Study of Human Secondary Sexual Characteristics* 5th edn (New York: Scribner's, 1914). See Anita Levy's discussion of Havelock Ellis, sexology and gender in her *Other Women: The Writing of Class, Race and Gender, 1832–1898* (Princeton, NJ: Princeton University Press, 1991).
32. 'Female Pretensions', *London Review of Politics, Society, Literature, Art and Science*, XI (1865): 139; Stendhal, *On Love* (1822) (New York: Doubleday, 1957), p. 23.
33. 'Relations of the Sexes', *Westminster Review*, 111 (1879): 322.
34. 'Our Single Women', *North British Review*, xxxvi (1862): 73.
35. Rev. W.B. Sprague, 'Advice to a Daughter', *Ladies Wreath*, 1 (1846): 237.
36. Kate Ellis, *The Contested Castle*, provides the best analysis of the literary consequences of this problem of ambivalence towards the home; Judith L. Newton notes: 'The familiarity of separate spheres ideology should not obscure for us the tensions which those ways of representing the world produced.... Home, indeed ... is not a place about which many reviewers feel at ease. It is another sphere in which boundaries must be drawn, fortified, and policed'; in 'Engendering History', pp. 9–10.
37. 'Home Life', in *The Queen*, is quoted in *Westminster Review*, 103 (1875): 173; 'instead of love', etc. is on p. 182.
38. 'Home, Its Institutions and Constitution', *Monthly Religious Magazine*, 27 (1862): 214–15 (emphasis added).
39. Branca, *Silent Sisterhood*, p. 8; and P. Branca, 'Myth of the Idle Victorian Woman', in *Clio's Consciousness Raised*, ed. M. Hartman and Lois Banner (New York: Octagon Books, 1976), pp. 186–9.
40. Sarah Ellis, *The Women of England: Their Social Duties and Domestic Habits* (London: Fisher, Son & Co., 1839).
41. 'Womanliness', *Sharpe's London Magazine* 43 (1866): 151.
42. See, for example, Nancy Cott, *Bonds of Womanhood*. The inconsistency of an ideology that described women as at once of a finer spiritual

fibre than men, yet weak and irrational, was a card well played by 'domestic feminists' of the nineteenth century: see also Joan Burstyn, *Victorian Education and the Ideal of Womanhood* (Totowa, NJ: Barnes & Noble, 1980); and Deborah Gorham, *The Victorian Girl and the Feminine Ideal* (Bloomington: Indiana University Press, 1982).

43. 'Modern Revolt', *Macmillan Magazine*, 23 (1870): 142.
44. 'The Wild Women as Social Insurgents', *Nineteenth Century*, 30 (1891): 599.
45. E. Linton, Introduction to *Modern Women and What is Said of Them* (New York: J.S. Redfield, 1870), p. 6.
46. *Robert Elsmere*, quoted in Brian Harrison, 'Girls' Friendly Society', *Past and Present* 61 (1973): 123.
47. Linda Gordon, *Woman's Body, Woman's Right*, Ch. 9. Howard Gadlin astutely remarked that 'it was precisely when women had begun to question the overriding social significance of gender that their erotic sexuality was rediscovered, encouraged and developed'; in 'Private Lives and Public Order: A Critical View of the History of Intimate Relations in the United States', *Massachusetts Review*, 17 (1976): 322. See Rosalind Coward's development of this point in *Female Desires* (New York: Grove Press, 1985).
48. *Cornhill* 3 (1861): 46.
49. 'Nine Scenes from Two Lives', *London Journal*, 33 (1861): 38.
50. 'The Girl We Leave Behind Us', *London Journal*, 34 (1861): 155.
51. Pierce Egan, 'The Wonder of Kingswood Chace', *London Journal* 33 (1861): 273.
52. William Leach in his chapter on 'The Vindication of Love', discusses the idealized nature of 'sentimental love' and shows the changing feminist relation to it: *True Love and Perfect Union: The Feminist Reform of Sex and Society* (New York: Basic, 1980); see also Ellen DuBois and Linda Gordon, 'Seeking Ecstasy on the Battlefield: Danger and Pleasure in Nineteenth Century Feminist Sexual Thought', in *Pleasure and Danger: Exploring Female Sexuality*, ed. Carol Vance.
53. Barthes, *A Lover's Discourse*, p. 10.
54. In his essay 'On Love', Georg Simmel notes that 'it is as if love were a kind of gripping or violent experience that *comes from the outside* ... as if love came from its object' (p. 163, my italics). *On Women, Sexuality and Love* (New Haven: Yale University Press, 1984).
55. Barthes, *A Lover's Discourse*, p. 226.
56. Erich Fromm, *The Art of Loving* (New York: Harper, 1956), p. 88.
57. Elaine Hoffman Baruch makes much the same argument from a psychoanalytic point of view in her *Women, Love and Power: Literary and Psychoanalytic Perspectives* (New York: New York University Press, 1991).
58. S. Ellis, *The Women of England*, p. 51.
59. H. Ellis, *Studies in the Psychology of Sex* (Philadelphia: F.A. Davis, 1912), Vol. 3, p. 199 (my italics).
60. Kate Linker, 'Representation and Sexuality', *Art After Modernism*, ed. Brian Wallis (Boston: David R. Godine, Publisher, Inc., 1984), p. 393.

CHAPTER 3 THE LIGHT IN THE CAVERN: SAMUEL RICHARDSON AND SEXUAL LOVE

1. Samuel Richardson, *Clarissa* (London: Everyman, 1962) III, p. 321. All further references to this edition will be found in the text.
2. Linda Abbandonato, for example, examines the dominant place of *Clarissa* in British literary history, especially in the ideology of romances: 'Richardson himself... perfectly symbolizes white patriarchy', 'A View from "Elsewhere": Subversive Sexuality and the Rewriting of the Heroine's Story in *The Color Purple*', *PMLA* 106 (1991): 1107. See also Nancy K. Miller, *The Heroine's Text*.
3. Two studies of *Clarissa* disagree on exactly this point: whose story is the 'correct' version? William Warner's *Reading Clarissa: The Struggles of Interpretation* (New Haven: Yale University Press, 1979) sees Lovelace as a modern man playing parts, and tends to 'side' with him as actor and interpreter; Terry Castle's *Clarissa's Ciphers: Meaning and Disruption in Richardson's Clarissa* (Ithaca, NY: Cornell University Press, 1982) vehemently disagrees with Warner's point of view and offers an alternative femininist reading of Clarissa as a heroine/victim not permitted to speak her own interpretation of events in the novel.
4. Lionel Trilling, *The Liberal Imagination* (New York: Doubleday, 1950), p. 250.
5. Michael McKeon traces the history of the novel as an attempt to give form to the revolutionary clash between inconsistent class and status by organizing a narrative of conflicting, schematic sets of oppositional forces which are themselves constructed categories, *The Origins of the English Novel, 1600–1740* (Baltimore: Johns Hopkins Press, 1987).
6. John Richetti, *Popular Fiction Before Richardson: Narrative Patterns, 1700–1739* (Oxford: Clarendon Press, 1969), p. 124; for Richardson's debt to eighteenth-century novelists, see Jerry Beasley, 'Rousseau and the "New" Novels of Richardson, Fielding and Smollett', *SEL* 16 (1976): 437–50, which identifies the qualities these authors shared with popular romances, and Margaret Doody's chapter on '*Clarissa* and Earlier Novels of Love and Seduction', in *A Natural Passion: A Study of the Novels of Samuel Richardson* (Oxford: Clarendon Press, 1974). For female novelists before Richardson, see Janet Todd, *The Sign of Angellica: Women, Writing and Fiction, 1661–1800* (London: Virago Press, 1989); Susan Lanser, *Fictions of Authority: Women Writers and Narrative Voice* (Ithaca, NY: Cornell University Press, 1992); and Ros Ballaster, *Seductive Forms: Women's Amatory Fiction from 1684 to 1749* (Oxford: Clarendon Press, 1992).
7. Richetti, *Popular Fiction before Richardson*, p. 162.
8. G.S. Rousseau and Roy Porter, eds., *Sexual Underworlds of the Enlightenment* (Chapel Hill: University of North Carolina Press, 1988); and G.J. Barker-Benfield, *The Culture of Sensibility: Sex and Society in Eighteenth Century Britain* (Chicago: University of Chicago Press, 1992).
9. See Jerry Beasley, *Novels of the 1840's* (Athens, Ga: University of Georgia, 1979); and Laura Brown, 'The Defenseless Woman and the Development of English Tragedy', *SEL* 22 (1982): 429–43 for the

tradition of joining chastity to helplessness in the eighteenth century. For Richardson's place in the Enlightenment, see Rita Goldberg's fine study, *Sex and Enlightenment: Women in Richardson and Diderot* (Cambridge: Cambridge University Press, 1984), especially pp. 18–23 on *Clarissa* as sexual myth and model. An earlier work is Robert Moynihan, 'Clarissa and the Enlightened Woman as Literary Heroine', *Journal of the History of Ideas* 36 (1975). Ellen Pollak offers an interesting analogical paradox in the work of Pope, in which the heroine is portrayed as the 'centre of its fictional romance', yet strives at the same time towards reifying the proposition that 'women are virginal beings', 'Rereading "The Rape of the Lock": Pope and the Paradox of Female Power', in *Studies in Eighteenth Century Culture*, 10 (1981): 429.

10. 'Review of *Clarissa*', *Gentleman's Magazine* XIX (1749): 246 and 346.
11. The *Oxford English Dictionary* lists a quotation from 1711 as the last example of the archaic meaning of 'honest' as 'chaste, virtuous, especially of a woman'.
12. *Pamela, or Virtue Rewarded* (New York: Norton, 1958), p. 141.
13. Denis Diderot, 'Eloge de Richardson', *Oeuvres Complètes* V (Paris, 1885), p. 215. The original is: 'Il porte le flambeau au fond de la caverne...'. For an analysis of the 'cult of Richardsonism' in eighteenth-century France, see Chapter 4 of Goldberg's *Sex and Enlightenment*.
14. Terry Eagleton discusses Clarissa as a 'transcendental subject' in *The Rape of Clarissa* (Oxford: Blackwell, 1982); for an analysis of fiction as a drama of self-realization, see Arnold Weinstein's *Fictions of the Self, 1550–1800* (Princeton, NJ: Princeton University Press, 1981), which locates Richardson at the border of a phase of fiction marked by the turning inward of selfhood. For Richardson's 'narrative transvestism', see Susan Lanser, *Fictions of Authority*; and Madeleine Kahn, *Narrative Transvestism: Rhetoric and Gender in the Eighteenth Century English Novel* (Ithaca, NY: Cornell University Press, 1991).
15. In her study of popular romance in the present day, Janice Radway finds that the first function in a structural analysis of the romance plot is the heroine's 'removal from a familiar comfortable realm usually associated with her childhood and family' (p. 134), whereupon she is 'thrust out into the public world' (p. 138) in *Reading the Romance: Women, Patriarchy and Popular Literature* (Chapel Hill: University of North Carolina Press, 1984). For female *Bildungsroman* in the British novel tradition, see Elizabeth Abel et al., *The Voyage In: Fictions of Female Development* (Hanover: University Press of New England, 1983); and Susan Fraiman, *Unbecoming Women: British Women Writers and the Novel of Development* (New York: Columbia University Press, 1993).
16. Judith Laurence-Anderson's 'Changing Affective Life in Eighteenth Century England: Richardson's *Pamela*', *Studies in Eighteenth Century Culture* 10 (1981): 445–56, traces the way in which Richardson's work reflects contemporary attitudes towards master–servant relations.
17. A.O.J. Cockshut considers the role of double standards of sexual

morality in Richardson in *Man and Woman: A Study of Love and the Novel* (London: Collins, 1977).

18. *The Rambler*, 97 (19 February 1751): 235.
19. Letter of 6 August 1750, A. Barbauld, ed., *Correspondence*, III (New York: Arno Press, 1966), pp. 278 and 280.
20. The classic work on this point are Ian Watt, *Rise of the Novel* (Berkeley: University of California, 1957), p. 148; and Christopher Hill, 'Clarissa Harlowe and her Times', *Puritanism and Revolution* (New York: Schocken, 1958). Tassie Gwilliam, *Samuel Richardson's Fictions of Gender* (Stanford: Stanford University Press, 1993), sees *Pamela* as a 'split' novel, in which Richardson 'reproduce[s] contradictory aspects of the ideology of femininity', p. 15.
21. Nancy Miller astutely observes that Pamela's reward is not just marriage but society's 'recognition of [the heroine's] *spiritual* superiority', in *The Heroine's Text*, p. 49.
22. *Pamela, or Virtue Rewarded* (New York: Norton, 1958), p. 262. All further references will be found in the text.
23. Mary Poovey's '*Persuasion* and the Promises of Love', though concerned with Jane Austen's novels, explores the idea that romantic love appears ' "outside" ideology', in *The Representation of Women in Fiction*, ed. Carolyn Heilbrun and Margaret Higonnet (Baltimore: Johns Hopkins Press, 1983), p. 172.
24. For Lovelace as a conventional eighteenth-century rake, see Penelope Bigges, 'Hunt, Conquest, Trial: Lovelace and the Metaphors of the Rake', *Studies in Eighteenth Century Culture* 11 (1982): 51–64; Carol Flynn's chapter on 'A Lovelace in Every Corner: The Rake Figure in Richardson's Novels', in her *Samuel Richardson: Man of Letters* (Princeton, NJ: University of Princeton Press, 1982); particularly fine is John Traugott's '*Clarissa*'s Richardson: An Essay to Find the Reader', in *English Literature in the Age of Enlightenment*, ed. M.E. Novak (Berkeley: University of California Press, 1977), pp. 157–208, which discusses the transmutation of Lovelace from stock figure of Restoration comedy to one of 'sentimental realism'.
25. Similarly, the rake Sir Hargrave in *Sir Charles Grandison* kisses the heroine Harriet's hand and remarks: 'You may be glad you have a hand left. By my soul, I could eat you' (Oxford: Shakespeare Head (1931), I, p. 150).
26. Christopher Hill sees *Clarissa* as the supreme criticism of property marriage; John Allen Stevenson, 'Courtship of the Family: Clarissa and the Harlowes Once More', *ELH* 48 (1981): 757–77, discusses the relations of family, courtship and endogamy; Leo Braudy studies the breakdown of institutional and familial authority and its effect on identity in 'Penetration and Impenetrability in *Clarissa*', in P. Harth, ed., *New Approaches to Eighteenth Century Literature* (New York: Columbia University Press, 1974); see also Tony Tanner on the importance of the father's authority in *Adultery in the Novel: Contract and Transgression* (Baltimore: Johns Hopkins Press, 1979), pp. 103–4; and Florian Stuber, 'On Fathers and Authority in *Clarissa*', *SEL* 25 (1985): 557–74. Louise Kibbie's 'Sentimental Properties: *Pamela* and *Memoirs*

of a Woman of Pleasure', *ELH* 58 (1991): 561–77, traces the relations between the Virgin, the 'slut' and the wife as emblems of male prerogative.
27. Hester Thrale Piozzi, *Thralania*, ed. Katharine Balderston (Oxford: Clarendon, 1951), p. 570.
28. *De la littérature* (1800).
29. Quoted in Richetti, *Popular Fiction before Richardson*, p. 202.
30. *Correspondence*, III, pp. 182 and 184.
31. Quoted in T.C.D. Eaves and B. Kimpel, *Samuel Richardson: A Biography* (Oxford: Clarendon Press, 1971), p. 52.
32. We can see the eighteenth-century alignment of romantic love with the reasonable pursuit of happiness by the individual in a comment by Mrs Thrale, who wrote in 1782 of her desire to marry for love: 'I married the first time to please my mother, I must marry for the second time to please my daughter – I have always sacrificed my own choice to that of others. . . . If I *have* superior Understanding, let me make use of it for once; and rise to the rank of a human being conscious of its own power to discern Good from Ill – that person who has uniformly acted by the will of others, has hardly that dignity to boast.' *Thraliana*, pp. 544–5.
33. Patricia Spacks, in 'The Dangerous Age', *Eighteenth Century Studies* 11 (1978): 417–38, points out that the decision to be a child or woman was often resolved by death; see Eagleton's comment on Clarissa's death on p. 76, which he believes signifies 'an absolute refusal of political society', while being 'submissive to patriarchal order'; see also Castle, p. 31, who sees her death as a rejection of language.
34. *The Living Novel* (New York: Reynal and Hitchcock, 1947), p. 25.

CHAPTER 4   THORNFIELD AND 'THE DREAM TO REPOSE ON': *JANE EYRE*

1. See Chapter 3, n. 15.
2. See Winifred Gerin, *Charlotte Brontë: Evolution of a Genius* (Oxford: Clarendon Press, 1967); and Fannie Ratchford, *The Brontës' Web of Childhood* (New York: Russell and Russell, 1964).
3. Ratchford, *ibid.*, pp. 108–9. See also Thomas Wise and J.A. Symington, eds., *The Brontës: Their Lives, Friendships and Correspondence* (Philadelphia: Porcupine Press, 1980) I, p. 123.
4. Letter of 10 May 1836 to Ellen Nussey, in Wise and Symington, I, p. 319; the second quotation is on p. 141.
5. Ratchford, *Web of Childhood*, pp. 109–10. See also Gerin, *Brontë*, pp. 103–4.
6. Ratchford, *Web of Childhood*, p. 114.
7. Gerin, *Brontë*, p. 106.
8. *Ibid.*, p. 104.
9. *Ibid.*, p. 106.
10. *Ibid.*, p. 103. See also Ratchford, *Web of Childhood*, p. 109.
11. Wise and Symington, *The Brontës*, I, p. 146.

12. *Ibid.*, p. 143.
13. Letter of 7 August 1841 in *ibid.*, p. 241.
14. *Ibid.*, p. 110.
15. *Ibid.*, p. 148.
16. C. Brontë, *Five Novelettes*, ed. Winifred Gerin (London: The Folio Press, 1971), p. 311. Subsequent references will appear in the text.
17. See Dianne Sadoff, *Monsters of Affection*, for an analysis of father-figures in Brontë's writing.
18. I disagree here with Helene Moglen, who in *Charlotte Brontë: The Self Conceived* (New York: Norton, 1978) discusses Charlotte's juvenilia in terms of her 'masochism', and her early heroines as 'submissive'. See Terry Eagleton, *Myths of Power: A Marxist Study of the Brontës* (London: Macmillan, 1975), pp. 29–30: 'The novels dramatise a society in which almost all human relations are power struggles'; the same may be said of the sexual world of the juvenilia.
19. Charlotte Brontë, *Jane Eyre* (Harmondsworth: Penguin, 1966), p. 47. Subsequent references appear in the text.
20. Jane's time at Gateshead, and particularly the episode of the imprisonment in the Red Room, has been effectively analysed by Elaine Showalter, *Literature of Their Own*, pp. 114–15, and Gilbert and Gubar, *Madwoman in the Attic,* pp. 339–41, who all emphasize the symbolic sexual imagery. Nancy Pell, 'Resistance, Rebellion and Marriage: Economics of *Jane Eyre*', *Nineteenth Century Fiction* 31 (1977): 397–420, concentrates on the aspects of rebellion in the text.
21. Helene Moglen, for example, says: 'Miss Temple and Helen Burns provide her with role models . . . a new universe of values and the opportunity to excel', p. 114.
22. The doubleness of the Victorian governess's status in the household and in the culture in general has been explored by M. Jeanne Peterson, 'The Victorian Governess: Status Incongruence in Family and Society', in *Suffer and Be Still: Women in the Victorian Age*, ed. Martha Vicinus (Bloomington: Indiana University Press, 1972); and Mary Poovey, 'The Anathematized Race: The Governess and *Jane Eyre*', in Richard Feldstein and Judith Roof, eds., *Feminism and Psychoanalysis* (Ithaca, NY: Cornell University Press, 1989), among others. The role of governess was constructed by two conflicting discourses: they were Ladies and they were maternal figures, policing the sexual desire of their charges yet potentially tempting upper-class men to desire themselves, thus providing a link between views of gender and class.
23. For an innovative reading of the meaning of 'desire' in Victorian fiction, see John Kucich, whose *Repression in Victorian Fiction* locates the repression of passion as a means to representing interiority.
24. Karen Chase observes in *Eros and Psyche: The Representation of Personality in Charlotte Brontë, Charles Dickens and George Eliot* (New York: Methuen, 1984) that a 'saving distance' is the 'stringent requirement of romantic love' for Brontë, p. 90.
25. Janice Radway's analysis of popular romance in *Reading the Romance*, which emphasizes the heroine's quest for mother-nurturance, is based to a large extent on the work of Nancy Chodorow, *The Reproduction*

of *Mothering: Psychoanalysis and the Sociology of Gender* (Berkeley: University of California Press, 1978); Adrienne Rich noticed Jane's mother-longing in 'Jane Eyre: Temptations of a Motherless Woman', *Ms* 2 (1973).

26. Michelle A. Masse, *In the Name of Love: Women, Masochism, and the Gothic* (Ithaca, NY: Cornell University Press, 1992), treats the Gothic as a kind of narrative therapy for women to work through the trauma created by the ideology of romance. She is most interesting on Jane Eyre's ability to resist the calls of masochism by her status as rational narrator.

27. See, for example, Gilbert and Gubar, *Madwoman in the Attic*, p. 358, who see the dream-child as the 'part of [Jane Eyre] which resists a marriage of inequality'; more recently, Mary Poovey has analysed these dreams as 'psychological gestures' which seek to 'eroticize economics' and overcome social difference, in 'The Anathematized Race', pp. 242–6.

28. Jean Kennard discusses what she calls the 'convention of the two suitors' in the British novel, of relevance particularly in *Jane Eyre*, *Villette*, *Wuthering Heights* and *Mill on the Floss* in *Victims of Convention* (Hamden, CT: Archon Press, 1978), especially pp. 10–20; see also H.M. Daleski, *The Divided Heroine: A Recurrent Pattern in Six English Novels* (New York: Holmes and Meier, 1983) for an account of how the heroine pulled between two kinds of lovers embodies the Pauline dichotomy of flesh and spirit.

29. These are the exact words used on p. 101 to describe Jane's reaction to Helen's admonition. Also compare Helen's 'you think too much of the love of human beings' (p. 101).

30. See, for example, Richard Chase, 'The Brontës: A Centennial Observance', *Kenyon Review* IX (1947), as representative of this point of view, as well as extremely influential in later Brontë criticism; Carolyn Heilbrun, in *Toward a Recognition of Androgeny* (New York: Knopf, 1973) offered an important political interpretation based on Jane's demand for autonomy and Rochester's necessary suffering in giving up his own; Maurianne Adams sees the resolution in terms of Jane's return to her psychic and spiritual 'estate' in '*Jane Eyre*: Woman's Estate', in *The Authority of Experience: Essays in Feminist Criticism*, ed. A. Diamond and Lee R. Edwards (Amherst: University of Massachusetts Press, 1977), pp. 137–59; Rachel Brownstein, *Becoming a Heroine*, sees the ending of the novel as affirming 'not the heroine's transformation but her remaining herself', p. 156; Dianne Sadoff has an unusual view in her lengthy argument in favour of interpreting the closure as a wish for castration on Brontë's apart; Shirley Foster, *Victorian Women's Fiction: Marriage, Freedom and the Individual* (London: Croom Helm, 1985) reads the ending two different ways, trying for a balanced view: Charlotte Brontë is neither 'conventional nor militantly feminist', p. 92. Some recent critics such as Pat MacPherson tend to a more flexible analysis of Brontë's relation to the feminist agenda of the present day, in *Jane Eyre* (London and New York: Routledge, 1989).

31. My reading here is similar to that of Rosemarie Bodenheimer, *The Politics of Story in Victorian Social Fiction* (Ithaca, NY: Cornell University Press, 1988), which sees novels as social texts reflecting the irresolvable contradictions of the nineteenth-century sex/gender system.

CHAPTER 5 DOWN THE FORBIDDEN PATH: *VILLETTE*

1. Letter of 11 March 1853, in Miriam Allott, ed., *The Brontës: The Critical Heritage* (London: Routledge and Kegan Paul, 1974), p. 197.
2. *Daily News*, 3 February 1853, quoted *ibid.*, p. 171.
3. Thomas Wise and J.A. Symington, eds., *The Brontës: Their Lives, Friendships and Correspondence* IV, p. 42. Charlotte's reaction was extreme: so outraged was she that she cut off the friendship between them.
4. Karen Lawrence develops some of these points at length in addressing the meaning of Lucy's selfhood as a 'cypher', denoting 'both meaning and absence of meaning', in 'The Cypher: Disclosure and Reticence in *Villette*', *Tradition and the Talents of Women*, ed. Florence Howe (Urbana and Chicago: University of Illinois Press, 1991), pp. 87–101.
5. *Villette* (London: Dent, 1972), p. 21. Lucy describes Polly with this phrase. All subsequent references appear in the text.
6. Monica Feinberg argues in 'Homesick: The Domestic Interiors of *Villette*', *Novel* (1993), that Lucy sees home and the domestic ideal as not necessarily implicated with romance or egocentric concerns of sexuality, but as something 'communitarian'. I would say rather that the description of Lucy's longing for a 'true home' reflects the double discourse about romance in the Victorian age.
7. Of course, the irony here is also on Lucy herself, who, in watching Polly and vicariously participating in her love for Graham, is doing just that. Kate Millett has memorably called Lucy 'a pair of eyes watching society: weighing, ridiculing, judging', in *Sexual Politics* (New York: Doubleday, 1970), p. 140, which puts a new slant on this watching.
8. In 'The Face in the Mirror: *Villette* and the Conventions of Autobiography', *ELH*, 46 (1979), Janice Carlisle uses a famous anecdote of the Brontë childhood (recounted in Mrs Gaskell's *Life of Charlotte Brontë*, p. 36), in which M.R. Brontë quizzed his children from behind a mask, to illustrate Charlotte's attraction to 'subversive modes of self-expression'; 'the form of this little drama would become the form of her art', p. 262. Lucy's outward self *is* masklike, a blank surface with eye-holes cut out for viewing. This speaking from behind a mask also has obvious implications for her later attraction to acting. The metaphor of the mask and its autobiographical importance for Charlotte Brontë is discussed at great length in Annette Tromly, *The Cover of the Mask: The Autobiographer in Charlotte Brontë's Fiction*, English Literature Studies 26 (University of Victoria, B.C., 1983). Luann M. Fletcher analyses *Villette* as a novel about surfaces, roles and assumed identities, in both senses of theatrical performance and the sense of

the hypothetical 'assumptions made about identity', 'Manufactured Marvels, Heretic Narratives and the Process of Interpretation in Villette', *SEL* 32 (1992): 725.

9. For a further elaboration of this idea, see Susan Ostrov Weisser, 'The Wonderful-Terrible Bitch Figure in Harlequin Novels', in Susan Ostrov Weisser and Jennifer Fleischner, eds., *Feminist Nightmares: Women at Odds* (New York: New York University Press, 1994): 269–84.

10. Though the character of Ginevra is often discussed in the critical literature, rarely is she satisfactorily explained. Gilbert and Gubar, for example, mention Lucy's attraction to her as an embodiment of 'self-indulgence and freedom' (p. 409), but give surprisingly little space to Lucy's play-acting her lover. Charles Burkhart, in his *Charlotte Brontë: A Psychosexual Study of her Novels* (London: Gollancz, 1973), p. 107, notes the 'polymorphous sexuality' of *Villette*, and sees Lucy's play-acting the male role as a sign of 'the depth of her sexuality', a phrase which one would like to see defined. Very possibly Lucy's ambiguous feelings towards Ginevra cause discomfort as well as puzzlement in critics, who tend to avoid the subject. Kate Millett, in *Sexual Politics*, p. 141, however, calls the play-acting episode, 'one of the most indecorous scenes in the entire Victorian novel', and says of Ginevra's involvement with Lucy that 'critical Lucy would be the best catch of all'; more recently, Christina Crosby discusses the blurring of sexual identities in 'Charlotte Brontë's Haunted Text', *SEL* 24 (1984): 701–15, and Brenda Silver explicates the play-acting scene as 'male discourse', in 'The Reflecting Reader in *Villette*', *The Voyage In*, p. 100.

11. Gilbert and Gubar see the nun in Villette as an embodiment of 'Lucy's anxiety, not only about the imagination and passion, but about her very right to exist' (p. 425). Two other articles on the subject of the apparition are E.D.H. Johnson, 'Daring the Dread Glance: Charlotte Brontë's Treatment of the Supernatural in *Villette*', *Nineteenth Century Fiction* XX (1966): 325–36, which opposes the empty selfhood of the nun to the passionate self-expression of acting, and Charles Burkhart's 'The Nuns of *Villette*', *Victorian Newsletter* 44 (1973): 8–12, which briefly examines the sexual significance of the nun-image in Lucy's psychological development; Mary Jacobus, '*Villette*'s Buried Letter', *Essays in Criticism*, 28 (1978), sees the nun as Lucy's 'psychic double', p. 238; Christina Crosby illuminatingly discusses the nun as an 'excess' or fragment signifying the search for identity and authority in 'Brontë's Haunted Text'.

12. Elaine Showalter's observation, in *A Literature of their Own: British Women Novelists from Brontë to Lessing* (Princeton, NJ: Princeton University Press, 1977), p. 136, that Victorian women writer's heroes are not so much fantasy lovers as 'women wishing they were men, with the greater freedom and range masculinity confers', seems particularly relevant here.

13. Joseph Boone speaks of the 'voyeuristic delight' in the text of *Villette* in 'Depolicing *Villette*: Surveillance, Invisibility, and the Female Erotics of "Heretic Narrative"', *Novel* 52 (1992): 20–42.

14. Julia Kristeva writes about 'The Carnival: A Homology between the Body, Dream, Linguistic Structure and the Structures of Desire': 'A participant is both actor and spectator; he loses his sense of individuality, passes through a zero point of carnivalesque activity, and splits into the subject of the spectacle and an object of the game...', *Desire in Language* (New York: Columbia University Press, 1980), p. 78. See also Terry Castle's work on masquerade, associated with sexual licence and urbanity, 'a bounded dreamscape of uncanny, disorienting power', *Masquerade and Civilization: the Carnivalesque in Eighteenth Century Culture and Fiction* (Stanford: Stanford University Press, 1986), p. 53.
15. However, it is worthwhile to note that this love, during this 'happiest period of Lucy's life', is expressed through letters, not through the body.
16. I am thinking here of one of Charlotte's letters to M. Heger, in which she reproaches him: 'Monsieur, the poor have not need of much to sustain them – they ask only for the crumbs that fall from the rich man's table. But if they are refused the crumbs, they die of hunger.' T. Wise and J.A. Symington, II, p. 23. 'Temperate draught' is from *Villette*: Lucy wished to 'be content with a temperate draught of this living stream' – the affection of Dr John and his mother (p. 160).
17. Elizabeth Langland makes the point that the destabilization of the conclusion to a novel about female desire resists the closure of transgression on which the expression of that desire depends, in 'The Voicing of Feminine Desire in Anne Brontë', in Harrison and Taylor, pp. 111–23. Earlier critics have found either a kind of healing (e.g. Russell Goldfarb, *Sexual Repression and Victorian Literature* (Lewisburg: Bucknell University Press, 1970); John Maynard, *Charlotte Brontë and Sexuality* (Cambridge: Cambridge University Press, 1984); Elaine Showalter) or else a radical ambiguity in the ending (Gilbert and Gubar; Patricia E. Johnson, '"This Heretic Narrative": The Strategy of the Split Narrative in *Villette*', *SEL* 30 (1990): 617–31). I would say that the theme of ambivalence over the efficacy of sexual love is expressed in the critics' diverse and contradictory reactions.
18. L.M. Fletcher finds in *Villette* a kind of argument against essentialism as a social concept used by society 'to define identity while believing it is merely discovering the "real" identities of its characters', p. 725. While the play of identities does seem to refer us to the power of language to create, the text also underlines that material reality is important: what underpins Ginevra's view is her economic relation to the world, her ambition to Ladyhood.

CHAPTER 6 WILD DESIRE AND QUENCHLESS WILL: *WUTHERING HEIGHTS*

1. Peter Garrett, *The Victorian Multiplot Novel: Studies in Dialogic Form* (New Haven: Yale University Press, 1980) argues for the coexistence of two plots in 'perpetual alternative', p. 19; Elizabeth Langland

essentially makes the same point in *Society and the Novel* (Chapel Hill: University of North Carolina Press, 1984), pp. 168–80; James Kavanaugh, in *Emily Brontë* (Oxford: Blackwell, 1985) sees Heathcliff as a figure for an Oedipal father in opposition to Nelly's 'phallic mother', a social power redirecting sexual energy to sexual/social reproduction, so that the text of *Wuthering Heights* is continually destabilized; J. Hillis Miller, in *Fiction and Repetition: Seven English Novels* (Cambridge, Mass.: Harvard University Press, 1982) writes persuasively that 'the secret truth about *Wuthering Heights* ... is that there is no secret truth [about it]', p. 51. For an excellent poststructuralist view of the narrative disjunctions of *Wuthering Heights*, see Carol Jacobs, *Uncontainable Romanticism: Shelley, Brontë, Kleist* (Baltimore: Johns Hopkins University Press, 1989).

2. Carol Jacobs, *Uncontainable Romanticism*, finds dreams at the heart of the text: '[Dreams are] the means by which *Wuthering Heights* speaks of its own textuality', p. 81.

3. Bersani uses the phrase 'a hole in being' to describe desire as growing from a lack in Catherine in *A Future for Astyanax: Character and Desire in Literature* (Boston: Little, Brown and Co., 1976), p. 213. Bersani sees the dispersal of unitary selfhood as the major problem of *Wuthering Heights*. See also Tony Tanner's analysis of Catherine's 'escape' from identity in 'Passion, Narrative and Identity in *Wuthering Heights* and *Jane Eyre*', in *Contemporary Approaches to Narrative*, ed. Anthony Mortimer (Tubingen: G. Narr, 1984).

4. J. Hillis Miller, *The Disappearance of God* (Cambridge, Mass.: Harvard University Press, 1963), p. 175.

5. Thus A.O.J. Cockshut tells us that 'All readers of *Wuthering Heights* are aware that the book presents two different kinds of love, the love between Heathcliff and Catherine, and the ordinary love which the world knows', *Man and Woman: A Study of Love and the Novel*, p. 107.

6. Thus we may place Irving Buchen's confident pronouncement that 'there is no sex [in *Wuthering Heights*]. To be sure, there is love ... but it is never corporeal [in kind]', 'Emily Brontë and the Metaphysics of Childhood and Love', *Nineteenth Century Fiction* 22 (1967): 63–70, esp. p. 113, next to Thomas Moser's detailed analysis of Heathcliff as the 'embodiment of sexual energy', in 'What Is the Matter with Emily Jane? Conflicting Impulses in *Wuthering Heights*', in *The Victorian Novel: Modern Essays in Criticism*, ed. Ian Watt (Oxford: Oxford University Press, 1971), p. 184. Moser's analysis of sexual imagery is used to little purpose other than to show that Brontë, 'whether she knew it or not', was writing 'a passionate paean to Eros', p. 191. See Carol Ohmann's denunciation of Moser and his view of the novel as trivialized by its 'feminine' (non-Heathcliffian) elements in her 'Emily Brontë in the Hands of Male Critics', *College English* 32 (1971): 906–13; the same criticism could be made of Richard Chase's view of the 'sheer dazzling sexual ... force' of *Wuthering Heights* as a male principle, in 'The Brontës, or Myth Domesticated', *Forms of Modern Fiction*, ed. William Van O'Connor (Minneapolis: University of Minnesota Press, 1948), p. 109. Then again, Eric Solomon's dismissive charge of

incest in 'The Incest Theme in *Wuthering Heights*', *Nineteenth Century Fiction* 14 (1959): 80–3, may be mated with Helene Moglen's conclusion that the love of Catherine and Heathcliff is 'auto-eroticism', in 'The Double Vision of *Wuthering Heights*: A Clarifying View of Female Development', *Centennial Review* 15 (1971): 391–405, esp. p. 394. Representative of the spiritual-mythical school, Evelyn J. Hinz locates the Catherine–Heathcliff pairing as a 'hierogamous' (sacred) marriage of a superior woman with a dark god, resulting in the 'regeneration of the cosmos', 'Hierogamy vs. Wedlock: Types of Marriage Plots and their Relationships to Genres of Prose Fiction', *PMLA* 91 (1976): 900–13, esp. p. 909.

To cite merely a handful of the proponents of the view that Catherine's and Heathcliff's love is not 'really' sexual, Dorothy Van Ghent states that the passion of Catherine and Heathcliff is neither romantic nor sexual love, because 'one cannot "mate" with oneself', *The English Novel: Form and Function* p. 158; V.S. Pritchett speaks of their 'sexless companionship', Introduction to *Wuthering Heights* (Boston: Houghton Mifflin, 1956), p. xiii; Q.D. Leavis explains that 'Catherine's feelings about Heathcliff are never sexual', 'A Fresh Approach to *Wuthering Heights*', p. 90; and A.O.J. Cockshut wishes us to believe that 'Though ... [Heathcliff] is intensely masculine, [Cathy] intensely feminine; and each is effortlessly attractive to members of the other sex', 'their love is sexless', in *Man and Woman: A Study of Love and the Novel*, p. 109. The generation of such radically different viewpoints forces a return to the question of what exactly is meant when we use such a broad term as 'sexuality': we might consider, for example, what happens to such distinctions if all sexuality is viewed as egoistic and narcissistic, infantile and/or 'incestuous' in some essential way.

7. Sandra Gilbert and Susan Gubar are representative of this point of view when they argue that Catherine is forced by 'reason, education and decorum to become a Lady', since she has 'no meaningful choices', in *The Madwoman in the Attic: The Woman Writer and the Nineteenth Century Literary Imagination* (New Haven: Yale University Press, 1979), p. 277.

8. See, for example, Helene Moglen's 'The Double Vision of *Wuthering Heights*', in which she speaks of the 'childish, narcissistic nature of Catherine and Heathcliff's relationship', p. 393.

9. The role of Heathcliff in the novel as a projection of female desires is taken up by Gilbert and Gubar, who argue that his character is 'gynandrous', p. 297, and more briefly, by Nina Auerbach, who speaks of him as 'half-create[d]' by the women of the novel, in *Woman and the Demon*. Both Brontës' relation to the figure of the male is taken up by Joanne Blum, who considers the role of male/female doubles in *Transcending Gender: The Male/Female Double in Women's Fiction* (Ann Arbor: UMI Research Press, 1988); and Irene Tayler, exploring the 'male muses' of the sisters in *Holy Ghosts: The Male Muses of Emily and Charlotte Brontë* (New York: Columbia University Press, 1990); Anita Levy analyses the way in which the doubling and splitting of

characters in the novel figures cultural strategies for naturalizing class and gender distinctions, *Other Women*, pp. 75–97.

10. Nancy Armstrong's *Desire and Domestic Fiction* traces the complex relation between the textual constructions of desire and the inscription of the female in the novel. See also Helena Michie's *The Flesh Made Word: Female Figures and Women's Bodies* (New York: Oxford University Press, 1987), which looks at Victorian and modern representations of women's bodies from a post-Foucault, feminist perspective.

11. Pritchett, p. xiii. The critic does not offer textual evidence that Heathcliff wishes to return either to childhood or to sexless companionship.

12. Among them are Irving Buchen, 'Emily Brontë and the Metaphysics of Childhood and Love', and Tom Winnifreth, *The Brontës and their Background* (London: Macmillan, 1973). See also Helene Moglen, 'The Double Vision of *Wuthering Heights*', p. 393; James Kincaid, in *Child Loving: The Erotic Child and Victorian Culture* (New York: Routledge, 1992) says, 'This great image of erotic passion in the modern Anglo-American imagination is put together out of childhood and emptiness', p. 12.

13. Ellen Moers comments in *Literary Women* (New York: Doubleday, 1976) that Catherine and Heathcliff's love is a childlike yet sexual one 'modeled after the brother–sister relationship', p. 106; Margaret Homans states that what the lovers seek is not primordial reunion, but a return to their 'invented origin' – their rebirth as friends/lovers, in *Women Writers and Poetic Identity: Dorothy Wordsworth, Emily Brontë and Emily Dickinson* (Princeton, NJ: Princeton University Press, 1980), p. 156. Jean Hagstrum analyses the lack of fit between Brontë's view of love and Romantic, Christian and Freudian discourses in *The Romantic Body: Love and Sexuality in Keats, Wordsworth, and Blake* (Knoxville: University of Tennessee Press, 1985): '*Wuthering Heights* absorbed only the spiritual side of the Shelleyan fusion [of body and spirit] and so denuded it of some of its palpability', while 'Freud surely would have seen immaturity here, and the unbreakable union of two such beings he would have regarded as an example of natural mysticism ... which does violence to the boundaries of a healthy ego and to the sense of reality by which we should order all our being and doing', pp. 38–9. It should be noted, however, that while Love is often taken to be identical with loss of self-consciousness and dissolution of identity, it also may be seen as an acute consciousness of the lover's Otherness.

14. Regina Barreca, ed., *Sex and Death in Victorian Literature* is a collection that links the two thematic structures; see Regina Barreca's own essay in that collection, 'The Power of Excommunication: Sex and the Feminine Text in *Wuthering Heights*', 227–40.

CHAPTER 7 GEORGE ELIOT AND THE 'HIDDEN WOUND'

1. Henry James, 'The Novels of George Eliot', *Notes and Reviews* (Cambridge, Mass.: Dunsler House, 1921), p. 204. Nearly a century after

this review of 1866, W.J. Harvey wrote that Eliot 'was unwilling or unable to treat fully and properly... romantic or passionate love between two adults', *The Art of George Eliot* (New York: Oxford University Press, 1961), p. 197. See Barbara Hardy's plea for the complexity of Eliot's treatment of this subject in '*Middlemarch* and the Passions', in *This Particular Web: Essays on Middlemarch*, ed. Ian Adam (Toronto: University of Toronto Press, 1975).

2. *Fiction and the Reading Public* (London: Chatto and Windus, 1932), pp. 128–30. Margaret Doody examines the influence of Richardson and the female novelists of this century on Eliot in 'George Eliot and the Eighteenth Century Novel', *Nineteenth Century Fiction* 30 (1980): 260–91.
3. Janice Carlyle is illuminating on Eliot's narrative technique in *The Sense of an Audience: Dickens, Thackeray and Eliot at Mid-Century* (Athens, Ga: University of Georgia Press, 1981); see also Barbara Hardy, 'The Reticent Narrator', in her *Particularities* (Athens, Ohio: Ohio University Press, 1982).
4. *The Mill on the Floss* (Harmondsworth: Penguin, 1982), p. 363. All further references to this edition will be cited in text.
5. Suzanne Graver analyses Eliot's themes of community in *George Eliot and Community: A Study in Social Theory and Fictional Form* (Berkeley: University of California Press, 1984).
6. *Letters*, VI, p. 162. Sally Shuttleworth provides useful background on this and related topics in *George Eliot and Nineteenth Century Science: The Make-Believe of a Beginning* (Cambridge: Cambridge University Press, 1984); William Myers has more general background in *The Teaching of George Eliot* (Leicester: Leicester University Press, 1984).
7. *Scenes of Clerical Life* (New York: Harper and Bros., n.d.), p. 179.
8. *Letters*, II, p. 344. Compare the comment of James T. Fields, editor of *The Atlantic Monthly* to the young Henry James in 1864: 'What we want', he complained, 'is short *cheerful* stories.' Quoted in Leon Edel, *Henry James*, Vol. I: *The Untried Years, 1843–1870* (New York: Avon, 1978), p. 204.
9. *Letters*, II, p. 386.
10. This distinction between the 'poetry' and 'prose' of life was one of Eliot's recurrent metaphors. Barbara Hardy discusses the use of the terms in 'The Moment of Disenchantment in George Eliot's Novels', in *George Eliot: A Collection of Critical Essays*, ed. George Creeger (Englewood Cliffs, NJ: Prentice-Hall, 1970), in which she quotes a letter of Eliot's: 'Alas for the fate of poor mortals which condemns them to wake up some fine morning and find all the poetry in which their world was bathed... utterly gone! – the hard, angular world of chairs and tables and looking-glasses staring at them in all its naked prose', p. 55.
11. *Letters*, II, p. 413.
12. She is, however, darkly beautiful, and, more ominously, called 'Gypsy' by her once-loving husband.
13. An astute Victorian critic observed in *The Saturday Review* of 1859 that the English clergyman is an ideal hero because 'he is a gentleman, he

is going to Heaven, [yet] he may make love. He has the attractions of both worlds', quoted in Showalter, *Literature of their Own*, p. 143. See her chapter on 'Feminine Heroes: The Woman's Man', pp. 133–52. George Eliot herself wrote a biting article on the subject, 'Silly Novels by Lady Novelists', published in the *Westminster Review* of 1856, in which she deplored the way in which 'questions as to the state of the heroine's affections are mingled with anxieties as to the state of her soul', in Pinion, *George Eliot Miscellany*, pp. 14–15. David Carroll suggests that Eliot dramatizes the myth of the organic 'by adapting the conventional triangle of romantic love to express the process of growth in the individual and in society', in 'Janet's Repentance and the Myth of the Organic', *Nineteenth Century Fiction* 35 (1980), p. 347, though he does not explore the attitudes toward romantic love underlying that adaptation.

14. Marion Shaw, '"To tell the truth of sex": Confession and abjection in late Victorian writing', relates confession to a deeper horror: 'The truth that is sought seems to be a perverse Darwinian sublime, a reaching out to the limits of the human state, what lies beyond the rational and civilized, the point where not only sexual proprieties disappear but meaning itself collapses', in Antony Harrison and Beverly Taylor, eds., *Gender and Discourse in Victorian Literature and Art*, p. 91.

15. Gilbert and Gubar argue that Milly's death is what 'represents her superiority' to the inadequacy of the public world and establishes her spiritual authority, p. 485.

16. *Adam Bede* (Harmondsworth: Penguin, 1982), p. 333. All further references will be cited in text.

17. See George Eliot's 'History of Adam Bede', reprinted in Haight's *Letters*, II, pp. 502–5.

18. *A Future for Astyanax*, p. 213. Bersani uses the term to describe Catherine Earnshaw.

19. If more iconographic evidence is needed, Seth is described as shorter than Adam, with stooped shoulders, thin hair and eyebrows of 'less prominence and more repose' (p. 50). The eyebrows give it away every time. In popular romantic fiction from its beginning to the present day, sexually attractive males are almost invariably tall, straight-backed and endowed with thick hair and prominent eyebrows. The irresistible Stephen Guest of *The Mill on the Floss* is said to have 'well-marked, horizontal eyebrows' (p. 470); Jane Eyre's Rochester had 'broad and jetty eyebrows', as well as a 'horizontal sweep of black hair' (p. 123).

20. This is not to say that the novel concentrates exclusively on Maggie's consciousness; it is part of Eliot's ironic humour that until the last two Books of the novel, there is a continual cutting between the world seen through Maggie's eyes and our own view of Maggie through the eyes of the world. Thus we see her father's predicament before she does, for example, so that her childish view of it appears even more distorted.

21. *Letters*, I, p. 127.

22. Gillian Beer finds that female desire can assume no place in a sequential ordering of plot, thus resulting in the circular plot of *Mill*, in 'Beyond Determinism: George Eliot and Virginia Woolf', in *Women Writing and Writing about Women*, ed. Mary Jacobus (New York: B & N Imports, 1979): Mary Jacobus shows how the text of *Mill* subverts the patriarchal maxims of female submission and renunciation in 'The Question of Language: Men of Maxims and *The Mill on the Floss*', in *Writing and Sexual Difference*, ed. Elizabeth Abel (Chicago: University of Chicago Press, 1982). Marianne Hirsch writes that Maggie's values 'profoundly challenge the values of her culture', providing a different paradigm of development, in 'Spiritual Bildung', in *The Voyage In*, p. 37; Jane McDonnell touches on the same points in '"Perfect Goodness" or "the Wider Life"': *The Mill on the Floss* as Bildungsroman', *Genre* 15 (1982).
23. 'Checked' is a word used often to describe Maggie, as on p. 117: '[Tom] checked her joy at his coming...' or 'Tom, who checked her and met her thought and feeling always by some thwarting difference...', p. 380.
24. This says a good deal, perhaps, about what constitutes male sexual attractiveness in our society; it could be argued, however, that those sexually attractive heroines we have just been considering also exhibit great strength of will, so that large desires and strong wills in general signify sexual attractiveness. But an examination of romantic literature written for women does turn up an amazing number of male heroes who are described, like Heathcliff, as 'devilish'. Tania Modleski discusses cruel heroes in popular romantic fiction in *Loving with a Vengeance: Mass-Produced Fantasies for Women* (Hamdon, CT: Archon Books, 1982). See also Jessica Benjamin, *The Bonds of Love*.
25. For the extreme reactions of some of Eliot's contemporaries see David Carroll's collection, *George Eliot: The Critical Heritage*; among our own contemporary critics, Leavis set the tone when he remarked, 'George Eliot shares to the full the sense of Stephen's irresistibleness... there is no suggestion of any antipathy between this fascination and Maggie's "higher faculties", apart from the moral veto that imposes renunciation', *The Great Tradition*, p. 44. Leavis does not distinguish here between Eliot's lack of awareness of Stephen's spiritual thinness and Maggie's: perhaps nothing less than a forthright denunciation on Maggie's part – something along the lines of, 'Why, Philip Wakem is worth ten of you!' – would have satisfied this critic. See David Carroll on the history of the critical reception of Maggie's love affair ('The Placing of Stephen Guest', printed as an appendix to *The Mill on the Floss*, op. cit.).
26. Nancy Miller, in 'Emphasis Added', recognizes that the 'repressed content' of women's novels is 'not erotic impulses, but an impulse to power', so that 'egoistic desires... assert themselves paratactically alongside erotic ones' (p. 41).
27. Margaret Homans, 'Dinah's Blush, Maggie's Arm: Class, Gender and Sexuality in George Eliot's Early Novels', *Victorian Studies* 36 (1993) argues persuasively that 'The narrative fetishizes Maggie's arm on

Stephen's behalf', in both senses of commodification and psychoanalytic fetishism, p. 175. See also Helena Michie, *The Flesh Made Word*, on women's bodies.

28. This statement is ironic in view of her use of this very phrase in her essay on Mackay: 'The master-key ... is the recognition of the presence of undeviating law in the material-moral world', Pinion, 'A George Eliot Miscellany', p. 5. Her own revision of this firm position did not go without comment in her own time: 'There *is* a master-key ... to the puzzles of life', protested the *Eclectic* after the publication of *The Mill on the Floss* (Carroll, *George Eliot: The Critical Heritage*, p. 15).

29. *Letters*, II, p. 324.

30. One of Eliot's earliest letters perhaps sheds light on this paradox. Some, she says, can maintain community with God while multiplying earthly ties 'powerful enough to detach their heart and thoughts from heaven', but she finds, as Dr Johnson said about wine, 'total abstinence much easier than moderation', *Letters*, I, p. 6.

31. Critics have long been divided as to the success of George Eliot's attempts to drown Maggie's troubles, though the bulk of opinion through Leavis seems to have gone against her. David Smith's 'In Their Death They Were Not Divided: The Form of Illicit Passion in *The Mill on the Floss*', *Literature and Psychology* (1965), attempted to view Maggie's and Tom's last embrace from an incestuous Cathy–Heathcliff point of view; David L. Higdon also discusses the final embrace, from the perspective indicated by the title of his article, 'Failure of Design in *The Mill on the Floss*', *Journal of Narrative Technique* 3 (1973): 183–92; there is also a more modern trend of defending the conclusion of *Mill*: R.H. Lee explains the 'Unity of *The Mill on the Floss*', *ESA* 7 (1964): 34–53; George Levine, in 'Intelligence as Deception: *The Mill on the Floss*', in Creeger, finds the ending appropriate to the intellectual scheme of the novel, though admitting that there is a 'difficulty' to the scheme itself; Elizabeth Ermarth in 'Maggie Tulliver's Long Suicide', *SEL* 14 (1974), identifies Maggie's 'weakness' as her desire to substitute another's will for her own (p. 598), but justifies the drowning by asserting that George Eliot meant for us to criticize Maggie's renunciation of Stephen; similarly, Sara M. Putzell, in 'An Antagonism of Valid Claims: The Dynamics of *The Mill on the Floss*', *Studies in the Novel, Texas State* 7 (1975), sees the drowning as a positive synthesis of irreconcilable conflicts; Elizabeth Weed's deconstructive reading explains how the 'ordered and meaningful discourse' of *Mill* is 'dismantled' by the ending, so that the novel is flooded by the process of creation, in 'The Liquidation of Maggie Tulliver', *Genre* 11 (1978): 443. One of the best pieces of criticism on *Mill* is Nina Auerbach's spirited defence of the novel against Leavis's onslaught, which had been supported by Laurence Lerner in *The Truthtellers* (New York: Schocken Books, 1967); and U.C. Knoepflmacher in *George Eliot's Early Novels*. Auerbach sees the 'emotional', 'immature', 'feminine' side of the novel that Leavis denigrated, as 'a loss of perspective that is in many ways a gain ... [as

Eliot] refuses to be our sage', and exchanges 'a clear vision for a swimming vision', pp. 150–1 of 'The Power of Hunger: Demonism and Maggie Tulliver', *Nineteenth Century Fiction* 30 (1975). The critical difficulty, it seems to me, is that George Eliot, as always, wanted to swim with her eyes open. A psychoanalytic contribution is Claire Kahane, 'The Aesthetic Politics of Rage', *LIT* 3 (1991), who sees symptoms of hysteria in certain Victorian novels, such as in the 'intermingling of desire and rage' in the climactic drowning scene of *Mill on the Floss*, p. 22.

32. Though Nina Auerbach devotes only one disappointing paragraph to *The Mill on the Floss* in *Woman and the Demon*, she had already argued in 'The Power of Hunger' that Maggie is a woman 'whose primordially feminine hunger for love is at one with her instinct to kill and to die', p. 171.

33. George Eliot, *Daniel Deronda*, ed. Barbara Hardy (Harmondsworth: Penguin, 1973), p. 114. All further references to this work will be found in the text.

34. Athena Vrettos, 'From Neurosis to Narrative: The Private Life of the Nerves in *Villette* and *Daniel Deronda*', *Victorian Studies* 33 (1990) finds a relation between these two heroines in that in both novels 'disorders of the nerves reveal disturbing fissures in the concept of self, challenging the assumed wholeness and continuity of identity', p. 562; see also Deirdre David, who sees Gwendolen as a victim of 'Pre-Oedipal sexual arrest', in *Fictions of Resolution in Three Victorian Novels* (New York: Macmillan, 1981), p. 178.

35. Barbara Hardy, *The Appropriate Form: An Essay on the Novel* (London: Athlone Press, 1964), pp. 110–11.

36. The subversive element of desire in Eliot's work is discussed by Dorothea Barrett in *Vocation and Desire in George Eliot's Heroines* (London and New York: Routledge, 1989).

37. Joanne Long Demaria, 'The Wondrous Marriages of Daniel Deronda: Gender, Work and Love', *Studies in the Novel* 22 (1990), tries to explain why George Eliot used a feminized male figure instead of drawing a 'strong' woman to 'counter the examples of Gwendolen and the Princess': Daniel Deronda 'marr[ies] masculine and feminine virtues without compromising the feminine', p. 411.

38. Philip Fisher points out the 'marriage'-relation between Daniel and Mordecai, in *Making Up Society: The Novels of George Eliot* (Pittsburgh: University of Pittsburgh Press, 1981), p. 226.

39. Marcia Midler has written of Eliot's 'restless female artists', who use art as 'an outlet for "unfeminine" impulses toward anger and defiance', 'George Eliot's Rebels: Portraits of the Artist as a Woman', *Women's Studies* 7 (1980): 99; see also Nina Auerbach on the actress-magdalen figure in Victorian literature, *Woman and the Demon*, pp. 203–7.

40. Judith Wilt has a somewhat different view in which she sees the characters' relation to destiny as the 'very hallmark of the Gothic', in *Ghosts of the Gothic: Austen, Eliot and Lawrence* (Princeton, NJ: Princeton University Press, 1980), p. 184. Cynthia Chase shows how the novel's

double plotting ensures the 'triumph of idealism over irony', while at the same time irony serves to deconstruct the narrator's story, and story in general, 'The Decomposition of the Elephants: Double Reading *Daniel Deronda*', *PMLA* 93 (1978): 215. Peter Garrett's view in *The Victorian Multiplot Novel* is that Daniel's heroic destiny at the expense of Gwendolen's results in a 'radical instability' between the novel's 'manifest intentions' and possible readings, pp. 176–9; Patricia McKee discusses Eliot's insistence on meaning as 'restoration' of 'what is perceived as already there', in *Heroic Commitment in Richardson, Eliot and James* (Princeton, NJ: Princeton University Press, 1986), p. 269.

CONCLUSION

1. T. Wise and J.A. Symington, eds., *Miscellaneous and Unpublished Works of Charlotte and Patrick Branwell Brontë* (Oxford: Shakespeare Head Press, 1934), III, p. 208, Letter of 11 February 1851.
2. Elizabeth Gaskell, *The Life of Charlotte Brontë* (London: Dent, 1971), p. 382.
3. Wise and Symington, *Miscellaneous and Unpublished Work*, III, p. 208.
4. *Middlemarch* (Harmondsworth: Penguin, 1970), p. 40.
5. *Theophrastus Such*, p. 178.
6. *The Spanish Gypsy*. In *The Works of George Eliot*, Vol. 17 (Boston: Jefferson Press, n.d.), p. 101.
7. Daniel Deronda advises Gwendolen Harleth to 'take the present suffering as a painful letting in of light', *Daniel Deronda*, p. 508.

Index

Armstrong, Nancy 4
Arnold, Matthew 54
artist, figure of 147, 186 n.39
Auerbach, Nina 4
Austen, Jane 72

Barreca, Regina 6
Barthes, Roland 4, 32
Bersani, Leo 127
Bildungsroman 64, 171 n.15, 184 n.22
Blackwell, John 119, 121
body, the xii, 5, 6, 10, 36, 45, 57, 85, 91, 104–5, 112, 123, 132, 143, 148, 153, 160 n.4, 162 n.16, 164 n.23, 178 n.15, 181 n.10
Branca, Patricia 29
Brontë, Charlotte ix–xii, 1, 4, 6, 11, 14, 34, 45, 52–91, 95, 97, 114–17, 120, 125, 130, 152–6
  Jane Eyre 12, 47, 53–72, 75, 82, 85, 88–9, 91, 93, 97–9, 111, 116, 117, 119, 131, 133, 136, 139, 140, 141, 154
  journal ix, 54–8, 75, 79, 151, 160 n.1
  juvenilia 57–8, 174 n.18
  Shirley 85, 97, 152
  Villette 17, 33, 52, 54, 58, 73–91, 93, 95, 97, 99, 119, 125, 131, 133, 136, 147, 151, 156
Brontë, Emily ix, x, xii, 1, 6, 11, 14, 34, 45, 54, 56, 92–113, 114–17, 125, 130, 152–6
  Wuthering Heights 12, 17, 51–2, 54, 92–113, 115, 116, 117, 125, 126, 133, 135, 136, 140, 144, 154–7

Carlyle, Thomas 25–6, 44, 54
Carson, Anne 20

chastity 7–10, 13, 27–8, 31, 39, 50–2, 87, 124, 138, 162 n.16, 170 n.9, 170 n.11
child(hood) 154, 173 n.33, 181 n.12, 181 n.13
  in Charlotte Brontë 54, 59, 63–8, 75–7, 81, 83, 91
  in Emily Brontë 97–9, 102–4, 109–10, 111–12
  in George Eliot 123, 125, 127, 130–4, 140
courtship 26, 31, 71, 102, 109, 165 n.3, 172 n.26

de Beauvoir, Simone 15
De Staël, Mme 47
Dickens, Charles 57, 72
Diderot, Denis 39

Eliot, George ix, xi, xii, 1, 6, 11, 34, 157
  Adam Bede 126–9, 135, 157
  Daniel Deronda 116, 141–9, 157
  Felix Holt 142, 157
  The Impressions of Theophrastus Such 157
  Middlemarch 141–2, 157
  Mill on the Floss 12, 13, 116, 127, 129–41, 157
  Scenes of Clerical Life 116, 118–26, 130, 140, 144, 145
  'The Spanish Gypsy' 157
Ellis, Havelock 1, 26, 34, 168 n.31
Ellis, Sarah 29, 33

femininity ix, 10, 11, 21, 24, 29, 41, 53, 59, 64, 91, 92, 97–104, 106, 108, 111, 127, 132, 133–5, 144, 146, 172 n.20, 186 n.32, 186 n.37
  see also Moral Femininity; womanhood; women, representations of

Index

Fielding, Henry 156
Foucault, Michel 3, 7, 9, 11, 19, 163 n.20
Freud, Sigmund 17, 163 n.17, 181 n.13
Fromm, Erich 33

gender xi, 1–5, 10, 11, 21, 33–4, 37, 39, 41–2, 45–6, 50, 92, 113, 132–5, 151–2, 155, 157–9, 160 n.1, 176 n.31, 180 n.9
gentleman 86, 148, 182 n.13

Hardy, Barbara 141
Haywood, Eliza 38, 48
heroine 12, 14, 35, 42, 49, 50–2, 54, 56–8, 62–3, 74–5, 77, 91, 97–8, 102, 109–14, 118, 121–5, 127, 130–1, 135, 140–9, 164 n.28, 170 n.3, 175 n.30, 184 n.24, 186 n.34
home 24–5, 27–9, 31, 33, 44, 54, 57, 59, 68, 86, 88–9, 131, 134, 136, 140, 154, 166 n.6, 168 n.36

incest 96, 179 n.6, 185 n.31

James, Henry 114, 115, 130

Lady 1, 13, 22–5, 29–30, 32, 158, 167 n.15, 167 n.16, 174 n.22, 178 n.18, 180 n.7
  in Charlotte Brontë 55–9, 61–2, 64, 66–7, 72, 78–9, 81–2
  in Emily Brontë 93, 97, 99, 100, 104–7, 109–11
  in George Eliot 118, 142, 148
  in Samuel Richardson 40–1, 43, 46–7, 52
Lawrence, D.H. 36–7, 75
Leavis, F.R. xi
Leavis, Q.D. 115
Linton, Eliza Lynn 21, 23–4, 30
love *see* romantic love

Manley, Mary 38
marriage 26, 32–3, 42–3, 46, 48, 59, 65–7, 71, 104, 109, 111, 128, 142–3, 146, 166 n.9, 172 n.21, 172 n.26, 173 n.32, 175 n.27
Martineau, Harriet 73–4, 152, 154–6, 176 n.3
Marx, Karl 5, 10
masculinity x, 9, 10, 11, 12, 14, 21, 33, 41, 62, 71, 91, 92, 98, 103, 133–5, 142, 177 n.12
Michelet, J. 3, 4
Miller, J. Hillis 94
Moral Femininity x, 11, 12, 13, 18, 19, 20, 22, 25, 27–32, 153–4, 158–9, 166 n.6, 167 n.15, 167 n.16
  in Charlotte Brontë 54, 56, 59–60, 64, 67–72, 76, 84, 86–7, 90
  in Emily Brontë 93, 97–8, 100, 105–6
  in George Eliot 118, 126, 141, 144, 145, 146, 149
  in Samuel Richardson 40–3, 46–7, 51–2

nature 1, 7, 8, 18, 33, 38, 46, 48–9, 65, 70–1, 74, 90, 113, 118, 120, 129, 131, 136, 138, 139, 160 n.1
New Woman 30, 158
Newton, Judith L. 5
nun, figure of 82, 84, 85–7, 95, 177 n.11

Patmore, Coventry 7–19, 90, 93, 166 n.7
Pitt-Rivers, Julian 19–20
Poovey, Mary 4
popular romance fiction 183 n.19
  contemporary 17, 158, 171 n.15, 174 n.25, 177 n.9, 184 n.24
  eighteenth-century 38, 155, 170 n.6, 182 n.2
  Victorian 31, 148, 175 n.26
Pritchett, V.S. 51, 102, 179 n.6, 181 n.11

Richardson, Samuel x, xi, xii, 1, 6, 14, 17, 34, 36–52, 94, 115, 117, 130, 138

Richardson, Samuel – *continued*
  The Apprentice's Vade Mecum 49
  Clarissa x, 36–8, 40–52, 54, 59, 91, 93–4, 105–8, 117, 136, 140, 153
  Pamela x, 37, 39–43, 45–7, 52, 57, 66, 72, 118, 119, 128, 153
romantic love x, xi, xii, 1, 3–5, 10, 13, 16, 18–20, 26, 31–4, 152, 158–9, 165 n.4, 166 n.9, 167 n.10, 167 n.12, 169 n.52, 172 n.23, 173 n.32, 174 n.24, 176 n.6, 179 n.6, 181 n.13, 181 n.1, 182 n.13
  in Charlotte Brontë 63, 67, 69–70, 73–5, 79–84, 88
  in Emily Brontë 94–7, 99–102, 111–12
  in George Eliot 126–8, 138, 141–5, 149
  in Samuel Richardson 41–3, 46–9
Ronsenfelt, Deborah 5
Ruddick, Sara 159

Scott, Sir Walter 126
self-denial 17, 51, 56, 61, 64, 68–72, 74, 76, 84, 87, 98, 101, 105–6, 115, 118, 124, 141, 143–5, 149, 153–4, 156, 158, 164 n.28, 173 n.32
Senelick, Lawrence 6

sexuality, defining importance of to literature ix–xii; relation to gender in Victorian age 15–35; relation to romantic love 1–14
  see also individual authors; women, representations of
Stendhal 26

Tess of the D'Urbervilles 54
Thackeray, William Makepeace 73–4, 156
Thompson, E.P. 26
Thrale, Hester 46
Trilling, Lionel 37

Vicinus, Martha 12
virgin, figure of 13, 14, 26, 36–8, 40, 44, 50–1, 54, 85, 144, 158, 172 n.26

Ward, Mrs Humphry 30
Westminster Review 7, 21, 26
womanhood x, xi, xii, 1, 2, 9, 12, 15, 16, 22, 24, 27, 29, 33–4, 49, 52, 59, 61, 74–6, 91, 96, 113, 137, 147, 149, 152, 156, 164 n.21, 173 n.33
  see also femininity; gender; women, representations of
women, representations of *see* artist; child; heroine; Lady; Moral Femininity; nun; virgin
Woolf, Virginia 73